The Intimate Lives of Disabled

Disabled people are routinely assumed to lack the capabilities and capacities to embody and experience sexuality and desire, as well as the agency to love and be loved by others and build their own families, if they so choose. Centring on the sexual, intimate and erotic lives of disabled people, this book presents a rare opportunity to understand and ask critical questions about such widely held assumptions.

In essence, this book is a collection of sexual stories, told by disabled people on their own terms and in their own ways – stories that shed light on areas of disability, love and life that are typically overlooked and ignored. A sociological analysis of these stories reveals the creative ways in which disabled people manage and negotiate their sexual and intimate lives in contexts where these are habitually denied. In its calls for disabled people's sexual and intimate citizenship, stories are drawn upon as the means to create social change and build more radically inclusive sexual cultures.

In this groundbreaking feminist critical disability studies text, *The Intimate Lives of Disabled People* introduces and contributes to contemporary debates around disability, sexuality and intimacy in the twenty-first century. Its arguments are relevant and accessible to researchers, academics, and students across a wide range of disciplines – such as sociology, gender studies, psychology, social work and philosophy – as well as disabled people, their families and allies, and the professionals who work with and for them.

Kirsty Liddiard is a Research Fellow in the School of Education at the University of Sheffield, where she also co-leads the Institute for the Study of the Human (iHuman). Prior to this, she was the inaugural Ethel Louise Armstrong Postdoctoral Fellow at the School of Disability Studies, Ryerson University, Toronto, Canada. Kirsty's research spans disability, gender, sexuality and intimacy and youth. As a disabled feminist, she has a particular interest in how disablism and ableism both inform and shape these experiences in the everyday lives of disabled people and their families. She tweets at @kirstyliddiard1

To read more about Kirsty's work, please visit kirstyliddiard.wordpress.com

The Intimate Lives of Disabled People

Kirsty Liddiard

 Routledge
Taylor & Francis Group

LONDON AND NEW YORK

First published 2018
by Routledge

2 Park Square, Milton Park, Abingdon, Oxfordshire OX14 4RN
52 Vanderbilt Avenue, New York, NY 10017

Routledge is an imprint of the Taylor & Francis Group, an informa business

First issued in paperback 2019

British Library Cataloguing in Publication Data
A catalogue record for this book is available from the British Library

Library of Congress Cataloging in Publication Data
Names: Liddiard, Kirsty, 1984– author.
Title: The intimate lives of disabled people / Kirsty Liddiard.
Description: New York : Routledge, 2018. | Includes bibliographical
references and index.
Identifiers: LCCN 2017033565| ISBN 9781409460909 (hardback) |
ISBN 9781315556598 (ebook)
Subjects: LCSH: People with disabilities–Marriage. | Interpersonal
relations. | Intimacy (Psychology)
Classification: LCC HQ1036 .L53 2018 | DDC 305.9/08–dc23
LC record available at https://lccn.loc.gov/2017033565

ISBN: 978-1-4094-6090-9 (hbk)
ISBN: 978-0-367-26537-3 (pbk)

Typeset in Times New Roman
by Wearset Ltd, Boldon, Tyne and Wear

This book is dedicated to Jacky Lee (1946–2011), who never got to read the final draft. You are the determination in every page.

Contents

Preface

'Right, imagine you're in Toronto in a bar. You're pissed [drunk], but not too pissed. How would you explain your research to someone?' This was the first question put to me by my then-external examiner, Professor Dan Goodley, in my viva voce (the thesis defence for North American readers). Thoughts of the viva had made my blood run cold for nigh on three years, but as soon as I heard that question, I knew all would be well. As someone who has since examined others' PhDs, I now see that was the point! But up until the viva, my PhD had been an empirical research project, which I had painfully 'written up' as a doctoral thesis. It is thanks to both of my examiners then, Dan Goodley and Cath Lambert, and their suggestion that my thesis already was a book, which caused it to be written at all.

I wrote most of my thesis from the tiny back room at my mum and dad's house – my partner and I had moved in with them, after years of having our own place, to save enough money to emigrate to Canada so that I could undertake the inaugural Ethel Louise Armstrong Postdoctoral Fellowship at the School of Disability Studies, Ryerson University. I had seen the advert randomly in the oddly warm spring of 2011 on the Disability Research Discussion email list run out of the Centre for Disability Research at Leeds. Upon seeing it, I immediately rang The Boy (my partner) and said, 'You could live in Canada, right?' Instantly he replied, 'Go on, then.' At that point, both of us would have struggled to point to Toronto on a map. Within a month I had applied for the position, survived a telephone interview and had got the job. Within two months we had packed up our little home and moved into the 'granny annexe' at Mum and Dad's, where they very kindly brought me cups of tea as I wrote. My father proofread every single page. A reserved English fellow – a man who oft takes the British stiff upper lip to the extreme – confessed me so much love and support with every slash of his red pen through my terrible grammar. We were to leave for Canada in January 2012, with me submitting my thesis in December 2011. I had just eight months to complete writing, and I did.

Turning my PhD thesis into this book has not been nearly as quick and easy: it has been an enormous challenge. I have struggled. Like so many 'early career' scholars, I have found the Academy a precarious place to work, which has meant shelving writing on more than a few occasions, despite lots of support from colleagues, friends and allies. I have also found the (neoliberal) Academy relatively precarious to one's sense of self and wellness, particularly in terms of self-confidence and esteem. Disablism, ableism and the Academy can be a toxic combination at times, and can erode self-confidence. As a disabled woman, gender and disability can intersect in ways that encourage an attrition of self-belief and pride, which gets magnified by the hypercompetitive and disabling environment that is higher education in the UK. Regardless, it is this shortage of confidence that proffers the (also helpful) 'disclaimer' below.

What this book isn't...

This book isn't a grandiose theoretical text, but a reporting of empirical research. This is not because I undervalue the transformative potential of theory, or that this book is atheoretical. As Braidotti (2013) says, if we can't do theory, then we are really just drowning in hard data; or as Goodley (2014) affirms, we should be able to draw upon social theory without apology. As both a disability studies scholar and a disabled woman, it is crucial for me to continually locate the lived and material realities of disability life into my theoretical reworkings. As such, the politics of location are very vital to my work (see Chapter 3). While I relish postconventional theory, at times I am unapologetically materialist: acknowledging that the richness of the stories in this book emanate from an understanding that they are lived, *felt*, experienced and ground in the mundane and everyday. Sometimes this brings inconsistencies and tensions. Instead of making attempts to write these out, I purposefully write them in and – as Mike Gill (2015: 8) artfully puts it – 'eagerly await challenges, complications, and expansions of my work here by others'.

This book isn't an all-encompassing text that covers *all* facets of sexual and intimate life: what is contained within the covers of this book emerges only from the stories disabled informants told. Informants were predominantly (though not exclusively) White British, cisgender and heterosexual and identified as having physical and/or sensory impairment. All lived within the community, although many had experienced institutionalisation in one way or another in the past and/or frequented respite care in hospices in the present. Therefore, the stories I interpret in this book are inherently shaped by these intersections, experiences and histories. They are further shaped by the context of doctoral research. Doctoral research is bound by time (UK PhD students have a maximum of three years and three months before funding stops), (a lack of) money and the emerging research skills of a PhD candidate, all of which I'm sure are imprinted on these sexual stories in some way. Further, the intimate politics of sexual storytelling in marginalised communities means that I am rightfully imbricated within and through these stories. In short, this book is also piece of me: as a researcher, scholar and disabled woman, it speaks to my life as well as the lives of informants.

This book isn't a complete lesson in co-production. While I am very proud that the doctoral research that underpins this book made use of participatory methods, being guided by a Research Advisory Group made up of local disabled people (or 'The Rag' as they preferred to be known), this participation was not a co-production in the purest or fullest sense. As a then-doctoral student, I was yet to discover and immerse myself fully in the democratisation of research as a collaborative and collective process, which has later become my passion as a scholar and researcher (see livinglifetothefullest.org; see also Runswick-Cole, Curran and Liddiard, in press).

What this book is…

This book is a collection of stories: stories of intimacy, affection, care, eroticism, desire and love, as well as stories of pain, oppression, exclusion, denial and abjection and rejection. It contains a faithful disabled feminist analysis (ground in social and intimate justice) of sexual and intimate life in times of extensive disablism and ableism. It offers a narrative thematic analysis of sexual stories that shed light on areas of disability, love and life typically overlooked and ignored.

Importantly, this book is an accessible piece of writing. In disability studies I have come to see accessible writing as strength, a skill and a quality that is necessary in order to speak to a range of communities and publics. I hope this book is accessible and readable. There are accessible versions of much of its contents on my website that are free to access (https://kirstyliddiard.wordpress.com) and I offer an accessible summary at the beginning of each chapter.

Finally, this book is a snapshot in time. The sociological research upon which this book is based took place across England, UK, between 2008 and 2011. If I were to carry out this research now, as I write in 2017, my approach, my relationships with disabled informants and my analysis would likely be different. It's been almost five years since the research ended and eight years since it began. I'm different. The world is different: a global financial crisis has happened; a cruel UK Liberal Democrat and Conservative Coalition Government has been and gone; an even crueller Tory-majority government has emerged in its place. As if these weren't enough, more recently Brexit and Trump have emerged as the inevitable-but-toxic results of a lying, scaremongering mistrustful establishment; a corrupt corporate right-wing press; and interminable global austerity. Each of these global events has happened since the research was carried out and each has understandably left its mark on disabled people's individual and collective lives and selves, largely in devastating ways (Goodley *et al*. 2014a). As such, disabled people's rights and access to civil, emotional, intimate and cultural life is *different*. Thus, this book can only ever be a snapshot in time, but this is not to say that its contents are no longer relevant. Far from it, the stories contained within these covers have much to tell us about access to love, life and self in the shadows of disablism and ableism – all of which connect deeply to the current state of disability life in the global step to the Right (Goodley *et al*. 2017: 3): conditions for living which define the current era as a time of great precarity for many people, but particularly marginalised others.

Acknowledgements

While my name may be alone on the front cover of this book, I am by no means its sole contributor. Rather, there are a number of people behind this piece of work who deserve to be both acknowledged and thanked here: kind informants; patient friends (especially Lucy, who regularly brought wine and smiles; I miss you every day); committed supervisors; generous research advisory group members; loyal colleagues and passionate comrades; an inspiring mother (who led me here); a committed father (who will always be my hero); bloody clever sisters (Drs Kim and Kate); and a fantastically supportive partner. I am very lucky.

I would like to thank my partner, The Boy, for his unremitting encouragement. Put simply, I have never met anyone who believes in me more. Thank you for making me more than I am. I love you, and that's the beginning and end of everything.

Big thanks to The Kid – my favourite comrade – who kept asking, 'Is that book you're writing done yet?' and 'Can I wear my suit to your book launch?' I love you more than you know – always keep looking forward, to your bright and brilliant future.

I am forever indebted to my academic supervisors, Dr Carol Wolkowitz and Dr Karen Throsby, for their enthusiasm, guidance and unrelenting support throughout my PhD at the University of Warwick. Each routinely went beyond their duties to fire fight my worries, concerns, and anxieties, and worked to instil great confidence in both my work and myself. In addition, both generously shared their passion for feminism, and their knowledges of sexualities and the body, which are to the great benefit of this book.

Thank you to the Ethel Louise Armstrong Foundation and all of my comrades at the School of Disability Studies at Ryerson University, Canada: Danielle Landry, Kathryn Church, Catherine Frazee, Paris Master-McRae, Eliza Chandler, Melanie Panitch, Jennifer Paterson, David Reville, Esther Ignagni, Kim Collins, Tanya Jivraj, Jijian Veronka and Sarah Wren. The postdoctoral fellowship you gave me was a life-changing and career-defining springboard to which, in a perfect world, all disabled women would have access. I have now been back in England more time than I spent in Toronto with you and I think of the School every single day (especially you, Paris, as I make my morning brew at work and miss your smiles). Esther, what I have learned from you can't be contained to just one sentence here, but know that I hope we will be lifelong friends and collaborators. The School of Disability Studies is a very special place that taught me the richness of disability and community and the art of combining activism, passion and scholarship. As they go hand in hand, I will never forget the vibrant Crip community in Toronto that embraced me without question, and from which I have been lucky enough to gain lifelong friends. I had been looking for you all my life.

To the brilliant folk at Project Revision – Carla Rice, Eliza Chandler, Fran Odette, Lindsay Fisher, Sheyfali Suajani, Elisabeth Harrison, Dawn Matheson, and so many fabulous others – thank you for allowing me to learn from and contribute to your love for stories and storytelling.

Thanks also to the Sexuality Alliance, and to the wonderful Maddie Blackburn at its helm; to the Rose Centre for Love, Sex and Disability for such opportunity and friendship; to my disabled sisters at Sisters of Frida for a collective voice; and to all of the organisations that supported this research in one way or another – Scope, Muscular Dystrophy UK, Royal National Institute for Blind People (RNIB), Royal National Institute for Deaf and hard of hearing people (RNID), Spinal Injuries Association (SIA), Deaf Village, The Stroke Association, Spokz and REGARD.

To my current colleagues and comrades, disability studies folk 'tup in the North of England and elsewhere: Dan, Katherine, Rebecca Lawthom, Jen Slater, Em Nunn, Jill Smith, China Mills, Marek Mackiewicz, Rebecca Mallett, Nick Hodge, Jack Levinson (our honorary Yorkshireman), and Jon Harvey (come to the North…), Tillie Curran, Alan Roulstone (for my library…) and so many others. Thank you for your passion, support, solidarity and, above all, kindness. Coming back to England (and all of the life changes this brought) was daunting, but the warmth and affection you've shown as a community has made everything possible. Jen Slater, I love being disruptive with you – let's keep doing it. Katherine Runswick-Cole, I'm so grateful to work with you, thank you for guiding me. Thanks also to Holly Burkinshaw, Antonios Ktenidis and Kholood Aljaser – I learn from each of you and supporting your PhD journeys is one of my favourite parts of my job.

To Dan Goodley: thank you for everything you've ever done for me, and we both know it's a lot. You're a brilliant ally, comrade and friend. I love working with you. Thank you for your endless support and for remembering the Liddiard-Disability-Studies-lineage(!), that meant more than you know. You're a true star.

Of course, big thanks to #ScholarTed. He wrote most of it.

Thank you to the School of Education and Institute for the Study of the Human (iHuman) at the University of Sheffield for the time, space, support and encouragement to write this book. Thanks also go to Claire Jarvis (for her immense patience!) and Georgia Priestley at Routledge for their support during publishing.

Thank you to the very kind people who read, edited and gave feedback on individual chapters: Rebecca Lawthom, Dan Goodley, Jen Slater, Jon Harvey, Esther Ignagni, Katherine Runswick-Cole and China Mills.

Most important of all, I show extensive gratitude to all of the people who warmly contributed their stories, histories and experiences to the research, and thus this book. Without this willingness to share, the research itself would not have even been possible. I hope that you find my treatment of your stories in this book honest, ethical and faithful. I was deeply touched by how much people shared with me, and how close to many informants I would become. In the same vein, I would like to extend great thanks to Research Advisory Group members who offered their time, support and commitment. I'm so grateful – you taught me so much. This piece of research looks very different because of The Rag's input, influence and expert knowledge.

Last, I thank the Economic and Social Sciences Research Council (ESRC), which provided a full ESRC 1+3 (MA and PhD) Studentship to both learn the skills and carry out the research that underpins this book (ES/F009151/1).

1 Exploring disability and sexuality

Accessible summary

- In this chapter I introduce the ways in which disabled people are denied access to their sexual lives, selves and bodies.
- I explain key concepts such as ableism, disablism and sexual normalcy.
- I introduce the empirical research that underpins this book, outlining the intimate politics of sexual storytelling.
- I offer a short history of existing research into disabled sexualities.
- I outline the contents of the chapters that follow in the remainder of the books.

Disabled people have a sexual history marked by oppression, suppression and violence, and much of this sexual history has, in the past, been overlooked within both academic and activist contexts in favour of a focus on disabled people's social and political histories (Finger 1992; Shakespeare *et al.* 1996). Through disability rights movements from the 1960s onwards, disabled people have fought for their rightful place within public life, campaigning for civil rights, anti-discrimination legislation, equal access to education, community integration and environmental accessibility. Characteristically, alongside these have been an appreciation of diversity and a vivid celebration of pride. This (necessary) structural focus upon disabling environments has left disabled people's sexual politics marginalised and has inadvertently created a significant dearth of knowledges around disabled people's private and intimate lives. Since the early work of some disabled activists, who powerfully spoke out about their sexual oppression as central to their dehumanisation (see Finger 1992), and publication of the influential text *Untold Desires: The Politics of Disabled Sexuality* (Shakespeare *et al.* 1996), explorations of the oppressions within disabled people's intimate lives have emerged, albeit slowly. Standing (and sometimes sitting – I get tired) on the shoulders of giants (see Garland-Thomson 2002 for a discussion on disability neologism), a key aim of this book is to contribute to these explorations.

Positioned largely as asexual, most disabled people are assumed to lack the capabilities and capacities to embody sexuality, sensuality, expression and desire.

For clarity, the asexuality I speak of here (and in the remainder of this book) differs from the emergent asexual identity category powerfully claimed by those who, for a variety of reasons, do 'not experience sexual attraction' (Scherrer 2008: 626), or those who assert a different engagement with attraction and desire, claiming a positive and prideful identity and finding home in asexual communities. Instead, the asexuality to which I refer is a set of processes purposefully imposed *upon* disabled bodies and minds through the processes of ableism and disablism (I define these terms below). However, this is not to negate the fact that, as Kim (2011) reminds us, disabled people can identify with an asexual identity, too. To assume that all disabled people are sexual 'denies that asexuality can be positively experienced by subjects with a disability' (Kim 2011: 482). Or, as Gill (2015: 17) rightfully posits, 'being sexual is not central to being human; certainly many people live satisfying lives without sexual activity'.

In contexts of disablism and ableism, disability and impairment trouble that which we have come to understand as '(hetero)sex': a naturalised mode of gendered sexual practices that privilege physicality, penetration, form and function. Lurking in the shadows of this standardised sexual mode is the normative, controlled and bound body and rational, sane and coherent mind. These are the necessary embodied qualities for claiming any kind of sexual selfhood in what are now deeply dis/ableist times. Yet at the same time, bodies and minds diagnosed, marked and labelled as impaired readily and forcefully disrupt or *crip* these prescribed sexual norms, for radical effect – a tension that I return to often through this book. To clarify my usage of the term crip at this early juncture, my understanding follows others (Clare 1999; McRuer 2006a; Sandahl 2003) to denote it as the desire to unsettle, to contest and challenge normalcy; or, as McRuer (2006b: 35) puts it when talking about crip theory, crip is that which 'questions – or takes a sledgehammer to – that which has been concretised' (see Chapter 2 for a full unpacking of crip).

Disabled people's sexual agency and selfhood is often stripped away through stereotypes of eternal innocence and passivity. Alternatively, they are cast as objects of fetish: exploited, abused – the vulnerable subjects of devotees. Devotees are people attracted to impairment and/or disability that, quite typically, are pathologised for their desires, which are routinely considered 'abhorrent'. Paradoxically, some disabled people – usually those with the label of intellectual impairment (North America) or people with the label of learning disability (UK) (I use the latter in this book) – are positioned as hypersexual and in need of containment (see Liddiard and Slater 2017; see also Gill 2015). This aberrant hypersexual subject is deemed to lack the capacity to understand sexuality and desire and its mechanics, or fully consent to sexual acts and relationships, making them inherently vulnerable to self and other. Quite often, the response is to *protect* and *shield* from the supposed perils of sexual and intimate life (Gill 2015). Such actions are built on the assumption that a lack of capacity risks *others*, in terms of both sexual health and sexual violence. Cast in binaries of vulnerable/dangerous, abused/abuser and protected/unprotected, then, sexual agency, pleasure and desire become, at best, secondary considerations to safety and safeguarding. People with particular mental health diagnoses often experience similar containment because they are considered hazardous, uncontrollable and ultimately harmful to themselves or others. A dangerous irony within and amongst such dis/ableist assumptions is that excluding and denying knowledge, information, support, space and access to sexuality increases disabled people's vulnerability – particularly people with the label of learning disability – putting them at a greater risk of sexual abuse and violence (Hollomotz 2011; see also Razack 1998).

Disabled sexualities quickly fall into a realm of deviancy simply because, to fit with dominant constructions of disabled people as passive, vulnerable and childlike, disabled people aren't supposed to be having or desiring sex at all. Consequently, disabled desires are cast as inappropriate and unruly because they can take different forms to established sexual norms, particularly where the support of others is required. For example, facilitated sex (Earle 1999: 312), or sexual support (the term I use in this book), in its most applied sense, is usually carried out by a personal assistant, carer, partner or other chosen person, and can encompass a wide range of practices:

> At a general level, it might mean that assistance is required to attend social events such as parties, or to go to pubs and clubs. It might also mean, as described by one individual in the study, that assistance is required to negotiate the price when using the services of a prostitute [sic]. More specifically, a person might be required to facilitate sexual intercourse between two or more individuals, to undress them for such a purpose, or to masturbate them when no other form of sexual relief is available.

Sexual support comes up a lot in this book, even though the disabled people in my research rarely labelled it as such (see Chapter 7). This is not surprising, given that sexual support is contentious because of the ways in which it exposes the ableist myth of the sexually self-sufficient and self-governing body. In doing so, it contradicts *the* fundamental norms of conventional sexual mores that are 'heterosexual, private, ideally reproductive, and above all autonomous' (Shildrick 2009: 70). I say myth, because all people need, use and desire support. As humans we are rooted in a multiplicity of connections – technology, family, and community – we individually and collectively rely upon too many services and structures to mention here. Humans aren't autonomous or independent; everyone is reliant, interdependent and subject to a range of supports that enable everyday life. In the context of disability, support can take on new meaning to emerge as a problem, burden or, where sexuality is concerned, a form of deviance. When sexual support comes in the form of a sex worker, for example, who might assist a disabled person to experience pleasure, disabled desires come to be at risk of criminalisation. This is reflected in British legal constructions of sex work, whereby both soliciting (a crime of the seller) and curb crawling (a crime of the buyer), amongst other aspects of the sale of sex, are punishable by law. Sexual support emerges as a key theme in Chapter 7, where I consider the commercial sale of sex in contexts of disability. Those in my research who did engage in the commercial sale of sex did so primarily as the buyer, but it's important to acknowledge that sex workers are often disabled people too (Fritsch *et al*. 2016). Regardless of who is selling or buying, it is important to recognise that both actions remain predominantly socially deviant and/or illegal activities, both in the UK and across the globe.

While I have merely sketched out descriptions of Brown's (1994: 125) categories of 'asexual, or oversexed, innocents or perverts' here, they are fully fleshed out between these covers. In the remainder of this chapter I introduce the concepts of disablism and ableism as governing forces within human, sexual and intimate life. I consider their impact upon disabled people's access to desire, pleasure and sexual agency and selfhood in these neoliberal-able times (Goodley 2014).[1] Later, I introduce the empirical sociological research that underpins this book. I begin with a short history of research into disabled people's sexual and intimate lives, before outlining the genesis of this study – the impetus for exploration of this kind, the specific areas in focus and the central questions that guided my research. In doing so, I outline the personal and political emphases of telling sexual stories (Plummer 1995) and detail how sexual stories were collected and co-produced. Throughout this chapter I briefly introduce the contents of each chapter, which I hope can act as some kind of road map to guide readers. I recap these at the end.

Dis/ableism and sexuality

The term *dis/ableism* is used within this book to refer to the dual processes of disablism and ableism. This is because, more often than not, they work in conjunction, supporting one another, always intimately connected. Where I refer specifically to ableism or disablism, I use the respective term. While there are contestations around the meanings of both disablism and ableism (particularly between British and North American disability scholars and activists), for the purposes of clarity I follow Fiona Kumari Campbell's (2001: 4, 44) definitions:

> Disablism: A set of assumptions (conscious or unconscious) and practices that promote the differential or unequal treatment of people because of actual or presumed disabilities.

> Ableism: A network of beliefs, processes and practices that produces a particular kind of self and body (the corporeal standard) that is projected as the perfect, species-typical and therefore essential and fully human. Disability then is cast as a diminished state of being human.

This 'corporeal standard' proliferates within ableism and underscores why medical models of disability forcefully prevail in Western cultures. In late modernity, biomedical paradigms continue to perceive and treat impairment only as physiological deficiency. This deficiency is typically hypermanaged through relentless surveillance, classification, intervention and treatment and, for some, eradication. For example, measures such as restricted access to sexual health and family planning for disabled people, legal abortions on disabled foetuses at any time during gestation (in UK law), much genetic and stem cell research, and assisted dying are considered by some to be contemporary forms of genocide (see Morris 1991; Rock 1996; Sobsey 1994; Waxman 1994). Therefore, the impaired body and disabled existence are firmly devalued and dehumanised within the medico-scientific contexts that proliferate through ableism. An ableist imperative deems impaired bodies and minds subsist only as *broken* and, as such, subject to a very different set of priorities than those considered 'able'. Mitchell Tepper (2000) argues that it is this 'brokenness' that significantly contributes to impaired bodies and minds being cast as not requiring – or failing to embody – sensuality, pleasure and desire.

Ableism also permeates at the roots of sexual normalcy. Heteronormative sexuality, the governing mode of sexual order, is a distinctly narrow and highly regulated mode of naturalised sexuality. It is, amongst other things, *rooted* in a gender binary that maintains a phallocentrism that propagates pleasure as always genitally focused and performance-orientated (Tepper 2000). Disabled people (regardless of their impairments/labels) are assumed to lack the bodily requirements to perform heteronormative sexuality in expected ways. Disability is unruly and disorderly. Scholar Tobin Siebers (2008: 133) suggests that alternative means of acquiring pleasure often remain unrecognisable and that such 'illiteracy about the minds and bodies of disabled people drapes their sexual practices in deviance and perversion'. Let's not forget that conventional heterosex remains definable in terms of a reproductive imperative. Within the tyranny of ableism, it is not surprising that such an imperative is strictly exclusive to bodies deemed able, where procreation is 'solely the province of the fittest' (Tepper 2000: 285). Or, as disabled feminist Waxman Fiduccia (2000: 169) simply puts, 'sexual rights have always and only been awarded to those who are proclaimed to deliver quality offspring'.

Without doubt, we are living in deeply dis/ableist times. Ableism and disablism are ever present within postmodern society, where neoliberal and scientific rationalist ideologies are thriving and, currently, where global capitalism and global austerity are routinely highlighting the *costs* and therefore undermining the (human) value of disabled people. I follow McRuer (2006a: 2) in my understanding of neoliberal capitalism: 'the dominant economic and cultural system in which, and against which, embodied and sexual identities have been imagined and composed over the last quarter century'. The current UK context from which I write this book is a very good example of the toxic combination of disability, austerity and dis/ableism (Goodley *et al.* 2015). Most disabled people in the UK live in continuing poverty (Parckar 2008). Many disabled people remain excluded from or poorly supported and protected within the British labour market (Wilton and Schuer 2006). Disability hate crimes remain seldom satisfactorily recognised and policed (despite having markedly increased during austerity) (Roulstone *et al.* 2011; Soorenian 2016). Disabled people (particularly women) experience higher rates of sexual, physical and emotional violence than non-disabled people (Thiara *et al.* 2011). Debates on assisted dying are dominated by privileged voices and (dangerous) quality of life measurements, as well as ableist constructions of dignity (Koch 2000), and 'eugenetics' movements (Armer 2007) and 'genetic fundamentalism' (Overboe 2007: 223) loiter at the forefront of bio-scientific advancement. Each of these factions of modern life routinely demand and circulate a compulsory 'ableness' that simultaneously devalues disabled people's very existence (Campbell 2009).

We know too that disabled people have suffered exponentially through the austerity politics of both the previous coalition Liberal Democrat–Conservative government (which came to power in the UK in 2010) and the current Conservative government in the UK – a very Tory Story. Significant cuts to a multitude of benefits and public services – a predictable and systematic rolling back of the State – have exacerbated existing disability oppressions, and have ontologically, psychically, symbolically, materially, emotionally and affectively stripped disabled people (amongst many other minorities) of their rights, access and self-worth. There are countless disabled activists, self-advocates, artists (see Crow 2015) and allies who are documenting and mapping the brutal ways in which austerity has been enacted since the recession (Loach 2016). This work has highlighted the present as a time in disabled people's history when they are striving, once again, for rights and access to civil life. And, of course, such a desire to reduce the economic costs of disability, sickness and illness is further intensified through myriad other austerity measures that have targeted the poor, insecurely housed, deprived and ill, many of who are disabled.

For me, love, sex, intimacy and emotion are central to these austerity politics: disabled people are currently fighting to remain part of their communities; to stay connected to their partners, children and families; to find and stay in meaningful work; to be appropriately housed; and participate in civil society – surviving on ever-shrinking incomes and real uncertainty around the provision of services upon which many depend. As austerity bites and welfare is rolled back, more emphasis is placed upon individuals to take care of themselves and their loved ones, revealing the extent to which austerity demands able and ableist citizens. We are yet to know the true impact of Brexit (or, across the pond, Trump), though we can imagine these to bring a multitude of new harms to marginalised people, especially those who are disabled, sick and ill.[2] Despite this changing global order, however, austerity is seldom an *explicit* feature in this book; rather it is quietly present, not overt in people's stories but lurking nonetheless. In essence, this is because the austerity agenda and subsequent scapegoating of disabled people in the UK was only really just beginning at the very *end* of the research. Back then the disabled people at the centre of this study hadn't yet felt the sheer wave of the cuts to benefits and services that was to continue for the next five years, and beyond.

But to speak in a more general sense, disablism and ableism – the privileging of ability, sanity, rationality, physicality and cognition (Braidotti 2013) – have long rendered disability as abject and Other. Disabled bodies and minds are actively sequestered from public view, space and culture: segregated in education; institutionalised in hospitals, homes and treatment units; detained in mental health units; criminalised in prisons; lost through child protection systems; and excluded from the popular cultures of perfection which dominate a globalised techno-media age (see Hevey 1992). As such, disabled people have seldom ever been considered, nor treated, as 'fully human' (Goodley, Lawthom and Runswick-Cole 2014b) and are situated, at best, at the margins of human sexuality. As I have argued elsewhere (Goodley *et al.* 2015: 11), disabled people's exclusion from the category of the human operates on a number of levels within sexual and intimate life, denying rights and access to intimate citizenship (Plummer 2003; see Chapter 4):

> it compromises entry into normative sexual and gender categories; refutes sexual agency and selfhood; and silences calls for sexual, reproductive and parenting rights and justice. It is not surprising, then, given that humanness, humanity and sexuality are so tightly bound in our cultures, that sexual normalcy subsists as a very powerful cultural and political category of which to gain entry.

Relatedly, contexts of dis/ableism have long disqualified disabled people from 'discourses of pleasure' (Shildrick 2007a: 58) – in focus in Chapter 6. Disabled desires are rendered dangerous in 'a cultural imaginary that privileges corporeal wholeness and predictability above any form of bodily anomaly, and that supports fears that non-normative sexuality is always a potential point of breakdown in a well-ordered society' (Shildrick 2007a: 54). Such a thirst for well-ordered society disqualifies myriad bodies from the realm of pleasure as fat people, women, queer and trans, and Black and people of colour (POC) are rendered disgusting and beyond control (Tepper 2000). Disqualification, however, proffers an absence, an end or exclusion; following Fiona Campbell (2009), I find it more politically useful to consider the ways in which disabled desires are *contoured* by disablism and ableism. This political positionality also centres lived experience as the location from which to begin theorising disabled people's sexual, intimate and erotic lives, a key aim of this book.

For many disabled people, pleasure is institutionalised through multiple forms of incarceration, as particular individualised regimes of care and a disciplining therapeutic surveillance disrupt opportunities for the expression of pleasure (see Siebers 2008; see also Liddiard and Goodley 2016). Even where institutional sexual supports for pleasure exist, they often succumb to the rules of the institution. In her book *Learning Difficulties and Sexual Vulnerability* (2011), the wonderful Andrea Hollomotz tells the story of Rachel, a woman with the label of learning disability denied access to her vibrator during the day – when she wanted it – because group home staff thought masturbation at night was more *appropriate*. This institutionalisation of pleasure both denied Rachel's sexual agency (the choice when to masturbate) and mediated her embodied experiences of pleasure (a dictated time and place). Through similar processes, pleasure has been colonised, co-opted and pathologised through the interventions of education, medical and social care professionals. For example, masturbation training, chemical castration and over-medicating are routinely used to assuage the assumed animalistic hypersexuality of learning disabled, Black and queer disabled people (primarily men) (Gill 2015). Paradoxically, at the same time, access to pleasure is denied (particularly to disabled women and queer people) through a *lack* of access to multiple forms of sexual and reproductive healthcare (Anderson and Kitchen 2000; Browne and Russell 2005; Wong 2000).

Sexual agency is further denied, as you will see throughout the following chapters: (i) through a lack of sex education – a silence in learning about the pleasured body (see Thompson *et al.* 2001); (ii) through segregation: the routine separation of bodies and their extensive surveillance; (iii) through infantilisation and paternalisation: to be rendered as child, is to be rendered *unable* to desire; (iv) through material deprivation: as poverty mitigates both opportunities for and desire for pleasure (see Ignagni *et al.* 2016); (v) through exposure to multiple forms of violence – most notably sexual violence (see Sherry 2004); and (vi) through the criminalisation of non-normative pleasures (see Liddiard 2014c). And then there are the emotional, psychic and affective politics of pleasure, which includes things like the relative absence of disabled sexuality and pleasure in the cultural sphere (film, TV, media); the endemic shaming of disabled people's sexual expression through oppressive care practices (Liddiard and Slater 2017); and psycho-emotional disablism – what Thomas (1999: 60) calls 'the socially engendered undermining of emotional well-being' – which can exacerbate the cultural and political denial of an erotic self (Liddiard 2014c); and internalised ableism – the insidious process of *learning* to hate ourselves (Stevens 2011). Sexologist Bethany Stevens (2011: 12) – a crip legend in her own time – describes this as not being able to 'muster the capacity to see love for my body'. Finally, Shildrick (2007a: 54) points to prescriptive and utilitarian social policy, which has 'grounded a sociopolitical economy of disability predicated on rehabilitation or compensation' – thus 'leaving no scope for considerations of affective differences in such realms as sexual expression'. She notes that this silence is deeply ironic, given that sexuality is 'a major site of state intervention and control, with a range of sociopolitical instruments regulating its permissible forms and location' (Shildrick 2007a: 54).

Researching disability and sexuality

Shakespeare *et al.*'s (1996: 1) text on disability and sexuality, *Untold Desires: The Sexual Politics of Disability*, was 'the first book to look at the sexual politics of disability from a disability rights perspective'. The distinctly atheoretical text (Shuttleworth and Sanders 2010) for the first time voiced disabled people's own sexual stories. Shakespeare *et al.*'s (1996) critique of the existing qualitative studies of the time centred on the ways in which such research discussed disabled people's married lives but left the sexual distinctly unattended (see Parker

1993; Seymour 1994). Prior to this, very little empirical research on disability and sexuality (from a disability studies perspective) had been carried out. Rather, attention to disabled people's sexual lives came primarily from psychological, medical and sexological backgrounds. This is why, even today, in comparison to other areas of inquiry, sexual and intimate life remains an under-researched area of disability life (see Shakespeare and Richardson, forthcoming). There have been, however, a few attempts to commence a dialogue about the sexualities of disabled people as early as the 1980s. For example, Hicks' (1981: 79) assessment of 'sexual problems and visual impairment' within Brechin, Liddiard and Swain's (1981) *Handicap in a Social World*, itself a leading early disability text, put sexuality on the agenda in ways not done elsewhere. Shakespeare and Richardson (forthcoming) have since carried out a follow-up study to *Untold Desires: The Sexual Politics of Disability* (Shakespeare *et al.* 1996), tracing some original informants to explore their experiences over the last 20 years, representing a rare example of longitudinal qualitative research in the field of sexuality and disability research. Shakespeare and Richardson (forthcoming: 2) suggest that, despite 20 years' worth of potential development, 'studies reporting on the lived experience of disability and sexuality continue to be thin on the ground'.

The mid-1990s saw the beginnings of empirical research into disabled people's intimate lives that looked at the social 'barriers' to disabled people's sexual expression. For example, areas included sexual life (Bonnie 2004; Crabtree 1997; Dune and Shuttleworth 2009; Guldin 2000; Kim 2011; McCabe 2003; McCabe *et al.* 2000 Pearson and Klook 1989; Sakellariou 2006; Shakespeare 2000; Shakespeare *et al.* 1996; Tepper 2000; Waxman Fiduccia 2000); sexual and reproductive health and family planning (Anderson and Kitchen 2000; Browne and Russell 2005; Welner 1999; Wong 2000); sexual and intimate rights (Abeyesekera 1997; Petchesky 2000); parenting/motherhood and reproductive justice (Kent 2002; O'Toole 2002; Prillelltensky 2003); sexual identity (Galvin 2006; Scherrer 2008); disabled sexualities in global contexts (Addlakha 2007; Cheausuwantavee 2002; Kohrman 2008; Li and Yau 2006; Villanueva 1997; Wazakili *et al.* 2006; Yoshida *et al.* 1999); disabled men's experiences (Blyth and Carson 2007; Ostrander 2009; Shakespeare 1999b; Shuttleworth 2000; Tepper 1999) and disabled women's experiences (Bryant and Howland and Rintala 2001; Leibowitz 2005; Mona *et al.* 1994; Parker and Yau 2012; Rintala *et al.* 1997; Schofield 2007). Focus on the sexual abuse and violence perpetrated against disabled people has also been prevalent: for example, intimate partner abuse (Hassouneh-Phillips and McNeff 2005); prevalence of abuse (Young *et al.* 1997); barriers and strategies in addressing abuse (Powers *et al.* 2002), (sexual) vulnerability (Hollomotz 2010; Milberger *et al.* 2003; Nosek *et al.* 2001), and care-related violence (Hassouneh-Phillips and McNeff 2004). Disability activists have stressed that an extensive focus on sexual violence 'can itself become oppressive' (Finger 1992: 9). Yet later works by Thiara *et al.* (2011, 2012) remind us of the importance of continuing to speak about sexual violence, particularly in the lives of disabled women. Disabled women, Thiara *et al.* (2011: 757) maintain, continue 'losing out in both counts' because of their significantly high rates of exposure to violence and their marked lack of protection through violence and abuse services and sectors, which offer little specialist and accessible provision (see Chapter 5).

In a more recent edited collection, *Sexuality and Disability: Politics, Identity, and Access*, edited by Russell Shuttleworth and Teela Sanders, Shuttleworth (2010: 4) proclaims that there is 'still a marked lack of innovative socio-political and cultural research in disability and sexuality', with the following areas of inquiry routinely overlooked:

> Much less investigated are the socio-political structures and cultural meanings that restrict disabled people's sexual expression and sexual opportunities, disabled people's modes of resistance and creative sexual agency in their search for sexual wellbeing, the sexual implications of the intersection of disability with identity categories such as gender, race and sexuality, the impact of different policy contexts on disability and sexuality issues, and other topics less concerned with normative functioning.
>
> (Shuttleworth 2010: 3)

When Shuttleworth (2010: 3) refers to 'creative sexual agency' he is referring, I suggest, to the absence from existing research of 'detailed descriptions of disabled people's actual sexual activities, how they, in fact, often do adapt their impairments using different positions and various sexual aids to facilitate sexual fulfilment' (see also Hamam *et al.* 2009). These are offered in abundance in Chapter 6, as disabled people share their lived and material experiences of the body, disability and sexual expression. Additionally, echoing the assumed heterosexuality of disabled people (Abbott 2015; Siebers 2008) is the absence of empirical research into the (sexual) lives of lesbian, gay, bisexual, trans, queer, questioning, two-spirit,[3] intersex, or asexual (LGBTQQ2SIA) disabled people, or those who find power and pleasure in BDSM and Kink (Abbott 2015; Appleby 1994; Brownworth and Raffo 1999; Corbett 1994; Courvant 1999; Davies 2010; Martino 2017; Sheppard 2017; Tremain 2000; Whitney 2006). There is a need for far more empirical work that interrogates the intersections of homophobia, biphobia, transphobia, heterosexism, ableism and disablism – particularly in contexts of race, class, gender and nation. This inevitably further extends to the lives of people with the label of learning disability, whose queer desires are often 'interpreted … as expressions of friendship, not sexual desire' (Löfgren-Mårtenson 2009: 23) and disabled trans people, who are significantly underrepresented in research, although there are exceptions (McClelland *et al.* 2012). Baril (2015: 35) draws our attention to part of the problem of a lack of crip and trans knowledges being due to an 'ableist bias in trans studies and a cis(gender) normative bias in disability studies'.

Furthermore, while there are notable exceptions (see Gillespie-Sells *et al.* 1998), there are few explorations of disabled people's intimate relationships – for example, their interpersonal relationships with sexual and intimate partners and experiences of and engagements with intimacy and love. I explore this in

Chapter 5, as disabled people story their emotional, intimate and love lives with chosen others. Another significantly under-researched area, possibly because its ability to 'evoke highly emotionally charged discussion within, without and across the disabled and non-disabled communities' (Kanguade 2010: 207), is disability, sex work and sexual support. British sociologist Teela Sanders (2010: 152) calls for more research into 'the moral, social, practical, financial, legal and emotional dynamics of buying a sexual service for people with impairments', particularly, she maintains, the ways in which local policies impact upon disabled people's accessing of sex workers and experiences of sexual support (Davies 2000; Earle 1999). In agreement, Shuttleworth (2010: 4) calls for exploration of the 'ethical dilemmas surrounding political and structural barriers to implementing sexual facilitation services'. These are, in part, offered in Chapter 7.

The sociological research upon which this book is based, then, took place across England between 2008 and 2011. The overarching aim was to explore disabled people's lived experiences of sex and sexuality, intimacy and love through their own sexual stories told on their own terms. More specifically, the doctoral research sought to understand the complex ways in which 25 disabled men and women (and one non-disabled partner, 26 people in total) managed and negotiated their sexual and intimate lives, selves, and bodies in contexts of dis/ableism. This ethos echoed initiatives found in feminist, anti-racist and disability research methodologies, which make space for and centre marginalised groups within inquiry in order to prioritise subjective experience and voice (Dei and Johal 2005). It was also purposeful towards countering the dominant voices within existing research into disabled people's sexual lives, which has mainly been with those who often regulate the sexual lives *of* disabled people – for example, health professionals, social work practitioners, educators and support workers (although much of this is credible work – see Blackburn (2002) and Lees (2016). Therefore, my intention was to situate disabled people's own voices as well as their lived, embodied and material experiences amongst the myriad stories already told about their lives by 'experts'. I considered this a way to disrupt, in part, the mundane paternalistic, professional, patriarchal and dis/ableist discourses that routinely pathologise, medicalise and psychologise disabled people's (sexual) lives and bodies (Shakespeare *et al.* 1996; Siebers 2008).

Conceptualising disabled people's stories as the means through which to explore the intersections of disability and sexuality, and the subsequent narrative and thematic analyses of sexual stories, was embedded in the potential personal and political empowerment of telling stories (Langellier 2001) and the broader notion of sexual stories as instrumental within claims for sexual citizenship (Plummer 1995). What British Sociologist Ken Plummer (1995: 15) calls 'sexual stories' are 'socially embedded in the daily practices and strategies of everyday life'. Personal empowerment is possible through storytelling, argues Langellier (2001: 700), because 'personal narrative responds to the disintegration of master narratives as people make sense of experience, claim identities, and "get a life" by telling and writing their stories'. As Plummer (1995: 150) advocates, the sexual empowerment and rights of Othered communities depends upon a community of stories to make rights imaginable and tenable. Thus, storytelling is instrumental within social and political change:

> Rights and responsibilities are not 'natural' or 'inalienable' but have to be invented through human activities and built into the notions of communities, citizenship and identities. Rights and responsibilities depend upon a community of stories which make those same rights plausible and possible. They accrue to people whose identities flow out of the self-same communities. Thus it is only as lesbian and gay communities started to develop and women's movements gathered strength that stories around a new kind of citizenship became more and more plausible. The nature of our communities – the languages they use, the stories they harbour, the identities they construct, the moral/political codes they champion – move to the centre stage of political thinking.
>
> (Plummer 1995: 150)

Thus, while the notion of 'empowerment' – particularly within the margins of disability research – remains both contested and contestable (Oliver 1992), the act of telling sexual stories was conceptualised within this study to be politically pertinent towards (re)claiming a sexual culture (Siebers 2008), community and sexual citizenship unconnected to existing disabled sexual cultures and histories. Such cultures and histories, as with those of other sexually Othered bodies which have been subjugated and subjected to discrimination and violence in multiple social and historical contexts (Chauncey 1995; Kennedy and Davis 1993; Schilt 2011), are 'characterized largely by oppression and discrimination' (Rembis 2010: 53).

While I offer a fuller reflexive account of my research in Chapter 3, I want to speak to its participatory nature at this early juncture because it remains a defining characteristic. Participatory research is essentially about 'giving more "say" in research to people who are more usually subjected to research' (Swain and French 2004: 10). With this sentiment, and being mindful of my own lived and embodied experiences of disabling environments and systemic ableism as a disabled woman, it was imperative for me that the research process – how to collect stories, how to treat them and what to do with them – be decided, developed and designed alongside fellow disabled people. Consequently, I established a Research Advisory Group (hereby RAG) prior to the beginning of the research. The RAG was a committed group of local disabled people who actively guided the research from its initial design to the co-production of a dissemination plan following the culmination of the research (see Kitchen 2000, 2001). Collectively, the RAG established its own role and aims. Group members favoured a supportive and collaborative role whereby they could impart expert knowledge, help set the research agenda and have 'the opportunity to correct misrepresentations and influence the direction of the research' (Kitchen 2000: 38) without taking on the responsibility or accountability of being a full partner. The group was invaluable in many ways, evidenced throughout this book. Even prior to the commence-ment of any fieldwork, the group's laughter, support, guidance and enthusiasm fostered a relaxed space through which I learned to speak to fellow disabled people (or anyone!) about sex and intimacy. In particular, some RAG members warmly shared their own stories as a prerequisite to designing how the stories of others could be collected and used. Therefore I was taught to *listen*. As Barton (2005: 325) reminds us: 'there is the need to increasingly recognise and more thoroughly understand and practice the art of "listening" to the voices of dis-abled people'. I develop these reflections in Chapter 3 through a reflexive account of the process that details the (necessary) messiness of carrying research of this kind.

Conclusion

Offering some semblance of a map throughout this chapter has, I hope, has primed readers to forge their own journey through this book. To recap, Chapter 2 provides a thorough overview of the theoretical perspectives that have con-tributed to existing critical knowledges of disability and sex, but also gender, sexuality, identity, embodiment and subjectivity. Chapter 3 introduces the perti-nent politics, practicalities and ethics of telling, hearing and collecting disabled people's sexual stories for the purposes of research. Chapter 4 – the first chapter to engage with empirical data – is purposefully broad and includes the themes of public life, surveillance, sexual citizenship and privacy as disabled informants' story their management and negotiation of sexual identity in the public sphere. Chapter 5 explores informants' experiences of love and self in current and past intimate relationships with others. Chapter 6 explores how the sexual pleasures, practices and interactions of disabled informants are shaped by both their 'anom-alous embodiment' (Shildrick 2009) and dominant discourses of heteronorma-tive sexuality. Chapter 7 focuses on informants' experiences of sexual support and sex work. The book culminates in a conclusion in Chapter 8, which sets the key findings in a wider context, moving beyond the research's theoretical, intel-lectual and political aims to ask critical questions of disabled people's sexual and intimate futures. To do so, I draw upon more recent developments to disabil-ity theory, namely posthuman disability studies and DisHuman studies (Goodley *et al.* 2014b; see also dishuman.com).

Notes

1 This refers to the merging of neoliberal discourses of progression, marketisation, per-formativity and austerity with the discourses of ableism (see Liddiard and Goodley 2016).
2 As I write this, Donald Trump has been president for just 168 days and we have already seen American disability rights activists being violently pulled from their wheelchairs and arrested at Senate majority leader Mitch McConnell's office, where they were peacefully protesting about cuts to Medicaid – cuts which will kill a wealth of disabled Americans (see Mills, in press).

3 '2S' – otherwise known as Two-Spirit or Two Spirit – 'refers broadly to Native Americans who were born with masculine and feminine spirits in one body' (Sheppard and Mayo 2013: 262). As Sheppard and Mayo (2013: 262) articulate, 'traditionally, many Native cultures acknowledged and accepted greater variation in how individuals expressed gender identification, which is in contrast with the Western tradition of adhering to a strict binary (male/female) conceptualization of gender'.

2 Theorising disabled sexualities

Constraints and possibilities

Accessible summary

- In this chapter I construct a theoretical framework for the empirical research that follows in the rest of this book.
- I make use of critical disability studies – a perspective that offers many perspectives and 'tools' through which to explore disability and sexuality.
- I talk about disability, ability, impairment, the body, pleasure and desire, as well as society, culture, biology and politics.
- I draw upon some key tensions between certain perspectives that are explored in disabled people's *own* stories in the following chapters.

Theory and theorising, quite rightly, can be messy jobs. In this chapter I create a real mess, applying myriad critical theories such as feminism, interactionism, phenomenology, poststructuralism, and crip, queer, postmodern and psychoanalytic approaches to disability, the body, gender, sexuality, identity, embodiment and subjectivity. This mess – to me – embodies critical disability studies, a theoretical movement that has unpacked the dominance of the social model in British Disability Studies and beyond. As Shakespeare and Watson (2001: 19) argue, 'a modernist theory of disability – seeking to provide an overarching meta-analysis covering all dimensions of every disabled person's experience – is not a useful or attainable concept'. Rather, critical disability studies form a politicised, ethical and transdisciplinary space – one that Goodley (2011a: 174) argues 'connects the aspirations and ambitions of disabled people with the transformative agendas of class, feminist, queer and postcolonial studies'. Critical disability studies enables focus, then, on the intersections of disability life, connecting disability with the politics of class, race, ethnicity, gender and sexuality. Moreover, they do so in ways that stay mindful of local, national and global economic contexts and the impact of these upon disabled people (Goodley 2014). It has been questioned whether a more critical disability studies does indeed constitute a 'radical paradigm shift or simply signifies a maturing of the discipline' (Meekosha and Shuttleworth 2009: 48). Either way, as Meekosha and Shuttleworth (2009: 49) suggest, critical disability studies seek to build upon, but not discard, materialist approaches. They state:

Use of CDS signifies an implicit understanding that the terms of engagement in disability studies have changed; that the struggle for social justice and diversity continues but on another plane of development – one that is not simply social, economic and political, but also psychological, cultural, discursive and carnal.

(Meekosha and Shuttleworth 2009: 50)

Key to critical disability studies, for me, is its commitment to destabilising and contesting dis/ableism: its acknowledgement that studies of disability and ability are always political; that theory is not divorced from the everyday lived realities of disabled people, but begins there. Disability politics, of course, do not exist in a vacuum, but are intimately connected to the wider hegemony of ableism. Thus, at particular junctures I follow others (Campbell 2001, 2009; Davis 2002; Goodley 2014; Rose 2001) in turning my attention away from disability and onto ableist hegemony or 'ableist-normativity' (Campbell 2008: 1) – something now known as critical ableism studies or ability studies (Wolbring 2008) – which disrupts 'those normative homelands that all of us are forced to populate' (Goodley 2014: 194). In this way, using critical disability studies offers me a comprehensive 'theoretical toolbox' through which to explore the shifting boundaries of dis/ability (ability and disability), intimacy and sexuality, as well as the liminal spaces between.

In this chapter, I offer the theoretical, intellectual and political context to the sociological research detailed in this book. Typically, this chapter asks more questions than it answers as it makes its way through a smorgasbord of theoretical approaches, considering their usefulness and applicability towards understanding the sexual, intimate and erotic lives of disabled people. The chapter is divided into three sections. In the first, I concentrate on the problems and possibilities in theorising disability. I position the social model of disability as an inadequate analytical tool with which to explore disabled sexualities, and argue for an alternative, embodied conceptualisation of disablement. In the second, I consider the re/makings of sexual bodies and selves, drawing upon biological essentialism, discourse and the role of power, and forms of interactionism and script theory to question what these offer to a sexual politics of disability. In the third and final section, I imagine otherwise through queer theory and crip theory, asking not only where one ends and the other begins, but questioning their ability to forge out a new sexual politics of disability that speaks to the everyday lived lives of disabled people. In doing so I demarcate a series of productive tensions that follow in the remainder of this book. I conclude by questioning whether critical social theories, as currently constructed, can adequately theorise the lived, embodied and material realities of disabled people's sexual, intimate and erotic lives.

Conceptualising disability: criticality, activism and justice

I begin, then, by detailing the history of social theories of disability that have preceded more critical approaches, namely the 'strong social model' (Shakespeare and Watson 2001), and I outline some problems with using this model as a theoretical underpinning for my explorations. Importantly, I do so not to denigrate the (pioneering) work of others, but in acknowledgement that theorising sexuality, intimacy and the body, quite simply, requires more than materialist approaches can provide. Next, I draw upon more recent literatures that have turned their attention away from disability and cast it onto ableist hegemony in order to proffer alternative means through which disability can come to be understood. Importantly, throughout this section, and chapter, I stress the importance of balancing the theoretical with the *lived* – between reimagining otherwise through the possibilities that theory brings and understanding the material, political and embodied relations of disability and sexuality. Both are in play throughout this book, and often rub up against one another. This is a tension that is not easily resolved – at least until much later (see Chapter 8). To keep the lived and material at the centre, then, in this section I make use of disabled feminist interjections to 'malestream' structural disability theory that have centred pain, the body, emotion, subjectivity and the intimacies of disability life. Such perspectives, I argue, give way to examining the ways in which disabled people negotiate their sexual lives and selves in disablist cultures and through ableist structures, as well as acknowledging the potential psycho-emotional consequences of this labour.

A social model of disabled sexuality?

The social model of disability (Oliver 1990) was born out the Union of the Physically Impaired Against Segregation (UPIAS), an early founding organisation of the British disability movement that radically shifted the meaning of 'disability' from the bodies of individuals to a product of the social world. The social model offers a predominantly Marxist and materialist-orientated approach to disability, laying 'the blame for disabled people's oppression clearly at the feet of economic relations in capitalistic society' (Meekosha and Shuttleworth 2009: 55). Within the social model, 'impairment' as the bodily bio-physiological condition of disability is determinedly marginalised in favour of a focus on 'disability' as a complex set of social relations that structure the experience of impairment. In this sense, the social model mirrors early (mainstream) feminist movements that distinguished between sex (as a 'natural' entity) and gender (the cultural construction of one's sex) (Rubin 1975). Such revolutionary redefinitions were rooted firmly within disabled people's self-organisation and mobilisation of independence and civil rights movements in Britain (Barton and Oliver 1997; Campbell and Oliver 1996). This purposeful redirection of focus towards exclusory social environments, which consisted of 'social and environmental barriers such as inaccessible buildings and transport, discriminatory attitudes and negative cultural stereotypes' (Barnes and Mercer 2003: 1), was intended to disassociate disabled people from medico-scientific models of disablement which, as Siebers states (2001: 738), 'situate disability exclusively in individual bodies and strives to cure them by particular treatment, isolating the patient as diseased or defective'. This was disabled people's and their movements' radical rejection of and resistance to their medicalised and pathologised existence. As disabled feminist and artist Liz Crow (1996: 207) states, the introduction of the social model enabled a 'vision of ourselves free from the constraints of disability (oppression) and provided a commitment for our social change – I don't think it's an exaggeration to say the social model has saved lives'.

The consequence of this 'strong social model' (Shakespeare and Watson 2001), with its unrelenting focus on civil rights and structural disablism, was that it simultaneously omitted equal political focus towards the private and intimate lives of disabled people. This omission was felt strongly within disability rights movements, although it was seldom publicly acknowledged; as activist Anne Finger (1992: 8) stated in an early edition of the *New Internationalist,*

> Sexuality is often the source of our deepest oppression; it is also often the source of our deepest pain. It's easier for us to talk about – and formulate strategies for changing – discrimination in employment, education, and housing than to talk about our exclusion from sexuality and reproduction.

Finger's words are reproduced in most scholarly writings on disability and sexuality, and this is no coincidence: her words reach the very heart of key problems within the disability rights movements of the era. The marginalisation of sexual politics in favour of a focus on 'survival level issues' (Waxman Fiduccia 2000: 168) has, Shakespeare (1999: 54) argues, been at the expense of the more 'personal and individual dimensions of oppression', such as lived experiences of impairment, sexuality and identity. The disinclination of rights movements and disability studies, as a scholarly discipline, to attend to matters of sexuality and relationships – something Margrit Shildrick (2007b: 226) calls the 'self-censorship of the disability movement itself' – has been attributed to early social model proponents (Finkelstein 1980; Hunt 1981; Oliver 1990) who, in their eagerness to see society and the state, rather than disabled people, as the problem, wrote both the material body and subjective experiences out of their theorisations. Such a silence has served only to reproduce society's attitudes and contribute to disabled people's lack of sexual culture (Shakespeare 1996; Siebers 2008). According to Shakespeare (2000: 159), the reluctance to discuss sexuality was primarily about prioritisation, but also because the movement in Britain at that time 'consciously tapped into the tradition of labour movement organizing and adopted the paradigms of trades unionism and socialism, rather than the paradigms of consciousness raising and feminism'. Fittingly, the 'Movement' at that time was predominantly led by disabled men (Morris 1991) who ratified hardline direct action, or 'macho politics' (Shakespeare 2000: 160), rather than a focus on more subjective and 'domestic' issues.

Such significant omissions has meant that the social model of disability has been subjected to a substantial amount of critique and debate (Begum 1992; Crow 1996; Gabel and Peters 2004; Hughes and Paterson 1997; Keith 1990; Light 2000; Lonsdale 1990; Meekosha 1998; Morris 1991, 1993; Rembis 2010; Shakespeare and Watson 2001, 2002; Shakespeare *et al.* 1996; Thomas 1999;

Wendell 1996). Wide-ranging critiques from feminist, critical realist, poststructural and postmodern theorists have challenged the social model on various grounds: its rigidity and anti-experiential nature (Corker and Thomas 2002); its masculinist and outdated principles (Crow 1996); its overlooking of the psycho-emotional consequences of disablement (Thomas 1999); its disembodied conceptualisation of disablement (Shakespeare and Watson 2001); its somatophobia (Williams 1999); and, perhaps most importantly for the explorations in this book, its 'inability to recognise sexual agency' (Gabel and Peters 2004: 594) and the way in which it has 'little or nothing to say on the subject of sexuality and has no place for the question of desire in particular' (Shildrick 2007b: 228).

Lives, selves and bodies

Critiques of the social model were initially articulated through disabled feminists talking openly about their own bodies and experiences of impairment (see Crow 1996; Lonsdale 1990; Thomas 1999; Wendell 1996). Doing so echoed the 'deconstruction of the public/private divides' (Sherry 2004: 776) advocated by mainstream feminist theorists of the time. It is important to state at this early juncture, however, that while the deconstruction of public/private was influenced by second wave feminism, it was disabled feminists' *own* engagement with these ideas that instigated important changes for disabled women, rather than via support from their non-disabled sisters whose 'narrow notions of womanhood' (Wilkerson 2002: 39) have largely excluded and overlooked the experiences of disabled women – something Sandoval (1991) labels 'hegemonic feminism' (Begum 1992; Fine and Asch 1988; Garland-Thomson 2002; Keith 1990; Lonsdale 1990; Morris 1991, 1993, 1996; Schriempft 2001; Thomas 1999; Wendell 1996). This is perplexing given that, as Jenny Morris (1996: 1) argues, 'disability is a women's issue – in that the majority of disabled people are women – yet the experiences of disabled women have been largely absent from feminism's concerns'. Indeed (mainstream) feminist explorations of reproductive rights, motherhood, and forms of violence, abuse and caring have predominantly excluded the experiences of disabled women from their analyses (Garland-Thomson 2002; Morris 1996). While there have been noteworthy exceptions of non-disabled feminists interrogating their own inherent ableism (see Lloyd 2001; Rohrer 2005), this is a critique extendable to social theory more generally, since disability is typically omitted from intersectional analyses of gender, race, sexuality, age, and class (see Kimberlé Crenshaw's work for an understanding of intersectionality, 1989, 1991). Or, as Davis (2002: 32) states, the 'majority of academics do not consider disability to be part of their social conscience' and this despite the fact that 'disability, like gender and race, is everywhere, once we know how to look for it' (Garland-Thomson 2002: 28).

As well as instigating recognition of impairment and the body, disabled feminists of this period made significant strides in locating gender within analyses of disability; a distinctly under-theorised dimension of disabled people's lives. Locating gender was important for multiple reasons: (i) to challenge the *degendered* identities of disabled people, the notion that disabled people are stripped of and/ or denied a gender identity (see Shakespeare 1997); (ii) to recognise that disabled women are relatively more disadvantaged than disabled men through patriarchy (Thomas 2006); and (iii) to establish that the powers and processes that construct both gender and disability are intimately connected and tightly bound (Thomas 2006). Early disabled feminist scholarship aimed to define experiences of gender and disability, and later race, as constituting multiple oppressions (see Begum 1992; Deegan 1995; Fine and Asch 1985). However, disabled feminist Jenny Morris (1998: 5) declared of such developments: 'I feel burdened by disadvantage and I feel a victim – such writings do not empower me.' Positioning the intersections of disability and gender in this way was argued to miss 'the social relational connections between them and the particular ways in which different configurations of disability and gender affect individual and group experiences' (Traustadóttir 2006: 82). Moreover, it has previously been argued in what Shakespeare (1999b: 57) calls 'the traditional account' that cultural constructions of disability conflict more with dominant constructions of masculinities than femininities (see Connell 1995; Murphy 1990): 'femininity and disability reinforce each other, [while] masculinity and disability conflict with each other' (Shakespeare 1999b: 57) – a crude assumption unpacked later.

However, later works offered more sophisticated analyses of disability and gender, and drew upon other axes of identity, such as sexual orientation and race, to show that disability influences, impacts and informs lived experiences of gender in myriad ways (Gerschick 2000). For example, Gerschick (2000) reminds us that the type, origin, effects, visibility and trajectory of impairment can further mediate experiences of gender and impact upon the ability (or desire) to perform socially and culturally 'appropriate' gender identities. Ultimately, patriarchy, sexism and misogyny ensure that the majority of disabled men have greater access to forms social, political and economic power than disabled women. As Goodley (2011a: 35) reminds us, disabled women are 'more likely to be poor than disabled men; are less likely to have access to rehabilitation and employment; are more likely to experience public space as threatening; and are more likely to live in the parental home and experience sexual abuse'. What is also important to recognise, however, within these early inclusions of gender is the extent to which they made use of binary distinctions – the binary (either/or) being a key characteristic of conceptualisations of the time: medical/social, able/ disabled and impairment/disability (see Fawcett 2000). Thus, initial disabled feminist contestations of gender unquestionably upheld the normative gender binary and what Butler (1990: 5) calls the heterosexual matrix: 'the grid of cultural intelligibility through which bodies, genders and desires are naturalised'. Thus, at this time, there was little recognition of gendered (sexual) lives that sat extraneous to the (naturalised) categories of male and female. I return to this critique later in the chapter.

In short, disabled feminists called for 'a renewed social model of disability' (Crow 1996: 218). Important within this struggle was the recognition of the differences between impairment and the embodiment of other oppressed groups, and the acknowledgement of impairment as a potentially negative bodily state. As Crow (1996: 209; original emphasis) states, 'sexuality, sex, and skin colour are neutral facts. In contrast, impairment means our experiences of our bodies *can* be unpleasant or difficult'. The (problematic) assertion of skin colour as a 'neutral fact' speaks to the inherent Whiteness of disabled feminism of the time (Abu-Habib 1997; Begum 1992). While I think there is space for more nuance here – particularly along the lines that impairment-only-as-negative is confining and exclusory (as I come onto later) – Crow's assertions highlighted the collective desire to bring the (gendered) body back into theories of disability, both reflecting and contributing to the trend within other areas of sociology to 'bring the body back' (which, ironically, have largely omitted the impaired body) (see Leder 1990; Shilling 2003), and acknowledging that for many the impaired body 'experiences real pain, nausea, fatigue and weakness' (Thomas 2002a: 69; see also Morris 1991). It is not by coincidence, however, that such calls were primarily from women with physical and sensory impairments, at the same time excluding the lives (and concerns) of women with the labels of learning disability and mental illness. As McCarthy (2009) states, learning disabled women are still 'regarded as fundamentally different from other women'. We can draw similarities here to the lives of Black women who, in contexts of slavery, were excluded from the category of 'woman' (as the subject), yet still allowed entry into the category of 'female' (Carby 1987, in Tremain 2000). The exclusion of *women* with learning disabilities from both feminist and disability rights analyses of the time is palpable (see also Rodgers 2001), and this remains prevalent today, despite the fact that the (sexual) lives, bodies and selves of learning-disabled women remain overtly targeted for many of the interventions disabled feminists protest (e.g. forced sterilisation; the removal of children), being routinely denied their reproductive and parenting rights (McCarthy 2009). The burgeoning psychiatric survivor movement, also known as the Mad movement, has offered similar critiques that speak to the lives of those who experience distress and/or live with mental illness diagnoses (see Beresford *et al.* 2010; LeFrançois *et al.* 2013).

Feminist developments of the 'strong' social model (Shakespeare and Watson 1997), then, which draw upon gender, subjectivity, embodiment and impairment not only permit a more helpful focus on sexuality and intimacy but enable an analytical focus on the intersections of disability with other social identity categories, currently missing from much disability and sexuality research (Shuttleworth 2010; see also Hughes and Paterson 1997; Kanguade 2010). As Goodley (2011a: 33) states, 'a body or mind that is disabled is also one that is raced, gendered, trans/nationally sited, aged, sexualized and classed'. Instead, disabled feminist developments of the social model avow an appreciation of the differences *between* disabled people (Thomas 2002a) – that disabled people are not a homogenous group – and thus enable inclusion of their multiple social identities (see Vernon 1999). Considering the intersections of gender and disability also offers opportunities to explore disabled men's (and others') experiences of masculine subjectivities and identities, which remains under-researched and undertheorised (Gerschick and Miller 1995; Shakespeare *et al.* 1996; Vernon 1999), while centring what are considered 'disabled women's issues' (namely sexuality, motherhood, reproduction, imagery, and relationships) that have been excluded from the 'malestream' of disability theory and political life (Deegan and Brooks 1985).

Furthermore, in advocating for gendered subjectivities and theorising through their own lived and embodied experiences, disabled feminists also reified the ways in which structural and patriarchal oppression *felt*. Related to one's lived experiences of the body, and of ableism, are the ways in which we feel about, relate to and care for our bodies. As Goodley (2011: 716) states,

> oppression is felt psychically, subjectively and emotionally but is always socially, cultural, politically and economically produced. And, as Thomas (2006: 182) proposes, psycho-emotional disablism is a mode of 'disablism that works with and upon gendered realities; it operates along psychological and emotional pathways and frequently results in disabled people being made to feel worthless, useless, of lesser value, unattractive, a burden'.

Central to this, then, are disabled people's psychic responses to living in disabling cultures: the psycho-emotional consequences of sexual oppression and the ways in which this may be internalised, managed, negotiated and resisted. As Marks (1999: 615) puts it, 'it is important to examine not just the relationship that people have with others, but also the relationship they have with themselves'.

Thus the disabled psyche, produced within an ableist cultural imaginary, is central to the lived, emotional and affective experiences of sexual and intimate life; it plays an important role within the re/construction of gendered sexual selves in dominant cultures where they are routinely disavowed. In her analysis of anxiety, desire and disability, Shildrick (2007b: 221) draws attention to Western anxiety at the expression of erotic desire that 'cannot be subsumed unproblematically under the rubric of the normative body'. Shildrick (2007b) suggests that the cultural imaginary closes down the possibilities of a disabled sexual self because the anomalously embodied disabled sexual subject represents the pinnacle of Western anxiety surrounding both the erotic and disablement. While the erotic, 'the coming together of any bodies and more specifically the intercorporeality of much sexuality', already causes anxiety within us all because of the 'loss of self-definition' such sexual relations entail, then this anxiety is at 'its most acute where the body of the other already breaches normative standards of embodiment' (Shildrick 2007b: 226). For disabled people, this results in disqualification from discourses of sexuality but also raises the 'contested question of who is to count as a *sexual* subject' (Shildrick 2007b: 221; original emphasis).

Therefore, disabled feminist calls for the consideration of disabled people's material, subjective, affective, embodied and gendered experiences proffer a crucial development, but one which remains politically contentious 'since it tugs – somewhat disconcertingly – at the key conceptual distinction which was at the heart of the transformation of disability discourse from medical problem to emancipatory politics' (Hughes and Paterson 1997: 326). Such theoretical developments have, as Goodley (2011a: 28) identifies, 'sparked outrage' from (some) male architects of the social model who have, without any hint of irony around their own sexism, called these 'sentimental biography' (Barnes 1998, in Goodley 2011a: 28). Or as Finkelstein (1996: 11) put it, 'finding insight in the experiences of discrimination is just a return to the old case file approach to oppression, dressed up as social model jargon'. Michael Oliver (1996: 52) has also criticised these intellectual developments, claiming that they 'stretch the social model further than it is intended to go'. Furthermore, it has been suggested by others (see Light 2000; Sheldon *et al.* 2007) that, rather than merely critiquing the social model, disability scholars should propose some meaningful alternatives. Critiques from poststructuralist disabled feminist Marian Corker (in Thomas and Corker 2002: 23) suggest that the inclusion of lived experiences of impairment within theorisations of disablement can mean that 'impairment is often conflated with personal experience and thus remains firmly located at the level of the individual'. Furthermore, she argues that embodying disability in such ways has shrouded impairment in negativity, and therefore dampened the potentially extraordinary, productive and pleasurable possibilities of impairment that more recent critical approaches now emphasise (Thomas and Corker 2002). I come on to detail these later in the third and final section of this chapter, where I get up close to crip and queer, exploring how these enable a revision of impairment. Other critiques centre on the notion that merely describing impairment and its bodily effects is to render it unproblematised, treating it only as 'biological' reality, and 'an objective, transhistorical and transcultural entity' (Tremain 2002: 34; see also Corker 1999; Hughes and Paterson 1997): an 'untouched, unchallenged; a taken-for-granted fixed corporeality' (Meekosha 1998: 175) rather than a relational, constructed and negotiable aspect of the human experience that is always historically and culturally located and produced.

What to do with 'impairment'?

I use the word 'impairment' throughout this book, more out of habit (and due to *growing up* in British Disability Studies, where it dominates) than because I equate 'impairment' with 'the state or fact of being impaired' (Oxford English Dictionary 2017), or because I see value in upholding the social modellist impairment/disability distinction whereby impairment constitutes some kind of biological truth. Quite the contrary, impairment requires as much political and theoretical debate as 'disability'. The *danger* of not sufficiently theorising impairment alongside disability in general terms, then, Marks (1999: 611) argues, means that 'a theoretical vacuum is left, which is filled by those who adopt an individualistic and decontextualised perspective'. Paterson and Hughes (1999: 597–598) suggest that disability studies' unembodied conceptualisations have overlooked bodily agency; that the 'Cartesianised subject it [disability studies] produces does not provide for an emancipatory politics of identity'. Carol Thomas (2002a: 20) argues that, not only does the *experience* of impairment need to be considered, but 'impairment effects', which she defines as 'the direct effects of impairment which differentiate bodily functioning from that which is socially construed to be normal or usual'. The rationale for considering 'impairment effects' is, as Thomas maintains (2002: 20), that 'in our society, these impairment effects generally, but not always, become the medium for the social relational enactment of disability: social exclusionary and discriminatory practices'. In short impairment effects contribute to people's lived and embodied experiences of disability, as well as their experiences of dis/ableism. There is, then, a need for a sociology or social theory of impairment *alongside* disablement, quite simply because the body and impairment do not exist outside of culture (Paterson and Hughes 1999; see also Goodley and Runswick-Cole 2012).

Hughes and Paterson (1999: 329) suggest that in order to move past social model perspectives which problematically construct the body as 'devoid of meaning, a dysfunctional, anatomical, corporeal mass obdurate in its resignification and phenomenologically dead, without intentionality or agency', phenomenology is the means through which to reconceptualise the impaired body as entwined with culture, the social and embodiment. Phenomenology proposes that our bodies are the means through which the outside world is experienced (Merleau-Ponty 1962). Davy (2010: 181) argues that this helps us to recognise the body/self as an overlapping totality, 'which rests upon, amongst other aspects, corporeal capacities and intentionality'. Following Merleau-Ponty (1962), intentionality, Davy (2010: 181) suggests, is defined as 'a consciousness about something in relation to the lived body and the world in which it dwells'. Paterson and Hughes (1999: 609) argue that impairment materialises through experience:

> Oppression is not simply produced by structural barriers, it is manifest in corporeal and intercorporeal norms and conventions, and can be read in and through the ways in which 'everyday encounters' can go astray. From this perspective we can begin to analyse how impairment is produced as experience.

Davy (2010) argues that, because of its focus on the corporeality of knowledge and experience, phenomenology has been overlooked by disability scholars who are cautious of its application to disability and impairment for fear of affirming individualising discourses or narratives of disability. However, she argues that 'disability scholars seem to be equating bodily capacities with those of a universalized normative (masculine) standard, which is not necessarily the case in phenomenological interpretations'. Rather, phenomenology can be used to 'decentralise the universalized non-disabled body and draw attention to gender relations and sexual difference, illustrating that it can be useful for understanding bodies from other than what is assumed' (Davy 2010: 181; see also Young 1990). However, disability theorist Shildrick (2009: 32) argues that mainstream phenomenology 'implies that those who do not seemingly intermesh with the world as embodied subjects experience bodily discontinuities as disruptions or blockages to their own self-possession'. Thus, she suggests, the body 'becomes an unwelcome presence which signals limitation and vulnerability' (Shildrick 2009: 32); therefore becoming a body that is treated only as a problem and thus always inherently pathologisable. While I have only just begun to sketch out some of the theoretical deliberations, dalliances and debates that surround impairment, I return to these later in the chapter. First, however, I move forward to look at the essentialist constructions of the *normative* sexual body (and by extension, its deviations), and their very constructed naturalness, before returning to explore (impaired) bodies as inherently social and discursive, produced through polymorphous power (Foucault 1976) and given meaning through the (dis/ableist) relations of everyday interactions (Brickell 2006).

The re/makings of sexual bodies and selves

Biological bodies

Early constructionism, which was rooted in phenomenological and interactionist sociology, redefined the scholarly field of sexualities from the 1960s onwards (see Gagnon and Simon 1973). Constructionism enabled a rejection of essentialist 'pre-social' notions of sexuality towards an understanding of sexuality as socially, politically, and culturally produced (Jackson and Scott 2010): 'shaped through a system of social, cultural and interpersonal processes' (Villanueva 1997: 18). Essentialist perspectives of sexuality root sexual expression and desire as purely biological in nature, which arguably denies human agency and autonomy (Jackson 1999). In this vein, sexuality emerges as an 'ethological fallacy' (Gagnon and Simon 1973: 3) that pays no heed to humans as 'complex, arbitrary and changeable creatures' (Weeks 1986: 46). Such conceptualisations of sexuality are rooted in a eurocentric and Humanist biological essentialism that posits human sexuality as 'the most spontaneously natural thing about us' (Weeks 1986: 13). Through such a lens, sexuality is 'innate, instinctual, animalistic, and physiological law' (Weeks 1986: 13). Biological approaches to sexuality both maintain and reproduce a heteronormative order based upon traditional binary modes of gender, from which disabled and myriad Othered bodies are routinely excluded (Liddiard 2014c). For example, the 'male' is situated as dominant, animalistic, and powerful: a reductionist phallocentrism places significant emphasis on stamina, performance, and bodily function, which can serve to emasculate disabled men and obstruct disabled masculinities (Drench 1992; Murphy 1990; Shakespeare 1996). Inevitably, such essentialist approaches put reproductive function at the heart of sexuality: for biological determinists, 'sexuality is both definable and explicable in terms of a reproductive imperative' (Jackson 1999: 5). Thus, in an ableist cultural imaginary where rights to reproduction are awarded only to those deemed the fittest (Tepper 2000), a mode of sexuality defined by reproduction is deeply problematic in contexts of disability. As Waxman Fiduccia (2000: 169) suggests, 'sexual rights have always and only been awarded to those who are proclaimed to deliver quality offspring'; thus biomedicine seeks to control and regulate the fertility of the dangerous disabled female. By regulating female sexuality and reproduction, as suggested by Waxman Fiduccia (2000) and others (e.g. Anderson and Kitchen 2000; Kent 2002; Lee and Heykyung 2005), the disabled female body is denied reproductive justice and freedom (Waxman and Finger 1991).

Biological essentialism is also central to the discipline of Sexology – an 'empiricist approach that focuses on the study and classification of sexual behaviours, identities and relations' (Bland and Doan 1998: 1) – which made sex an 'object of study' for the first time (Hawkes 1996: 56). For example, the works of Kinsey (1948, 1953), Chesser (1950), and Masters and Johnson (1966) espoused biomedical sexological knowledges of human sexuality that made visible and measurable what came to be known as the key stages of the archetypal human sexual experience. Such physiological norms, established by sexual medicine, are problematic for a majority of bodies, but particularly for those labelled impaired. For example, Masters and Johnson's (1966) sexual response cycle quantified and charted the physiological aspects of sexuality – a normative, linear trajectory of pleasure: attraction, arousal, climax, orgasm and resolution. Through interviews, statistical tests and the direct observation of manual masturbation and intercourse, collected physiological and anatomical data became the benchmark for new scientific and cultural understandings of human sexuality. Such study firmly established a 'physiological norm' of the sexually able body, legitimised through expert clinical and scientific knowledges. Such homogenising material norms firmly rooted the ability and necessity to 'achieve', reach and strive for orgasm (Tepper 2002) as central to sexuality in ways that rendered alternative experiences of pleasure as dysfunctional, inadequate and in need of treatment (Bullough 1994; Hawkes 1996). Masters and Johnson (1974: 28) asserted the orgasm as 'authentic, abiding satisfaction that makes us feel like complete human beings', establishing what Tepper (2000: 287) calls the 'orgasm imperative in our culture' and the common anthropocentric, self-aggrandising notion that to orgasm is to be human (see Chapter 6).

The construction of a functionally normative sexual body – re/produced through what Tepper (2000: 288) calls 'a genitally focused and performance orientated conception of sexuality' – devalues the potentialities of impairment for sexual pleasure, expression and desire. A relentless focus on body *function* means that sexuality becomes the province of doctors and other related professionals who become 'gate-keepers' within sexual and intimate life (Shakespeare *et al.* 1996). For disabled people, it places the fate of a sexual self at the mercy of a paradigm that devalues the possibilities of their bodies (Anderson and Kitchen 2000; Hahn 1981; Milligan and Naudfeldt 2001; Tepper 1999, 2000), serving to (further) medicalise their lives and bodies and place the onus of disability (and sexual 'failure') back onto the individual. Medicine's propagation of the physiological norm of the sexually able body, Shakespeare *et al.* (1996: 66) argue, invites a biomedical gaze which reinforces and advocates the need for sexual treatments and therapies, and serves to contribute to the medical voyeurism of disabled people as 'subjects and fetishized objects' (Shakespeare *et al.* 1996: 3; see also Solvang 2007; Waxman Fiduccia 1999).

Social bodies: discourse and power

Disability theorists have long utilised poststructuralism, particularly Foucauldian theory and the role of discourse, applying it to critically examine both disability and impairment (see Shildrick and Price 1996; Tremain 2000, 2002). Michel Foucault (1976: 136) proposes that power operates between and through bodies via mechanisms of self-discipline, rather than through repressive powers in the form of physical forces extraneous to the body. Thus, for Foucault (1976: 136), the body is rendered 'docile', 'subjected, used, transformed, and improved'. However, although Foucault's docile body is problematically degendered (Bartky 1990; Jackson 1999; Marshall and Katz 2002; Ramazanoglu 1993; Smart 1992), and has been argued to portray 'disabled people as largely passive witnesses to discursive practices' (Barnes and Mercer 2003: 86; see also Thomas 2006), Foucauldian theory has inevitable uses towards interrogating what constitutes impairment and its inherent naturalness (Tremain 2000). From a discursive point of view, as Tremain (2000: 296) suggests,

'The body' has no pre-given materiality, structure, or meaning prior to its articulation in discourse. Rather, the very articulation of 'a (material) body' in discourse is a dimension of what materializes that 'body' in the first place.

For example, Foucault's (1976: 140) biopower, defined as 'an explosion of numerous and diverse techniques for achieving the subjugations of bodies and the control of populations', is relevant to the ways in which the impaired body, as naturalised through discourse, has been observed, treated, and eradicated through the contemporary and historic eugenicist efforts that surround impaired bodies, minds and people (Morris 1991; Sobsey 1994; Tremain 2005; Waxman 1994). As an entity that is 'educated, parented, observed, tested, measured, treated, psychologised' (Goodley 2011a: 114), the impaired body materialises through a host of disciplinary practices and institutional discourses. Hughes and Paterson (1997: 332) assert that even 'somatic sensations themselves are discursively constructed', because the meaning of such corporeal experience is articulated through language.

Not surprisingly, this discursive body is heavily contested within certain critical realist corners of disability studies. Critical realism defines the body as 'a *real* entity, no matter what we call it or how we observe it. It also, like all other social and natural domains, has its own mind-independent generative structures and causal mechanisms' (Williams 1999: 806). While this runs counter to my own ways of thinking about bodies, it is important to consider the consequences of what it *means* to consider impairment as predominately discursive – or, rather, the (disability) politics of positioning impairment as that which doesn't exist outside of discourse. One argument, of course, is that this denies the body's materiality and people's lived and embodied experiences of impairment, which may include pain, exhaustion, and immobility. For example, disability activist, writer and performer Cheryl Marie Wade (1994: 88–89) emphasises this position:

> To put it bluntly – because this is as blunt as it gets – we must have our arse cleaned after we shit and pee, or we have others' fingers inserted into our rectums to assist shitting. The blunt, crude realities… If we are ever to really be at home in the world and in ourselves, then we must say these things out loud. And we must say them with real language.

Thus the primary concern is that, as Wendell (1996: 45) argues, 'in post-modern cultural theorising about the body, there is no recognition of the hard physical realities faced by disabled people'. In this sense, overlooking the role of such 'hard physical realities' counters the notion that impairment (and its bodily effects) may play an integral role within disabled people's interpretations of their own gendered sexual bodies and identities. Thus, while impairment is produced and materialised through discourse (Tremain 2000), postmodern discursive theory fails to give enough credence to the pragmatic gritty realities of impairment and, more importantly, the meanings of such realities to disabled people. The tension between these ways-of-thinking-through-bodies is woven through most chapters of this book, as disabled informants centre lived experiences of their bodies in their sexual stories. However, while it is imperative to recognise and acknowledge such theoretical tensions, it is not to say that these differing perspectives cannot be applied in an additive manner, or that they both propose totalising ideologies that cannot be viewed through a more nuanced lens. As Thomas (2006: 60) proposes, the challenge in building a 'non-reductionist materialist ontology of the body and of impairment' is to move beyond the dualisms that plague our thinking, 'especially essentialism/constructionist; biology/society; nature/culture'.

Importantly, Foucauldian perspectives open up consideration of the ways in which sexuality, the body and desire are discursively constructed and maintained in contexts of dis/ability. Through his rejection of the repressive hypothesis in the first volume of his *History of Sexuality*, Foucault (1976) positions sexuality as a discursive and historical construct, suggesting that the apparent 'repression' of the sexual in Victorian society was underwritten by proliferation of and incitement to discourse – a 'discursive explosion' – which paradoxically produced sexualities, constructing them through emerging knowledges of the body, self and sexual behaviour, which instigated intimate lives and bodies to be further observed, scrutinised, pathologised – a legitimised form of surveillance enacted through social institutions such as Sexology, pedagogy, medicine, psychiatry, social welfare and law. In the context of sexual life, biopower is both executed and enabled through the very act of defining, labelling and categorising sexual behaviour. Foucault's primary concern, then, was not *what* was spoken about sex or necessarily its public prohibition, but,

> To account for the fact that it is spoken about, to discover who does the speaking, the positions and viewpoints from which they speak, the institutions which prompt people to speak about it and which store and distribute

the things that are said. What is at issue [is] the way in which sex is put into discourse.

(Foucault 1976: 11)

This makes space for consideration of the ways in which disabled desires come to be Othered, policed through a variety of social institutions, practices, and bodies – education, segregation, material deprivation, criminalisation, shame and psycho-emotional disablism, and prescriptive and utilitarian social policy, amongst others (Shildrick 2007b; see also Liddiard and Slater 2017) – which render disabled people and bodies at the margins of human sexuality. As Kafer (2003: 85) suggests, 'while the sexuality of disabled people may be denied in conversations, it is being denied loudly and repeatedly, not silently' (see also McRuer 2006a). Such *volume* is inevitably made possible by disablism and ableism, which are imposed upon self and society, as Foucault would argue, through 'a multiplicity of discourses produced by a whole series of mechanisms operating in different institutions'.

In this way, for Foucault power is 'the tangible but forceful reality of social existence and of all social relations' (Weeks 1986: 7). Rather than purely repressive, power is 'polymorphous' (Foucault 1976: 11); it is negotiable and interchangeable, and can take a variety of forms. Meekosha and Shuttleworth (2009: 57) argue that Foucault's perspective on power is of great value to critical disability studies because it 'performs a radical de-familiarisation of modern institutions and practices as caring and benevolent and reveals technologies and procedures that classify, normalise, manage, and control anomalous body-subjects'. They argue that it moves disability studies to consider 'not only legitimate and overt forms of control, but also a micropolitics of power in which modern human beings are complicit with their subjection' (Meekosha and Shuttleworth 2009: 57). Crucially, such flows of power demarcate the ways in which disabled people (and those who care for them) may (un/knowingly) act as their own oppressors, being complicit in their own suppression through internalised ableism: the emotional, psychological and psychic barriers that serve to subjugate the self and encourage, as Campbell (2009) suggests, the disabled individual to emulate the norm; a form of 'epistemic invalidation' (Goodley 2014: 97; see also Marks 1999). At the same time, however, Gabel and Peters (2004: 592) suggest that 'the circulation of power through social relations' can make space for forms of resistance. Indeed, the very idea of power as polymorphous makes space for thinking about the ways in which disability and sexuality are contoured by (dis/ableist) social and political processes, but more importantly the ways in which disabled people might enact, claim or assert sexual agency when negotiating a sexual self and identity.

Yet Foucault's undervaluing of structural and political power is important to consider, particularly in the context of disability. The assumption that disciplinary powers are more *containing* than political powers is to 'ignore important political transformations' (Weeks 1986: 9). As proponents of sexual citizenship claim, sexual citizenship and civil citizenship are interlaced and mutually dependent (e.g. see Giddens 1992; Plummer 1995; Richardson 1998; Weeks 1998). For disability theorist Abby Wilkerson (2002: 33, 35), 'sexual agency is integral to political agency' – we can't imagine one without the other: they are interlaced and mutually dependent – and thus 'sexual democracy should be recognised as a key political struggle' of disabled people. Therefore, as Siebers (2008: 154) contests, if we are 'to liberate disabled sexuality and give to disabled people a sexual culture of their own, their status as sexual minority requires the protection of citizenship rights similar to those being claimed by other sexual minorities'. It is also pertinent, as Jackson and Scott (2010: 17) remind us, to acknowledge that Foucault's privileging of juridico-discursive models of power over patriarchal power 'leaves us without the means of effectively analysing power over others and the production of systematic inequalities – including those of gender'. For example, discursive constructions of (sexual) competence, the act of being a sexual pleasure provider, of desire and the naturalisation of sex, and the need for sexual skill and introspection, are all gendered discourses (Jackson and Scott 1997). Inevitably, sexual competence – the necessity of being a 'skilled' lover – they state, is highly gendered:

> Where women are seen as candidates for therapeutic intervention this is still largely seen as a problem 'in their heads', a mental 'block' to be overcome. The model is one of repression causing 'impaired desire' or 'orgasmic dysfunction' from which women need to be 'liberated'. Male 'dysfunctionality' is more likely to be located in the body, localised in the penis. However elaborate and varied the sexual practices recommended in modern sex manuals have become, the syntax of heterosexual sex has largely remained unaltered: increasingly elaborate foreplay still leads to coitus. However skilled a man might be with hands or tongue, if his penis isn't up to it, he has failed in his performance.
>
> (Jackson and Scott 1997: 563)

Discursive constructionism, then, in a Foucauldian formation, doesn't offer much scope with which to explore the gendered dimensions of disabled sexualities, or the relative sexual power between disabled men, women and others who aren't situated within this binary. Failing to acknowledge or appreciate gender as a locus of power means ignoring the complexities at the intersections of gender, impairment and disability, as disabled feminists have long advocated (Morris 1989).

Intimate encounters and interactions

Jackson and Scott (2010) argue that a more proficient lens through which to explore the relationships between gender and sexuality is a symbolic interactionist one, on the grounds that it offers worthy possibilities for feminist analysis. While Foucauldian and other poststructuralist approaches to sexuality envision mass networks of disciplinary power as discursively constituting sexual life, they offer far less focus upon the everyday interactions through which meaning is experienced. In contrast, symbolic interactionist perspectives draw attention to subjective experiences of sexual identity to reinstate the 'significant dimensions of sexual life that are missing from Foucauldian approaches: everyday interpersonal interaction, the meanings deployed within it and the agency and reflexivity it entails' (Jackson and Scott 2010: 36).

Inevitably, disabled people's experiences of sexual opportunities, identities and encounters are not only re/produced through discourse engendered from a variety of (dis/ableist) social institutions, but emanate within and through their interpersonal interactions with others (although often these relationships are bound to institutions). In contexts of disability, sexual partners, teachers, personal assistants, parents, friends, peers, carers, doctors, physiotherapists and support staff can, knowingly and unknowingly, have a significant role in the shaping of disabled sexual subjectivities as well as disabled people's sexual access to and expressions of desire, sensuality and pleasure. As Jackson and Scott (1996: 97) suggest, the meaningful social reality of embodied sexual encounters are constituted through the 'meaning-making emergent from, and negotiated within, situated everyday interaction'.

According to Brickell (2006: 417), symbolic interactionism

> is used to explore how meanings are created, assembled, negotiated and modified by members of a society. It presumes meaning to be an emergent property of human interactions, not something intrinsic to an individual or a situation. Accordingly, we construct the meaning of our social world and our own lives through our interactions with other people, gathering together and negotiating meaning as we participate in social life. Our interpretations about what constitutes 'reality' are worked and reworked within multiple 'interaction orders': the domains of face-to-face interaction between people in given contexts, domains whose communications are governed by particular rules and conditions.

Thus, focusing upon the micro-sociological and the ways in which 'members of a society manipulate cultural resources – meanings and symbols – in order to construct a common world and their place in that world' (Brickell 2006: 416) facilitates a view of disabled people as active subjects, architects and negotiators of their sexual and gendered selves, and the meanings attached to such experiences (see Chapter 5). For Ken Plummer (1975: 13), interactionism focuses upon 'emergence and negotiation – the processes by which social action (in groups, organisations and societies) is constantly being constructed, modified, selected, checked, suspended, terminated and recommenced in everyday life'. Inevitably, such interactions do not take place in isolation and are always in relation to the other: 'interactionism highlights the ongoing construction of symbolic social worlds by men [sic] in *interaction with each other*' (Plummer 1975: 19, emphasis added). According to Brickell (2006: 416), it is through these 'meaning laden interactions that individual and collective identities develop'. For example, in the account below Katie Ball (2002: 170), an Australian grassroots disability rights activist who published the powerful essay 'Who'd Fuck an Ableist', describes how her sexual identity and self emerged in relation to interactions with others:

> Talk about close encounters of an ableist kind. I've been told by men that my vagina is ugly, that they can't fuck me because of my disability, that fucking me must be like fucking a rag doll, that they'd love to have a relationship with me, but that they can't handle the sight of my body. Most guys say they'll come over, and never show up. I've had guys come over, stand around in obvious discomfort, and then invent some lame excuse to go back to their car, never to be seen again. Two of them turned up one night. They rang me from their car, got me to come out into the street, and then shot through [left] as soon as they saw me.

While Ball's account doesn't speak explicitly to the impact such interactions have on her (she merely describes the interactions), she illustrates the critical relationships between interaction, self and Other, as we come to view such (brutal) interactions as the products of, and given meaning by, the intersections of misogyny, sexism, disablism and ableism. Ball's sexual self was, at that point in her life, constructed and located within and through these negative interactions with non-disabled men. The inherent dis/ableism within these everyday social interactions had significant psycho-emotional consequences that shaped her sexual self for the majority of her young adulthood (see Chapter 4). Furthermore, one cannot separate Ball's experience from her identity as a disabled *woman*. The fact her impaired body was objectified and ridiculed for its deviation from normative feminine and hegemonic Euro-American bodily beauty aesthetics marks how her gender is a part of her everyday reality and her experiences of disablism in this context (Thomas 2006). Therefore, while this is a literal example of the ways in which we collate, organise and mediate meaning through participation in the social world, it does once again emphasise the acute gendered experiences of living in contexts of dis/ableist sexual normalcy that not only serve to Other disabled sexualities, but which contribute to the makings of disabled sexual subjectivities.

The meanings of (crip) scripts?

> Without the proper elements of a script that defines the situation, names the actors, and plots the behaviour, nothing sexual is likely to happen.
>
> (Gagnon and Simon 1973: 19)

Emerging from symbolic interactionist perspectives is script theory (Simon and Gagnon 1969). Gagnon and Simon (1973: 19) propose that sexual scripts are 'involved in learning the meaning of internal states, organizing the sequences of specifically sexual acts, decoding novel situations, setting the limits on sexual responses, and linking meanings from non-sexual aspects of life to specifically sexual experience'. In short, this pertains to socially imbued scripts that act as guidelines that people use to direct their behaviour and social experiences (Dune and Shuttleworth 2009: 98). Gagnon and Simon (1973) propose three levels of script: cultural scenarios, interpersonal scripts and intrapsychic scripts. Cultural scenarios provide the 'larger frameworks and roles through which sex is experienced' (Kimmel 2007: xii). Interpersonal scripts 'represent the routine patterns of social interaction that guide behaviours in specific settings' (Kimmel 2007: xii). Intrapsychic scripts assume that 'social action is always conducted with an on-going internal dialogue about internalized cultural expectations' (Kimmel 2007: xii). Jackson (1999: 41) argues that scripting is inherently gendered: 'men and women have learnt to be sexual in different ways, sexual drama are scripted for actors who have different sexual vocabularies of motive and different orientations to and expectations of sexual relationships'. Thus, Jackson suggests (1999: 9), where other forms of social constructionism have largely written out gender, script theory foregrounds gender as 'central to the scripting of sexuality, the complex co-ordination of bodies and meanings which sexual relations entail' (see also Ramazanoglu 1993).

To 'insert' disability once again, then (in another space where it is omitted), means asking critical questions about how dominant scripts come into being, how they are made comprehensible and therefore accessed, and upon which types of bodies and selves they rest. If sexual scripting is based upon a notion of normative (gendered) sexual socialisation or the learning of sexual behaviours mediated through normative bodies, encounters and interactions, then it is likely that disabled people may have been denied access. Therefore, disabled sexualities (and the multifarious forms they can take) may conflict with or be unintelligible to dominant 'traditional sexual scripts' (Denov 2003) or, more likely, may remain 'unscripted' (Laws and Schwartz 1977). For example, Jackson (1999: 39) demarcates youth as *the* key time in which people learn the dominant scripts that 'govern adult sexual behaviour' and provide them 'a sexual vocabulary of motives'. The significant exclusion of disabled young people from the dominant cultures of youth (see Slater 2016), where such scripts are likely to be learned, organised and internalised can be understood, through a symbolic interactionist account, of why many disabled people grow up – as Shakespeare *et al.* (1996) phrase it – to lack the language of sex and love (see Chapter 4).

Dominant sexual scripts, then, seemingly perpetuate normative ideals and thus, I suggest, are 'written' for non-impaired bodies and minds. For example, Sakellariou's (2006: 108) research with spinal-cord-injured men found that following injury men struggled to articulate their new sexual identity within the dominant scripts of conventional male sexualities: 'they are torn between a social script that does not bear any resemblance to their life and a personal will that contradicts the social imperative of asexuality'. Similarly, Dune and Shuttleworth (2009: 100) identify what they call the dominant 'sexual script of spontaneity', which views spontaneity as *necessary* for *successful* sexual satisfaction and which may lead to dissatisfaction if spontaneity is absent. This negatively impacts upon a range of people who may have difficulty experiencing spontaneous sex (and overlooks that most of us are not swinging off the chandeliers when we get in from work) – but particularly those who live with particular impairments, pain or chronic illness (Dune and Shuttleworth 2009; see Gillespie-Sells *et al.* 1998), or who need care and support to access pleasure and intimacy with themselves and/or others. Thus, 'hegemonic sexual scripts and efforts to fulfill the expectations of sexual spontaneity can produce barriers to the expression of their sexuality' (Dune and Shuttleworth 2009: 105) (see Chapter 6).

'Queering the Crip or Cripping the Queer?' (Sandahl 2003)

Queering the other

As I stated at the outset of this chapter, critical disability studies interrogate and problematise hegemonic normalcy, its politics, its power, its language and its identity (Wilchins 2004) – in ways similar to queer theory's political project to de-essentialise identity (see Halperin 1995). Many disability scholars have acknowledged queer theory's contribution to a radical disability studies agenda (Breckenridge and Vogler 2001; Corbett 1994; McRuer 2006a; Sherry 2004; Sinecka 2008), acknowledging 'a synthesis of queer and disability theories' (Goodley 2011a: 41). Within this final section of the chapter, I work through my understandings of queer and crip, exploring where queer ends and crip begins. Whether they even have distinct and discrete borders remains unknown (see McRuer 2006a); as Carrie Sandahl (2003: 27) states, 'the fluidity of both terms makes it likely that their boundaries will dissolve'. Disability studies scholar Mark Sherry (2004: 769) identifies the similarities between the experiences of queer people and disabled people: 'familial isolation, high rates of violence, stereotypes and discrimination, and the difficulties associated with passing and coming out'. Relatedly, crip and queer share distinct theoretical overlap: 'their debt to feminism, their opposition to hegemonic normalcy, their strategic use of universalist and minority discourses, their deconstruction of essentialist identity categories and their use of concepts such as performativity'. Sandahl (2004: 769) reminds us that 'as academic corollaries of minority civil rights movements, queer theory and disability studies both have origins in and commitments to activism'. As Sherry (2004: 769) clarifies, queer and crip activist movements both 'flaunt', that is, seek to reclaim and redefine the language that at the same time oppresses them (see Clare 1999) and staunchly 'reject pathologisation, politicise access, and use humour and parody as political tools'. Sandahl (2003: 27) details this common ground:

> Both [disability and queer communities] have been pathologised by medicine; demonised by religion; discriminated against in housing, employment and education; stereotyped in representation; victimised by hate groups; and isolated socially, often in their families of origin. Both constituencies are diverse and therefore share many members, as well as allies. Both have self-consciously created their own enclaves and vibrant sub-cultural practices.

While these overlaps are important to keep in view, it's important to recognise that queer theory, in its purest sense, is by no means a 'unified perspective' (Jackson and Scott 2010: 19). It is also pertinent to be cautious of the myriad critiques of queer theory. For example, queer theory has been accused of overlooking the specifically gendered experience of sexual dissidents; neglecting the material conditions of women's lives through ignoring material and structural inequalities (Jackson 1999); overlooking the oppression of lesbians and 'discriminating against the interests of lesbians' (Jeffreys 1994: 459); acting as masculinist theory in costume (Smyth 1992); reducing gender to lexicon and overlooking embodiment (Bordo 1993); and distancing the category of woman from everyday lived reality (Fraser 1999).

Despite these important critiques – and they are important – as the (gendered) sexual stories in the remainder of this book will show, for me, queer offers a conversation about bodies, boundaries and binaries that cannot be ignored when theorising disabled, or crip, sexualities. Like crip, queer contests norms along multiple registers: 'corporeal, mental, sexual, social, cultural, subcultural' (Sandahl 2003: 26). Where sexuality is concerned, this comes in its attempts to reject the strict boundaries of hegemonic pleasure, desire and sexuality and its commitment to shatter the naturalised binaries of sex and gender – both of which alienate and Other disabled people with impaired bodies (amongst many others). Shildrick (2009: 85) states that theorists who engage with *queered* disability studies 'are increasingly problematising the conventional parameters of sexuality, in order to explore non-normative constructions of sexual identities, pleasures and agency that more adequately encompass multifarious forms of embodied difference'. Thus, *thinking through* queer facilitates thinking about disability, sex and gender in terms of their revolutionary potential, which is lost through other approaches (Rembis 2010: 54):

> Ironically, much of the social research on disabled sexuality and many of the pronouncements of disabled subjects, both of which have been concerned with 'defying sex/gender stereotypes' and challenging powerful cultural myths concerning disabled people, have served to reinforce, rather than challenge the heterosexual matrix.

Instead, making use of a queered critical disability studies enables us to challenge taken-for-granted hegemonies where sex and gender are concerned, positioning disability as a productive and vital threat to – or emancipation from – the heterosexual matrix (Butler 1990, 1993). As Rembis (2010) proposes, the sexual futures of disabled people must be based upon Davis's (2002: 31) notion of 'dismodernism' whereby 'impairment is the rule and normalcy is the fantasy':

> By loosening the conceptual ties that bind our perception of 'normal' relationships, we in turn open up new ways of thinking about sex and beauty. 'Dismodernism' has the potential to transform a society where people are expected to live a life free of pain and discomfort, a society where strict

social norms concerning beauty and physical fitness compel people to alter their bodies in drastic, often violent ways, through surgery, dieting, exercise, and other 'cosmetic' procedures, a society where youth, physical prowess and a very narrow idealization of heteronormative sexual allure are highly valued and sexual performance is wedded to one's physicality. Sex, eroticism, and desire, will look very different in a 'dismodern' world where 'cosmopolitanism,' interdependence and a reliance on technology are the 'norm.' In a 'dismodern' world, dis/abled bodies will become 'sexy' bodies.

Therefore it is not enough to merely assimilate disabled people, their (possible) alternative sexual practices, and their anomalous embodiment (Shildrick 2009) into a (hegemonic) heteronormativity that refuses to house them. Instead, disabled people's erotic freedom and their intimate futures must begin with exploring human sexuality according to a dismodernist ideology. By its very nature, a dismodernist society would emancipate the sexualities of *all* people: a sexual utopia.

Rather than settling for Sherry's (2004: 770) definition of queer as 'a range of sexual identities and practices which do not conform to heteronormativity', then, I acknowledge queer for its possibilities as a mode of transgression that produces (necessary) forms of disruption to the categories of 'able' 'sexual' and 'normal'. To use Goodley *et al.*'s (2017: 53) phraseology, 'queer contests the able individual, disputes the psychological, geographical and cultural normative centre and breaks fixed binaries'. I do so while recognising, as Alison Kafer reminds us (2013: 16), that queer is 'contested terrain, with theorists and activists continuing to debate what and (whom) the term encompasses or excludes'. For McRuer (2002: 222) queer theory emerges 'a diverse array of projects that explore the construction and shifting contemporary meanings of sexuality'. Importantly, critical disability studies interrogate the dis/ableist institutions and practices that re/produce the necessity and naturalness of the 'able' body and which contribute to thanatopolitics, defined by Rose (2001) as the increasingly ableist-obsessed nature of everyday life. It is through the construction of the disabled body as Other, grotesque and monstrous (see Goodley *et al.* 2015) that hegemonic normalcy is upheld (Davis 1995). Thus, not only does normalcy, as currently constructed, make possible disability, race, class and gender, but the construction of these Othered states legitimates and provides authority to notions of normalcy. Other theorists (see Michalko 2002) have highlighted the fragility of the non-impaired body by using the term TAB, or Temporarily Able Bodied, as a means through which to destabilise the apparent boundaries of dis/abled and normal/other. Helpfully, McRuer (2006a: 2) puts forward the concept of 'compulsory able-bodiedness' based upon feminist/queer notions of 'compulsory heterosexuality' (Rich 1989):

The system of compulsory able-bodiedness which in a sense produces disability, is thoroughly interwoven with the system of compulsory heterosexuality that produces queerness: that, in fact, compulsory heterosexuality is contingent on compulsory able-bodiedness and vice versa.

Thus an 'able' body is not a queer one, and a queered body is one that is 'disabled'. In much the same way that Butler (1990) posits heterosexual hegemony as maintained through repetitive performances of heterosexuality and heteronormativity, McRuer (2006a: 9) contends that 'institutions in our culture are showcases for able-bodied performance'. He maintains:

> The culture asking such questions assumes in advance that we all agree: able-bodied identities, able-bodied perspectives are preferable and that we all, collectively, are aiming for. A system of compulsory able-bodiedness repeatedly demands that people with disabilities embody for others an affirmative answer to the unspoken question, 'Yes, but in the end, wouldn't you rather be more like me?'
>
> (McRuer 2006a: 9)

Perhaps more importantly, McRuer (2006a: 9) suggests that, despite routine repetition of the heterosexual and able-bodied identity, both are doomed to fail: 'they are incomprehensible in that each is an identity that is simultaneously the ground on which all identities supposedly rest and an impressive achievement that is always deferred and thus never really guaranteed'. Therefore, based upon what he labels 'ability trouble' (extended from Butler's concept of 'gender trouble'), McRuer (2006a) proposes that, despite its compulsory nature, able-bodiedness is impossibility, therefore making everyone 'virtually disabled' (Goodley 2011a: 41).

Pulling in crip: or already present?

The fact that I've already used the word 'crip' multiple times throughout this section affirms that that crip and queer are indeed fluid categories that merge and converge. As I said in Chapter 1, McRuer (2006a: 35) positions crip theory as that which 'questions – or takes a sledgehammer to – that which has been concretised'. Crip doesn't just look inwards, but outwards: speaking back (see Rice *et al.* 2015, 2016, 2017) to non-disabled and disabled liberalism and non-disabled and disabled *neoliberalism*: 'crip experiences and epistemologies should be central to our efforts to counter neoliberalism and access alternative ways of being' (McRuer 2006a: 41). Embracing crip aids ways of thinking about impairment as more than just an 'unwelcome presence' (Shildrick 2009: 32). Crip shifts pathological discourses of disability that render bodies only as unintelligible and undesirable and makes space for considering the pleasurable and erotic possibilities of the (crip) body – for example, the ways in which disabled people and bodies can acknowledge or utilise impairment *for* pleasure and fulfilment (see Shuttleworth 2010) to potentially 'open up new (sexual) horizons' (Shildrick 2009: 36) in ways that exceed normative expectations and boundaries of what we have come to know as 'the body', 'sex' and the 'sexy body'. Assimilation is never the goal; 'passing' – performing normal – is counterintuitive. Crip doesn't seek to normalise or individualise disability or desire, but seeks to draw upon and centre its very queerness as a moment of reflection – making possible, as McRuer (2006a: 71) puts it, 'that a disabled world is possible and desirable'.

Thus, crip bodies are dynamic in their non-normativity: casting away medically imposed notions of deficit to reimagine bodies that may be ill, sick and impaired as transgressive and vital. This 'new mode of representation' (Siebers 2008: 54) of the crip sexual body has, in part, been realised through a hybrid of disabled/crip queer activism (McRuer 2006a). For example, sentiments such as: 'trached dykes eat pussy all night without coming up for air' (O'Toole 2000: 212) exemplify the productive realities of crip bodies within the confines of pleasure and sexuality. Other theorists, such as Sparkes and Smith (2002, 2003), have redefined bodies after injury as bodies that are capable of being revised and rewired; and philosopher Abby Wilkerson (2002: 48) emphasises the promises of the crip body: 'diffused sensuality, including orgasms centered in earlobes, nipples, sensitive areas of the neck, and else'.

Crip bodies can fuse with multiple technologies for maximum effect. Feminist postmodernists who have examined the role of technology in the making of the body have also emphasised the possibilities of crip (although they haven't labelled it as such), for example, Haraway's (1991) cyborg metaphor. Haraway (1991: 178) herself delineates a possible cyborg as 'perhaps paraplegics and other severely handicapped [*sic*] people can (and sometimes do) have the most intense experiences of complex hybridisation with other communication devices'. While it is important not to forget the largely oppressive historical influence of technology upon the impaired body and disabled identity, emerging technologies enable an exciting redefinition of conventional bodily boundaries and body politics. As Meekosha and Shuttleworth (2009: 60) suggest,

> The possibility that we could reconstitute our bodies, both as mechanical and organic, with the aid of prostheses and other mechanical devices means that we can embrace new technologies with positive identities rather than feeling victims of inadequate functioning.

Such transgression of the naturalised body is powerfully transformative and can be richly applied to the project of exploring and theorising disabled sexualities. However, a certain degree of caution is necessary, or at least some critical questions. Do crip and queer give enough consideration to the social and institutional conditions in which the majority of disabled people live? How might we use crip theory to politicise the lives of people with the label of learning disability? Who is included and who is excluded? We might question their relevance or proximity: particularly, the ways in which such perspectives remain largely out of reach of disabled people outside of the Academy and beyond spaces of queer and/or radical politics (see Liddiard and Slater 2017; see also Bone 2017). For example, while Rembis (2010) and others imagine alternative sexual modes that run counter to dualistic binaries (male/female, masculine/feminine, adult/childlike, independent/dependent, non-disabled/disabled, sexual/asexual, straight/gay) and thus contest sexual normalcy on this basis, few strategies are offered through which disabled people might emancipate themselves – today, *now*, in context of their lived realities. I'm being deliberately provocative here, of course, but my point is that it is imperative to ask critical questions of such propositions that are rooted in and faithful to the everyday realities of disabled people's lives. Or at least recognise, as Sandahl (2003: 50) does, that 'neither crip culture nor queer culture offers utopian spaces free from the need to perform stigma management'. One could also ask – as I do in later chapters – whether destabilising gender is an altogether helpful project when theorising the sexual lives of disabled people, many of who are, as their stories emphasise, striving for entry into the seemingly 'fixed' and 'stable' normative sex and gender categories that dis/ableist cultures routinely deny them (even though these are experienced as deeply oppressive) (see Chapter 8; see also Goodley *et al.* 2015). What, then, if the binary is desired, yearned for, lusted after? Where can *this* desire be located? How does the meaning of the norm change when we want to live within it? Thus, there may be costs to such radical and transgressive sexual politics in contexts of disability – a sentence that admittedly sounds deeply conservative and erotophobic (Wilkerson 2002). What I mean, to rephrase, is that it's critical to stay mindful of the material realities in which the majority of disabled people live: institutionalised, segregated, criminalised, infantilised and pathologised. This is a neoliberal-able (Goodley 2014) time when disabled people (amongst many marginalised others) are fighting for rights to life, to care and to love, all the while being re/cast as burden, problem and excess (Ignagni *et al.* 2016). Such tensions are woven through this book, in part because they (rightly) just won't go away. Thus, in the chapters that follow I critically explore these 'rubs' through disabled people's own stories of sexual and intimate life.

Conclusion

In sum, this chapter has sketched out the diverse theoretical, intellectual and political foundations upon which the sociological research in this book is based. The messy way in which I have made use of theory, drawing upon critical explorations of sexuality, pleasure, gender, the body and embodiment in contexts of dis/ability and dis/ableism, supports Shakespeare and Corker's (2002: 15) assertion that 'the global experience of disabled people is too complex to be rendered within one unitary model or set of ideas'. As my dad would say, 'Fetch me that toolbox!' In opening the toolbox, then, I have outlined the contributions of a range of theoretical perspectives and have highlighted the tensions and synergies between them, at the same time as considering their usefulness and applicability towards understanding the sexual, intimate and erotic lives of disabled people. Utilising a range of critical social theories in this way ensures that I remain politically aligned to critical disability studies, a framing that includes the multiple dimensions of disability: social, political and economic, psychic, cultural, discursive and carnal (Meekosha and Shuttleworth 2009). In the chapters that follow, I unpack disabled people's sexual stories in the context of this framing and question the application of certain critical approaches to disabled sexualities in isolation, for fear of privileging theory, intellectualism and radicalism over the everyday, the lived and the mundane. While Goodley (2016: viii) reminds us that we should never apologise for our use of theory, and indeed that 'contemporary times demand contemporaneous theories', as scholars interested in disability and disabled people it is our political, ethical and moral responsibility to remain faithful to the realities of disabled people's everyday lives.

3 Reflections on the process of researching disabled people's sexual lives

Accessible summary

- This chapter offers a reflexive account of storying disabled people's sexual and intimate lives for the purposes of sociological research.
- I consider how my identity, subjectivity and embodiment are interwoven within and through informants' sexual stories.
- I identify a number of reflexive dilemmas that make important methodological contributions to disability studies scholarship and research, and how qualitative researchers know and feel about their field.

It may already be relatively transparent the extent to which the research that informs this book, and its epistemological, ontological and political underpinnings, are embedded in my own disabled identity and subjectivity (and, unexpectedly to me, my lived experiences of disablism and ableism). In this chapter I delve deeper into the processes, politics, problems, practicalities and pleasures of co-constructing disabled people's sexual stories for the purposes of research. In doing so, I offer a reflexive but critical account of the research process. I seek to 'demystify the research activity' (Barton 2005: 319), a practice central to feminist and disability research methodologies whereby 'strong reflexivity' (McCorkel and Myers 2003: 203) 'attends to the diversity of informants and explicates the ways that differences between researchers and respondents shape research processes' (Rice 2009: 246; see also Goodley 1999; Haraway 1988; Reinharz 1992). Importantly, this chapter is neither narcissistic nor self-indulgent 'vanity reflexivity' (Kenway and McLeod 2004: 527), but seeks to take the legitimate stance of Bourdieu's reflexive sociology which calls 'less for intellectual introspection than for permanent sociological analysis and control of sociological practice' (Bourdieu and Wacquant 1992: 40). Thus, I stay mindful of Bourdieu's suggested three main reflexive concerns: 'my personal identity'; my location within the field; and my 'scholastic fallacy', the acknowledgement that my interpretation of the social world as an (intellectual) researcher is produced through the ' "collective unconscious" of an academic field' (Kenway and McLeod 2004: 529). My reflexivity in this chapter, then, is *purposeful*, and seeks to make important epistemological, ontological and methodological contributions.

To embody these aims, I write chronologically through the research process. I detail the significant political, ethical, material, emotional and methodological dilemmas which surrounded co-constructing the stories that disabled informants told about their (sexual) lives. Integral to this discussion are my explorations of the ways in which my identity, subjectivity and embodiment as a White, British, young, heterosexual, disabled, cisgender woman with congenital and (often, but not always) visible impairment were interwoven within the research process and informants' sexual storytelling. Rather than occupying an 'objective, disembodied voice, without any particular vantage point or value' (Rice 2009: 249), as proclaimed in traditional positivist social research (Rice 2009), I critically consider the role of my inner and outer (embodied) self, applying a self-conscious and self-reflexive lens to the research process and beyond.

Further, as Dickson-Smith *et al.* (2009: 61) suggest, 'undertaking qualitative research is an embodied experience and that researchers may be emotionally affected by the work that they do' (see also Davidson 2011; Woodby 2011). Thus later in this chapter, I (tentatively) turn the focus towards my own emotional experiences of carrying out research of this kind in my bid to show 'the real story behind the finished product' (Bennet deMarrais 1998: xi). Such a focus on the 'embodied work' of researchers undoubtedly flows from sociology of work theories of the emotional labours of employees in paid employment (note that emotional labour also gets taken up in Chapter 5 in relation to intimate relationships with others). To clarify, 'emotional work' and 'emotional labour' are terms coined by Arlie Hochschild (1983: 7) to represent the 'labour [which] one is required to induce or suppress feeling in order to sustain the outward countenance that produces the proper state of mind to others' within the labour market. Thus, such explorations have predominantly taken place through empirical work on occupations which require 'customer interactions' such as call centres (Korczynski 2003), flight attendants (Hochschild 1983), nursing (Henderson 2001), beauty therapy (Sharma and Black 2001) and university lecturers (Ogbonna and Harris 2004). Utilising Exley and Letherby's (2001: 115) definition of emotional work as the 'effort and skill required to deal with one's own feelings', I examine the ways in which my own lived and embodied experiences, relationships with the Research Advisory Group (RAG) and informants, as well as the process more broadly, built into the emotional work required of me as a (then novice) researcher. I do this not only because my 'emotional work' (Hochschild 1983) was both intensive and extensive, but because the emotional work of researchers is seldom theoretically or empirically investigated (Carroll 2012; Dickson-Smith *et al.* 2009; Woodby *et al.* 2011). I conclude this chapter, then, by considering the important contributions to feminist and disability research methodologies that can be drawn from my reflections.

Co-constructing sexual stories: a dialogical process

While multiple standard ethical guidelines were adhered to throughout the research process, the act of *collecting* disabled people's sexual stories for the purposes of research couldn't be detached from the ways in which their lives and bodies are routinely objectified, harmed and denied privacy through oppressive social and cultural practices (Sandahl 2003). Research 'on' disabled people has been labelled 'voyeuristic', and such critiques are, rather misguidedly, aimed only at non-disabled researchers (see Bury 2001). Shakespeare (1997: 177–178) highlights how researching disabled people's sexual lives offers the potential for such narratives to be used and abused by 'unscrupulous readers [who] might find the description of disabled sex titillating'. He asserts that, while it is important 'to capture the creativity and energy of disabled people's sexual expression' – omitted within much disability and sexuality research (Shuttleworth 2010; Tepper 2000) – that 'doing so runs the risk of supplying non-disabled voyeurs with material for erotic fantasies (not a usual danger of academic writing)' (Shakespeare 1997: 177–178). For me, there was a very real tension between eliciting the required data by enabling disabled people to speak about their sexual lives, and subjecting their lived experiences to a lack of privacy experienced throughout public and private life (see Chapter 4); thus serving to objectify their sexual selves and desires. Consequently, the path to analysis (and beyond) was a bumpy one, usually lined with political, ethical, material, emotional and methodological concerns. In this section of the chapter, I explicate these concerns, also revealing where and how my identity, embodiment and subjectivity were intertwined with the stories people told about their lives.

Sexual stories: material misgivings

Although *not* identifying as a disabled person to informants during the research process was not an option due to the visible nature of my impairment, (attempting to 'pass' would also have been contrary to my personal disability politics), my body was undeniably an asset to the acquisition of knowledge (Engelsrud 2005). In hindsight, it's clear to me now that both my disabled identity and material and physical embodiment of impairment were ever present within the research context (Reich 2003), from accessing and recruiting informants, to the stories they told about their lives. In short these aspects of my outer self facilitated access to informants in a number of different ways. I utilised my existing network of disabled colleagues, activists, friends and their groups and organisations to access fruitful spaces in order to recruit informants. I allowed a story of 'young-disabled-girl-done-good' to be written about me for a national charity magazine in order to get publicity for my research and put a nationwide call out for informants. I was (purposefully) transparent when identifying as disabled (including naming my impairment through a diagnostic label) on all advertising and informational literature sent to prospective informants. One organisation that distributed my call for informants to its members even requested that I make my disability (and impairment) status more explicit on advertising literature for fear that it would get a negative reaction from its members who are regularly 'called upon' by non-disabled researchers – thus reflecting the politically contentious history within disability research of non-disabled researchers conducting research on disabled people (Goodley and Tregaskis 2006; Stone and Priestley 1996; see also Branfield 1998).

While 'impairment does not automatically give someone an affinity with disabled people' (Barnes 1992: 121), prospective informants may have assumed that, as a fellow disabled person with lived experience of impairment and a subjective 'knowing' of being disabled, I had a more embodied understanding of the issues faced or shared their experiences. Or, that I was more trustworthy, ethical or aligned to disability politics than other professionals in their lives. Johnson-Bailey (1999) speaks of similar fears as a Black woman interviewing other Black women. She states, 'there were instances where the Black women being interviewed assumed that the interviewer's status as a Black and a woman assured not only understanding but also empathy on race and gender issues' (Johnson-Bailey 1999: 659). Additionally, it's quite likely that my disabled identity and feminine subjectivity fruitfully eclipsed my 'researcher persona' in this phase of the research, a role of which most people are 'probably already wary' (Bury 1996: 111). Markedly, many informants openly stated at the beginning of their participation that they would not have taken part in the research at all, or be prepared to share as much, had I identified as, or 'been', non-disabled.

The influence of my identity and embodiment in this 'phase' of the research process, then, explicitly reveals the power of occupying a disabled identity in disability research. As Goodley and Tregaskis (2006: 637) suggest, my disabled identity and material embodiment offer a 'privileged position within disability research'. Occupying this privileged position not only bears ethical consideration when recruiting prospective informants, it – in part – comprises my ability to avoid affecting the traditional power imbalances within the researcher/researched relationship. This is because my researcher influence over informants' participation (and, more broadly, their storytelling) is – quite literally – inscribed in, on and through my material embodiment. Rice (2009) explores similar ethical concerns as a normatively sized culturally attractive woman researching diversely embodied women's lives. She asks, 'when studying sensitive subject matters such as body image where issues of appearance cannot be overlooked, how do we account for the influence of our physicalities?' (Rice 2009: 246). Further, occupying this privileged position in disability research potentially compromises the inquiry of non-disabled researchers whose unimpaired bodies can mark them as 'outsider' within the discipline; and more importantly, within the communities they research (Goodley and Tregaskis 2006).

However, 'naming' my disability and impairment status without any further context as to how these mark my life could be problematic. The term 'Muscular Dystrophy' refers to a wide variety of conditions that are (mostly, though not always) characterised by a degeneration of muscle in the body over time, also known as progressive impairment. Forms of the condition differ in terms of speed of progression, 'level' of impairment, particular muscles, time of onset and trajectory. Many types are life-shortening, though many are not. The substantial heterogeneity of the condition is often misunderstood through its popularised cultural understanding as 'severe', 'muscle-wasting' and 'life-threatening' (although, I don't deny for some, it is each of these). My 'type' is identified in medical circles as 'mild' and, so far, relatively static. Thus, some informants, particularly those with 'severe' or 'progressed' forms of Muscular Dystrophy and other neuromuscular conditions, sometimes assumed prior to meeting me that I had greater impairment than in reality. On a couple of occasions, this instigated noticeably awkward introductions when it was apparent that informants had anticipated that I would be 'more disabled'. Therefore, the reality of my material embodiment could potentially disrupt, as much as ensure, informants' participation in the research.

Sexual stories: materialising methodology

I made a decision to facilitate data collection methods that were not only accessible, but also sensitive to informants' own bodily experiences and interactions with disabling environments. This decision was rooted in the materiality of my impaired body – a body which routinely experiences restricted mobility, fatigue and pain – combined with my deep frustrations of living in an ableist social world which projects and thus perpetuates 'a corporeal standard' when it comes to bodies (Campbell 2009: 44). A multi-method and multi-format methodology, co-designed with the RAG, enabled informants to tell their sexual stories through face-to-face interviews ($n=10$), via email ($n=4$) and via new social technologies, such as Skype ($n=2$), instant messaging (e.g. MSN) ($n=4$) or a combination ($n=2$) (total $n=22/27$). The remaining five informants ($n=5/27$) chose to write their own stories through keeping a 'journal', often kept (privately from me) over several months. This design had both practical and political underpinnings. Practical, because it centred informants' comfort; offered choice; and ensured the research process was as accessible as possible. Political, because – as the RAG stressed – it was important to recognise the diverse ways in which (disabled) people communicate, but also because research should be designed with informants' needs and preferences at the forefront (rather than those of the researcher).

Such a design created considerable labour for me as a researcher – namely because it produced disparate 'styles' of data that could be technically complex to manage and code. However, the approach enabled the surfacing of stories from those who, if only conventional research methods had been available, are unlikely to have participated. For example, storytelling via email and instant messaging enabled the participation of those who, for multiple reasons (likely fear or embarrassment), didn't feel able to speak about their sexual lives in person. Storytelling via instant messaging (e.g. MSN) and/or Skype were often chosen by informants who experienced pain, speech difficulties and/or fatigue, or who just couldn't get to a face-to-face interview because of accessibility or institutional constraints. Storytelling via email was beneficial where informants didn't want to meet in person, but for reasons of limited manual dexterity didn't want to be interviewed via instant messaging technology (which requires good typing skills). Storytelling via writing a journal enabled Grace – a 58-year-old

Deaf woman who was concerned at having a British Sign Language (hereby BSL) interpreter present at a face-to-face interview (because of the impact on confidentiality) – to participate, because no BSL interpreter was needed. Not surprisingly, as part of the 'Facebook generation' (Meadows-Klue 2008: 245), 'online methods' were most popular with younger informants (30 years and under) (*n*=5). Significantly, these online methods offered a further informality that put younger informants at ease, at the same time as providing absolute anonymity, even to the researcher. Tellingly, many informants made method and format choices purely out of or due to preference (rather than for accessibility reasons), highlighting that social research methodology generally could benefit from privileging informant preferences and comfort. This is particularly so within the researching of sensitive topics 'where research intrudes into the private sphere or delves into some deeply personal experience' (Lee and Renzetti 1993: 6).

The utilisation of new social technologies and online methods within qualitative research remains cautious, and markedly in the shadows of the face-to-face encounter, which is 'the quintessence of qualitative research' (Seymour 2001: 155). However, such data collection methods are, I suggest, of significant value to existing and emerging disability research methodologies. First, because they are malleable to a multitude of different bodies, embodiment, and bodily capabilities: as Seymour (2001: 149) argues, 'information technology promises to bypass aspects of bodily function enabling participation in previously inaccessible domains'. Second, because online spaces can offer greater accessibility and privacy. And third, new social technologies *can* provide a means of disabled people participating in research without this becoming known to personal assistants, carers, partners and parents. This was particularly pertinent within this study, given that lacking privacy, an often-routine experience for disabled people, was at the heart of many informants' sexual stories – specifically, because 'disabled people face a considerable amount of curiosity and voyeurism' (Shakespeare 1996: 66) combined with 'a lack of sexual privacy' (Siebers 2008: 138) (see Chapter 4).

Sexual stories: telling and identity

Nowhere were my identity, subjectivity and embodiment more important in the dialogical process of sexual storytelling than in my role as an interlocutor and co-constructor of informants' stories. Importantly, my age, class, gender, sexual orientation, Whiteness and disability were determining factors that influenced the power dynamics of the researcher/researched relationship and thus contoured the ways in which stories were told – often quite literally. For example, older informants (I was just 24 when the research commenced) could be very 'protective' of me (despite my traditional authority and privilege as a researcher), initially shielding me from 'rude' words and sexually explicit details in the telling of their stories (this was likely further compounded by my gender). Another older informant said that he initially felt very uncomfortable talking about sex to a woman '*his daughter's age*'. In this case, I affirmed his existing feelings of inappropriateness surrounding his sexuality, a common psycho-emotional impact of disabled people's cultural desexualisation (Reeve 2002). Another informant, Bob, an older man with physical and sensory impairment, switched from telling his story in person to via email (after arranging and can-celling two meetings) because, he said, meeting me in a public place would have meant reliving bad memories whereby he had arranged to meet prospective part-ners ('dates') who had either not turned up or left after seeing him. Therefore, even an informant's choice of storytelling medium could rest precariously at the intersections of (most clearly) my gender and sexual identities.

Troubling Whiteness

Song and Parker (1995: 24) assert, 'where two people may claim commonality on one dimension, they may fall apart on another'. Thus, I found that the shared experiences of disability, impairment and ableism I had with certain informants could, at points, be interrupted by cross race positionality. While I was conscious of Black feminist and womanist critiques of White feminist scholarship (see bell hooks 1981), and had made concerted efforts to attract a diverse sample (particu-larly along the lines of sexual orientation and race), I had not critically con-sidered the ways in which my ethnic origin might impact upon the research process and informants' sexual storytelling. Thus, the invisibility of my White-ness *to me* – indistinctness undoubtedly afforded to me by my White privilege – meant that I seldom interrogated and problematised my racial identity to the same extent as other facets of my identity. As uncomfortable as it is now to admit, my Whiteness (and, surprisingly, my 'Britishness') only became clearly apparent to me upon hearing the sexual stories of informants from ethnic minority groups ($n=4/26$, all men), whose stories of sexual oppression were fre-quently further layered by their cultural, religious and racial identities.

Further, I was taken aback during analysis by the extent to which my White-ness had informed my then-knowledges of disability and sexuality. Hearing these informant's stories, which were distinctly told *around* their racial and cul-tural identities in a way not visible (at least to me at that time) in the stories of White informants, enabled me to ruminate cross-culturally and consider the role of the family, tradition, community, and faith in the making of disabled sexuali-ties. In hindsight, more could have been done to recruit informants from ethnic minority groups; particularly ethnic minority women, whose experiences of gender would have provided an interesting comparison to other women in the sample, all of who were White (see Egharevba 2001). Thus, my social, cultural and scholarly knowledges of disability rested not only upon my own embodied Whiteness, but were inevitably exacerbated by the stark Whiteness of disability studies a discipline (Bell 2010). My insufficient knowledge of the complex inter-sections of race, sexuality and disability, then, are imprinted upon these inform-ant's stories and, as some Black feminists have argued (see Hill-Collins 2000), this cross race positionality vis-à-vis these research subjects has produced certain kinds of knowledge. These intersections strongly affirm the necessity of self-reflexivity towards negating the ethnocentrism and (unconscious) racism within White feminist and disability research (Reinharz 1992).

Troubling gender, heterosexuality and intimacy

Moving forward, it was not uncommon that the interview setting was the first space in which some informants had ever talked about issues such as sex and love with another person. Many had been ridiculed, humiliated or chastised when raising such topics within their own familial and social networks (Shakespeare *et al.* 1996). This inevitably brought significant responsibility when managing informants' participation in a way that would not quash the confidence it took for them to participate. The intimate nature of the research topic combined with the sense of speaking about sex and love without fear or judgement created some strong researcher/researched relationships. In addition, the extensive work it took to ensure informants made it to participation (for example, regular conversations about access, informants outlining their life stories in order to determine 'eligibility', and the regular reassurance and contact required) meant that these relationships could already be developed prior to participation. This suggests, then, that in the researching of sensitive topics it is likely that relationships between researcher and researched may become close prior to an informant's actual participation in the research. At times, such relationships became ethically complex to manage. For example, in order to protect informants I had to maintain a 'professional distance' (Fetterman 1991: 94) while at the same time constructing a supportive environment conducive to eliciting intimate experiences. This could be further complicated for informants who experienced considerable social isolation in their lives. For example, a few informants became very dependent on the research relationship as a means of contact with another person. This highlighted the ethical circumstances of facilitating this relationship (for the elicitation of data) and, more importantly, how to end it without causing considerable harm. Upon ending the research relationship with these informants, I remained in 'light contact' for a while following their participation – which came to an organic end – rather than simply ending the researcher/researched relationship abruptly.

Undeniably, my heterosexual identity could further complicate this process (see Poulton 2012). Drawing upon her research with divorced fathers, Arundell (1997: 364–365) found 'that the norms of the situation of the research interview did not override or displace those of a gender stratified society; gender work was ever present and predominant'. Similarly, some male informants seldom abstained from performing typical heterosexual scripts, and thus keenly reaffirmed 'the conventional gender hierarchy as they told about their experiences' (Arundell 1997: 364). Some male informants could confuse the open, supportive and gentle context of the interview and pre- and post-participation contact with romantic or sexual feelings. Some men openly flirted throughout the interview (possibly enacting a sexualised and gendered identity they couldn't perform elsewhere). While sometimes this was in the context of asking questions about my own sexuality or sexual life, other times it was far more overt. Four male informants (*n*=4/16) asked to meet again in a social/sexual context following participation, which created a predicament whereby I had to decline such an offer without affecting their self-esteem or affirming their experiences of rejection, which were often central to their stories.

At other times, a few informants (who were later excluded) could be sexually objectifying and sometimes frightening through exhibiting inappropriate behaviour before, during and after participation (see Peng 2007; Sanders 2008). As a young, female researcher embarking on her first piece of 'proper' research, at the time this was very upsetting – not least in its immediacy, but also because it served as a stark reminder of the objectifying sexism which plagues women's lives, even within research contexts (Pierce 1995; Poulton 2012). Other feminist scholars have reflected on the sexism and objectification they've experienced in the field, revealing how sexism is often part and parcel of doing research as a woman interviewer/ethnographer (Kang 2010; Pierce 1995). In these moments, when men sent constant texts to my research phone number offering me sex, insisted I needed 'a good fuck' to loosen up or left me voicemails messages in which they would describe in graphic detail what they wanted to do to me, I was reduced to a sexual object. My worst experience was with a male informant – who was withdrawn following interview – whom I felt 'duped me', with me setting up, paying for and travelling 250 kilometres to the agreed venue under the guise that he had a sexual story to tell. In reality, the meaning of the interview to him was merely an opportunity to speak about his (what I deem) abusive, exploitative and violent acts with sex workers, simultaneously getting aroused at the same time and violating my bodily boundaries. Sanders (2008: 23–24) speaks of similar experiences when researching men who buy sex. She claims:

> it was a recurring theme that men would go about arranging our meeting (both practically and emotionally) in the same way that they had done many times with sex workers. Importantly, the research context masked what I would have seen, in any other context, as a form of sexual assault, meaning withdrawing the informant was my only action.

This again affirms the importance of reflexivity for women researchers towards calling out such behaviours for what they are, regardless of context and professional role, as well as the need to safeguard within the research process.

The emotional work of hearing stories

Hard work

Listening to the stories of others, through which tales of isolation, loneliness, self-hatred and abuse were not uncommon, was often gruelling (see Kleinman and Copp 1993). Many of the stories told were ones of pride, self-confidence, resistance and personal strength. Others embodied the oppression, discrimination and prejudice many disabled people face in their daily lives. Importantly, my own biography and subjectivity were complicit in my emotional work, as my own lived experiences were repeatedly echoed in the stories of others (Davidson 2011). At points, hearing informants' stories caused the surfacing of irrational fears:

> Hearing Julie's sad story of her husband rejecting her at the onset of her impairment because he 'didn't want a disabled wife' was probably one of the most disturbing things I have heard. She hid nothing from me and it upset me greatly. Later that evening at home I broke down to my partner, part through relief that the day was over, but more out of insecurity that he could leave me in much the same way. Julie reported a strong relationship, a great man who loved her very much, yet I had all of these things... I was firing such accusations at my partner with incredible speed, 'What makes us so different?'... Realistically and logically, I don't think that will ever be my life. I genuinely believe in, and have more faith in my partner than that, but when it's emotively in front of you all day it's impossible not to be affected by it.
>
> It was at this juncture that I suddenly realised that my research could be harmful. Not just for those whose stories I hoped to hear, but harmful to me, my sense of self, my relationships, and those around me. As I heard Julie's words I realised that she was voicing my worst fears. I may find elements of stories that remind me of my worst fears, or echo my feelings about myself and my body on the darkest days... How will I deal with this?
>
> (Research diary, 4 June 2009)

The above account was written in my research diary following a particularly bad day 'in the field' after which, as Davidson (2011: 5.12) aptly states, 'I wanted to cocoon myself for days'. My words here are indicative of the impact of hearing certain stories, but more importantly show how my own lived and embodied experiences built into my emotional working. Thus, such fears were also rational, in that they were underpinned by my shared identities and marginalities with informants. Significantly, this emotional work was not only realised upon hearing stories, but served as an unceasing anxiety which could resurface at particular times throughout the research process; for example, when transcribing interviews and coding and analysing informants' narratives. This was likely because these activities involved a more convoluted and exhaustive engagement with individual stories. Further, this emotional engagement was compounded by the very nature of doctoral study: inquiry carried out primarily alone (rather than as part of a research team), by novice researchers who are 'particularly vulnerable to the emotional challenges' (Woodby et al. 2011: 830), and who have little awareness of the self-care practices which may reduce researcher distress when researching sensitive topics (Woodby et al. 2011). In this instance, keeping a research diary was a (self-discovered) self-care strategy implemented promptly upon encountering the above emotions in the field.

Another form of considerable emotional work was in managing the sexist, disablist and racist language and beliefs voiced by some informants. Due to the need to elicit data, these were prejudices to which I could neither react nor object. It was at these points I had to *perform* a presentation of myself as a professional researcher (see Poulton 2012). For example, it was troublesome to hear some disabled men's opinions on disabled and/or fat women, who were routinely positioned as objects of disgust (affirming the cultural messages which are readily ascribed to my body as a disabled woman). Similarly, disabled male informants who had paid for sex often constructed sex workers in very particular ways when telling their stories. For example, many were fatphobic, dehumanising (*'it was a choice of two, a Polish or an English'*), racist, deeply sexist and placed these women's bodies and behaviours under significant scrutiny (see Chapter 7). These moments made for some difficult listening and revealed, in very raw ways, the problematic tensions that subsist between my liberal feminist and disability politics (see Lloyd 2001; O'Connell Davidson 1998; Sanders 2008). To clarify, I accept sex work as both a form of embodied labour for sex workers (see Boris *et al.* 2010) and as a legitimate means of sexual access for disabled people (Sanders 2008). However, the *act* of (mentally and emotionally) negotiating the rights, perspectives and politics of both of these marginalised groups (see Wotten and Isbister 2010) explicitly *at* the juncture of hearing (some) men's sex work stories was often a conflicting task which, at points, required considerable effort to remain sympathetic to disabled men's plights.

However, possibly the most distressing aspect of listening to stories was hearing the extent of informants' internalised oppression and experiencing of psycho-emotional disablism (Reeve 2002), defined by Thomas (1999: 60) as 'the socially engendered undermining of emotional well-being'. For example, some informants (and a research advisory group member) expressed that, although they respected my efforts, politicising disabled people's oppression was meaningless because disability is a biological, natural and genetic inferiority of which social oppression is both justified and inherent to human nature (see Campbell 2009). Beyond internalised oppressions, it was also difficult to hear about the sexual, emotional and physical violence that featured in informants' stories with striking frequency. Another struggle was acknowledging both the silence around and negative experiences within motherhood for many disabled women in the research (see Kent 2002; O'Toole 2002). Just three of the nine disabled women who participated were mothers, and each of these women told stories of the discrimination and prejudice to which they were subjected by strangers, medical professionals, family planning clinics, and friends and family members within their mothering experiences. Female informants without children either quickly changed the subject when the topic of motherhood arose, or categorically stated that their experiences of both impairment and disability heavily contributed to their decision not to become mothers (see Thomas 1997). As a disabled woman (who wants to be a mother), hearing the impact of such experiences led to considerable emotional distress – not least because such stories embodied the notion that motherhood remains an area of social life through which disabled women are at best excluded and at worst abused (Prilleltensky 2003).

Providing emotional support? The role of the RAG

In addition to keeping a research diary, another self-care strategy emerged from my engagement with the RAG. Even prior to the commencement of any field-work, the group's laughter, support, guidance and enthusiasm fostered a relaxed space through which I learned to speak to fellow disabled people about sex and intimacy. Regular discussion with the RAG constructed a safe space through which I 'practised' both asking questions and listening, and where I was (often brutally and crudely, but with much laughter) taught the intricacies of impair-ment and sexual practice and pleasure (for example, knowing about medications, medical equipment, personal assistants/care and bodily processes such as incon-tinence). Such knowledge was fundamental towards learning how to 'deal with' the materialities and realities of sexual stories. Such access to expert and lived knowledge was *the* major benefit of establishing and maintaining the RAG. In fact, there were few drawbacks to the group: there was no contention amongst group members; once the group was established, it took little 'extra' work; and it enabled a solid, rather than tokenistic, participatory process to take place (Barton 2005). Further, having to 'report' to the RAG (while sometimes stressful) was not only impetus to keep the research process constantly moving forward at times when I just wanted to give up, but served as a way to habitually keep reflecting upon each stage of the process. Ultimately, the RAG kept the research grounded in the everyday realities of disabled people's lives. Questions asked by group members within meetings disrupted much of my intellectual and theoret-ical romanticism and idealism; for example, questions such as *'What difference does that make?'* and *'So what?'* enabled me to keep the (political) purpose of the research in view.

However, while my relationships with group members (and theirs to one another) were warm, they were ultimately professional. Thus, I seldom utilised the RAG explicitly for emotional support, for a number of reasons. First, I didn't want to disrupt the goodwill of the group, or make unreasonable demands in terms of individual group members' time and engagement with the process. Second, I wasn't emotionally close enough to group members to aid disclosure; this not to denigrate the group but speaks to the deeply personal engagement I had with stories. Last, I was conscious I had to be the competent and capable (researcher) 'glue' that held the group (and the broader process) together. Thus, I felt that disclosing my emotional distress would compromise this professional performance (see Woodby *et al.* 2011). Paradoxically, I thought it was better to (physically and emotionally) 'mask it' via enacting the appropriate 'display work' that Hochschild (1983, 10) centres within her theorising of emotional labour.

Pleasurable work

While I have documented the adverse and oft-painful emotional work of the research process, as other empirical investigations into the emotional experiences of researchers have done (Carroll 2012; Woodby *et al.* 2011), my emotional investment with informants' storied lives was sometimes pleasurable (see Davidson 2011). For some informants, taking part in the research and 'speaking out' about their experiences was part of a wider narrative of emancipation in other areas of their lives. Thus, their participation was underpinned by significant and poignant personal motivations and could be a catalyst for other changes in their lives. For example, Lucille, a married 36-year-old woman with an acquired spinal injury, experienced writing her sexual story as a cathartic activity which allowed her to explore fragments of her life she had '*shut down*' after injury. On our last contact, she told me that telling her story had empowered her in ways she hadn't imagined possible; for example, she'd worn a skirt for the first time since her accident (10 years previous) because she '*finally felt comfortable as a disabled woman*'. More than this, Lucille had returned to study, enrolling in a PhD, a significant personal and career goal. Lucille's journey to self-acceptance as a proud disabled woman, which I saw emotively unfold throughout her journal, empowered me considerably. As a young disabled woman I seldom had access to strong and visible disabled female role models (other than disabled feminist scholars) (see Gillespie-Sells *et al.* 1998). Therefore, far from the artifice of objectivity, such stories of emancipation – which embodied the (potential) empowerment of personal narrative (Langellier 2001) – were very impactful and instigated strong emotional bonds. Had I continued contact with Lucille and other informants following their participation I've no doubt that these relationships would have grown to become strong friendships (see Zajano and Edelsberg 1993).

Drawing some conclusions

To sum up, then, this chapter has offered the ' "warts and all" admissions which are all too often absent from the usual research methods textbooks and "impact driven" research chapters which usually present "sanitised" accounts of methodological processes and practice' (Poulton 2012: 1.2). I hope this reflexive practice will prove useful for readers who can learn from my (frequent) reflexive dilemmas. Importantly, my reflections affirm feminist epistemologies that situate reflexivity, accountability and positionality as central to creating certain kinds of knowledge (Walby 2011). Thus, this chapter has explicitly shown the ways in which researcher identity, subjectivity, embodiment and lived experience are not merely *parts* of research, but instead may be the *sum* of it.

Undoubtedly, accounting for my many research dilemmas has revealed my complex positionality; how facets of my identity were manifest in different ways – and in distinct moments – dependent upon encounters with informant's identities (see England 1994). These moments have illuminated 'the ways that differences between researchers and respondents shape research processes' (Rice 2009: 246). Further, I have shown the ways in which multiple aspects of the research process – research design; informant recruitment; researcher/researched relationships; and data collection – were/are embedded in my identity, subjectivity and embodiment as a White, British, young, heterosexual, cisgender disabled woman with congenital impairment. Thus, I hope I have articulated fully the ways in which my inner and outer selves and representations have strengthened the research, rather than weakened it (as is propositioned within positivistic assumptions). Thus, by examining the connections between the process and myself – or through 'demystifying the research activity' (Barton 2005: 319) – I have painted a far richer picture of researching disabled people's sexual lives. This richer picture not only benefits readers who may want to carry out similar research, or use similar methodologies, but (rightly and publically) holds my researcher ethics, politics and actions to account (Bennet deMarrais 1998; England 1994).

Moving forward, providing a reflexive account has enabled me to identify and reconsider layers of identity privilege (e.g. my Whiteness) that I had overlooked in comparison to other facets of my identity which seldom invite such privilege (e.g. my disabled identity). I suggest that this omission may be a common occurrence within disability research, and that this in turn exacerbates the marked Whiteness of disability scholarship (Bell 2010); an interdisciplinary space which has only recently made a commitment towards theorising 'disability' in the Global South (Meekosha and Soldatic 2011). Thus, for Disability Studies specifically, the act of 'doing' reflexivity offers (White) disability scholars a means through which to (re)configure an understanding of Whiteness (and race and ethnicity generally) at a time of emerging intersectional and global knowledges of disability. However, as England (1994: 86) argues, while reflexivity 'can make us more aware of asymmetrical or exploitative relationships [within research], it cannot remove them'. Thus, while it is pertinent that the reflexivity of White disability studies scholars better extends to race, there is far more to be done to counter the entrenched Whiteness within 'White Disability Studies' (Bell 2010: 374), highlighting, then, some very real limits of reflexivity as an epistemological practice (England 1994).

Finally, through critically exploring my own emotional engagement with the research process, I have contributed to others' calls (see Carroll 2012; Dickson-Smith *et al.* 2009) for the inclusion of researchers' emotions to the process. As Carroll (2012: 13) states, 'the incorporation of emotions and their analysis into theoretical study on the sociology of emotion can be crucial to extending theory'. Thus, I suggest that the emotional engagement of researchers isn't just 'there' – to be excused – but is legitimate and productive. As Liddiard and Jones (2017) question, rather than writing this emotion out, what happens when we centre it? What happens to/for researchers when we conceptualise emotion and feeling not as barriers 'to clear reflexive thought' (Burkitt 2012: 458), but as necessary forms of affective labour for reflexivity itself (Liddiard and Jones 2017)? Thus, alongside 'doing' reflexivity, researcher emotion can become a crucial instrument 'for conducting qualitative research on emotional topics' (Carroll 2012:

13). My own embodied experiences of emotional work reveal the ways in which researcher identity, subjectivity and embodiment can contour, compound and contribute to the emotional work experienced by qualitative researchers. This is, undoubtedly, of prominence for disability and feminist scholarship where researchers and research informants are likely to occupy similar social locations, oppressions and embodied knowledges. A further reason behind (publicly) sharing this very private and personal part of the process was to highlight the specific circumstances around those new to qualitative research; for example, doctoral students, whose experiences of emotional work are potentially intensified and augmented by their relative lack of field experience. By 'speaking out' about my experiences I invite further dialogue in the hope that collectively sharing emotions, research journeys and strategies of management and self-care may be one answer towards lessening the burden of emotional work which, 'as a community, we often fail to openly discuss' (Woodby *et al.* 2011: 838).

4 '*Can you have sex?*'

Intimate citizens and intimate selves

Accessible summary

- In this chapter I unpack and explore sociologist Ken Plummer's (2003) 'intimate citizenship'.
- I explore various spaces within disabled people's lives – education and learning about sexuality and the body, the social and sexual context of (normative) youth, and the marked intrusion and lack of privacy endemic to disabled bodies and selves in dis/ableist cultures.
- I problematise the *absence* of rights to intimate citizenship for disabled people and explore the labour, or management strategies, employed by informants to claim it.
- I conclude that disabled people in my research routinely lacked many of the essential ingredients of intimate citizenship, and that this entailed significant psycho-emotional labour to survive, negotiate or resist.

One-way to characterise the sexual oppression experienced by disabled people is through the absence of what sociologist Ken Plummer (2003) calls 'intimate citizenship'. For Plummer (2003), 'intimate citizenship' is different from 'sexual citizenship' (see D. Richardson 2000; J. Richardson 1996; Weeks 1998), a claim to rights that sexual minorities are making, because it focuses on claims to rights of public and private intimacies that extend beyond the erotic and the sexual (see Smyth 2009). Broadly, intimate citizenship refers to the rights of people to choose how they organise their personal lives and claim sexual and other intimate identities (De Graeve 2010; Plummer 2003). In Chapter 1, I articulated the ways in which austerity politics have come to routinely compromise disabled people's intimate citizenship in contemporary Britain (see also Ignagni *et al.* 2016). Plummer (2003: 14; original emphasis) defines intimate citizenship as:

> *the control (or not)* over one's body, feelings, relationships; *access (or not)* to representations, relationships, public spaces, etc; and *socially grounded choices (or not)* about identities, gender experiences, erotic experiences. It does not imply one model, one pattern or one way.

Put another way, as Ignagni *et al.* (2016: 132) clarify, 'intimate citizenship concerns our rights and responsibilities to make personal and private decisions about with whom and how we are in intimate relations'. Within our intimate citizenship, Plummer (2003: 14) identifies the distinct multiple 'intimate zones' of 'self, relationships, gender, sexuality, the family, the body, emotional life, the sense, identity, and spirituality'. These intimate zones demarcate the areas of our lives upon which our intimate citizenship depends in postmodern times. As Plummer (2003) muses, the term 'intimate citizenship' appears an oxymoron. The term 'intimacy' refers to *closeness*, be it emotional, sexual or proximate; it is a bond with another person, thing or place; it is something we have with ourselves as much as it is that which we share with close others. But, this is not to say it is not social, for 'intimacies are lodged in worldwide inequalities of class, gender, age, race and the like' (Plummer 2015: 145). Traditionally our 'citizenship' refers to the opposite. While there are many contested theories of citizenship across the social sciences and humanities, in its most traditional and elemental meaning citizenship serves as public, legal and cultural affirmation and legitimation of a sovereign selfhood; access to our rights, to equality and to justice. It is also a feeling of *belonging*, whether this is to place, context or time. Intimate citizenship, then, explores the relationship between the public and private worlds on the grounds that, as Plummer maintains, there is a marked *blurring* of the private and the public in the late modern world, 'where the personal invades the public and the public invades the personal' (Plummer 2003: 68; see also Reynolds 2010). It is these eroding boundaries between the private and public that Reynolds (2010) argues give birth to a transformation of intimacy in advanced capitalist times (Braidotti 2012).

While Plummer's (2003) primary concern is upon emerging and new forms of intimate rights and new theories of citizenship that legitimate them, in this chapter I problematise the *absence* of rights to intimate citizenship for disabled people. Such rights are seldom challenged despite the fact that 'disabled people experience sexual repression, possess little or no sexual autonomy, and tolerate institutional and legal restrictions on their intimate contact' (Siebers 2008: 136). Many also 'face restrictions, penalties, and coercion, and are denied access to important information, all in relation to their sexuality' (Wilkerson 2002: 41–42). As Ignagni *et al.* (2016: 132) state:

> Intimate citizenship is fragile in the lives of labelled [disabled] people, despite the fact that rights to pursue several spheres of intimate life, including sexual identity and expression, friendship, marriage and cohabitation, family life and parenthood, are enshrined in the UN Convention of the Rights of Persons with Disabilities (UN General Assembly 2007). These rights matter because intimate relationships establish the social networks necessary to support employment, educational success, secure housing, family stability, sexual health and well being, and build resilience against the deleterious effects of structural and interpersonal ableism. Barriers to intimate ties lead to social and economic costs associated with vulnerability

to abuse and violence, child welfare involvement, trans-institutionalization and reliance on private and social care resources.

Importantly, Ignagni *et al.* (2016: 132) also draw our attention to the fact that little detailed exploration of disabled people's experiences of intimate citizenship has been undertaken, and that our 'knowledge rarely includes labelled [disabled] people as competent commentators on their own life conditions':

> We know little about the spaces people may easily access and claim, and how these may shape intimate subjectivities, relations and practice; nor do we know what new ableisms (the exclusions, disadvantages and silencing of people with impairments) or other barriers are encountered within the exercise of intimate rights.
>
> (Ignagni *et al.* 2016: 132)

Drawing upon disabled informants' experiences of managing and negotiating their sexual identities within particular public moments, contexts and interactions, then, in this chapter I explore the three main themes of intimate citizenship; (i) *the control (or not)* over one's body, feelings, relationships; (ii) *access (or not)* to representations, relationships, public spaces; and (iii) *socially grounded choices (or not)* about identities, gender experiences, erotic experiences (Plummer 2003: 14; original emphasis). My interview schedule started by exploring the formation of a sexual self as a key issue, and within that there were a number of recurrent concerns expressed by informants that centred on their public image and the ways in which others perceived their sexual selves. I explore these with reference to the forms of management and negotiation disabled informants carried out in order to carve out a *desired* public sexual self. I focus initially on what informants said in relation to their experiences of learning about sex through formal and informal means, and more broadly their experiences of youth, before exploring the ways in which they said they lacked privacy and autonomy within spaces where they received personal care. In the final section of this chapter, I examine informants' experiences of non-disabled gazes across different social contexts. In doing so, I question the ways in which disabled people's ascribed *asexual* identities contribute to their lack of rights to intimate citizenship. Thus, I consider the relationship between the experience of occupying a public asexual identity, which informants described as restrictive and required work to 'correct', and their lack of rights to intimate citizenship.

'Learning' and the expectations of youth

GRACE: We watched films on menstruation and reproduction. That was about it. I read women's magazines but they did not tell you much. Sex was not talked about at home. I really knew hardly anything. I was curious but ignorant!

In the above account, Grace is reflecting back on her experiences of sex education at school in the 1970s. She told how '*watching films*' was the extent of the
(passive) teaching offered, leaving her '*curious but ignorant*'. Sex education has
undoubtedly moved on, but still remains contested terrain. In the present day,
sex education is compulsory under the national curriculum from the age of 11 in
the UK, from where I write, but it is permissible for parents and carers to remove
their children from particular aspects of it. Sex and relationships education
(SRE) – part of PSHE: personal, social, health and economic education – has
been long fought for across four parliamentary committees in the House of
Commons. Importantly, the last Conservative Party Cabinet refused this appeal.
The legislation is infamously confusing: in England the law allows primary
schools, academies and free schools to choose not to teach pupils about sex and
relationships. These schools usually offer some basic biological and developmental information, such as content on puberty and the reproductive system.
This is part of the National Curriculum in England – but academies and free
schools are not required to teach it. The result, perhaps not surprisingly, is that
young people leave compulsory education with fragmented knowledges of
sexual health, intimacy, sex and gender.

This is exacerbated by the fact that knowledges around sex, particularly those
surrounding young people (see Holland *et al.* 1998), are already markedly
shaped by conservatism, morality and erotophobia. For example, in recent years
in the UK we have seen moral panics about sexual health 'epidemics' in young
people (despite the fact that the rates of STIs – sexually transmitted infections –
are increasing most sharply in the over 50s); moralistic indignation around
young people as porn-obsessed and sexually 'out of control' (evidenced clearly
in the UK with media storms around teenage pregnancy rates); and increasing
cultural anxieties around paedophilia and childhood innocence. Theorist Abby
Wilkerson (2002: 41) defines erotophobia as:

> not merely a general taboo against open discussions of sexuality, and dis-
> plays of sexual behaviour, but a very effective means of creating and main-
> taining social hierarchies, not only those of sexuality, but those of gender,
> race, class, age, and physical and mental ability.

Much of this panic is rooted in the idea that, as Slater (2015: 14) maintains,
'youth unnerves us'. By this, Slater (2015: 14; see also Slater 2016) is referring
to the way in which youth subsists not merely as a temporal space between
'childhood' and 'adulthood' but as a space where ' "non-normativity" emerges
as a place allowed, indeed expected, as a stage of "normative development" '.
Rather, 'adolescence' is demarcated as *the* time for permissible rebellion, abnormality – an abandonment of the rules – and a lack of governability and reason,
yet only for those who have the privilege of culturally sanctioned identities
(Slater 2015). At the same time, young people are deemed to be growing up
within and through 'overtly sexualised environments' consisting of 'sexualised
images in advertisements and the media' (Wilkerson 2002: 40–41). Some feminists

(e.g. Rossi 2007) label this the 'pornification of everyday life' – a term used to describe what 'scholars, pundits, and journalists began noticing in the mid-1990s and [were] later characterizing as the ways in which the gestures, styles, and aesthetics of pornographic media had entered into the non-pornographic landscape of the culture' (in Schuchardt 2012: pagination unknown). Importantly, however, Lees (2000: 3) argues that the connections between education and the formation of sexual identity are pertinent to the issue of citizenship rights. Using gender, she proposes that the omission from sex education of 'how the double standard operates and how gender relations are constructed' ensures that schools 'maintain the heterosexist gender order, which leads to bullying and the denial of citizenship rights' for women and LGBTQQ2SIA communities (Lees 2000: 9). Thus, this emphasises that sex education and the will to claim for rights to intimate or sexual citizenship are tightly bound (Lees 2000).

Davies (2000: 181) argues that disabled people are 'excluded from most of the dominant socialisation processes that help teach and prepare people for love, sex and intimacy'. Sex education has notoriously been denied to disabled people in the past, and for many disabled people this remains the norm. Shakespeare *et al.* (1996) and others (Garbutt 2010; Hollomotz 2010) argue that the denial of even the basic anatomical knowledge of reproduction to disabled young people remains embedded in their infantilisation. This is further exacerbated for people with the label of learning disability who, as I suggested in Chapter 1, are routinely positioned as 'incapable of forming substantial life preferences, learning the skills necessary to negotiate sexual choices, or making meaningful decisions in general' (Wilkerson 2002: 43; see also Brown 1994). Thus, widespread dis/ableist constructions of disability continue to shape the extent to which disabled young people acquire knowledge about sex and sex-related topics such as contraception, sexual health, reproduction and intimate relationships. Such an absence of (quality) sex education has a range of consequences. These range from the internalisation of feelings of inappropriateness and shame, to contributing to the harmful discourses of 'vulnerability' which plague disabled people. Such discourses are not only deeply disempowering, but also dangerous (Waxman 1991; Hollomotz 2010).

Informants' learning about sex was through a variety of formal and informal means; for example, knowledges of sex were learned through sex education, playground jokes, innuendo within teenage friendship groups, the media and, of course, from older siblings (for me, my older sister Kim held nothing back). Many said that matters of sex were seldom discussed at home, and some said this was because their parents considered it unnecessary knowledge for disabled children. While conversations about sex are customarily difficult between *any* parent and child, parents of disabled children can face 'complex challenges in understanding and addressing young people's needs' (Swain 1996: 58) regarding sexual life, which may exacerbate the problem. A few male informants said that they knew so little that upon entering puberty that upon ejaculating for the first time they thought they had a serious illness and were going to die. Most informants said that formal sex education was unhelpful because it was offered 'too late' and that its focus was too biological, clinical or just too narrow (see Corlyon and McGuire 1997; Holland *et al.* 1998; Jackson 1999), having little relevance to their lived experiences.

Terry, a 20-year-old wheelchair user who had been educated in mainstream schools, was segregated for PSHE education and placed in a class with other disabled students. This was – as Terry explained – considered progressive by the school, on the grounds that disabled young people needed 'special' knowledges of sex and sexuality. While Terry acknowledged that attention to the specialist knowledge he received in the class was beneficial, and considered radical by the school, he withdrew from the class because he felt that this overt segregation would only serve to affirm peers' assumptions about his (a)sexuality. Terry said that teaching all students together about the sexualities of *all* people would be far more radical. He said that, even within the special session (taught by a non-disabled person), there was little practical and informed advice on issues relating to the interrelationship of impairment and sexual life:

TERRY: 'Today we're going to learn how people with muscle weakness are going to put a condom on'. I remember saying – 'to be fair you're talking to someone who can't even open a chocolate wrapper, so I haven't got much hope, have I?' I remember it was almost like a shock because he [teacher] said 'does that mean you're not going to use contraception?!' and I said 'well no, obviously I'd just ask the other person to put the condom on'.

Terry's experience shows that, even within educational spaces where disability/ impairment-specific knowledges are offered, disabled people's learning about sex can remain defined by its deviation from dominant ableist sexual cultures and practices. Therefore, a focus on normative bodies and normative bodily experiences alienated Terry in his sexual learning. Thus, the heteronormative sex education that he and other informants described serves, I suggest, to affirm the compulsory ways in which sexual interactions take place, and that the absence of impairment in this space – or as Plummer (2003: 14) asserts, the 'lack of representation' – confirms that heteronormative sexuality remains exclusive to non-impaired sexually 'able' bodies. Thus, mainstream sex education continues to promulgate myths such as '"disability implies asexuality"' (Thompson *et al.* 2001: 59) because, as Blyth and Carson (2007: 37) found in their research into the sexual inequalities experienced by disabled young gay men, young disabled people 'internalise and use language that reinforces the heteronormative dominant discourses relating to what constitutes "natural" and "normal"' (see also Gillespie-Sells *et al.* 1998; Waxman Fiduccia 2000). Thus, for many informants, sex education served as a reproduction of their Otherness.

Learning about sexuality only through an ableist and heteronormative lens reinforced dominant expectations of 'teenage sexuality' for most informants with congenital impairments. Not meeting such expectations caused feelings of anxiety and failure (see Anderson and Clarke 1982). This was often expressed in relation to feelings of failure in other areas of adolescent life – for example, social life. The majority of these informants (most of who were under 25 at the time of interview) felt they had 'missed out' on much of the formative teenage experiences such as getting drunk, going to parties and having fleeting sexual encounters, because of issues with access, transport and non-disabled peers' attitudes. Being ostracised within and excluded from these key social spaces contributed to feelings of low self-worth and esteem and further exacerbated their feelings of frustration and isolation. Many said that prior to entering secondary education (as children) they'd had many friends, felt included within social networks and were less aware of 'being disabled' (see Tamm and Prellwitz 1999). Younger informants also said that, until this age, they had always presumed that they would have the makings of a (desired) normative heterosexual life and future – a 'healthy' sex life; an intimate partner to whom they would commit or marry; and their own (biological) family – expectations of an idealised, neoliberal adulthood (see Liddiard and Slater 2017).

However, such normative expectations shifted dramatically during their time in secondary education where exclusion from young people's social and sexual spaces confirmed their status as Other. For informants with neuromuscular conditions with pre-teen/teenage onsets, being a young person included a difficult negotiation of coming to terms with a newly acquired impairment and disabled identity at the same time as dealing with the typical tumult of teenage life and the formation of a sexual identity (see Galvin 2005). These were often highly conflicting, and the transition from non-disabled to a disabled identity was explicitly said to hinder social and sexual opportunities. For example, Helen said that her rapid accession to a wheelchair alienated her from her peers: *'Once you've passed that barrier [entering the wheelchair] you can't just ... they've made up their minds and it's quite hard to come back from it'*.

Many informants felt inadequate during youth because their sexual experiences came later than those of non-disabled peers and in different forms (see Howland and Rintala 2001). For example, many did not experience penetrative sex during their youth, often because of factors such as logistics, access and a lack of privacy. Jane described herself as a 'slow starter' and said hearing friends' sexual stories made her feel left behind. Kadeem (and many others) thought sex was something unavailable and out of reach. Robert worried if he'd ever lose his virginity, and Rhona said that if she weren't disabled she would have been *'sexually active at a much younger age'*. Interestingly, Rhona said that she would *'get off with men in clubs'* but that the most important part of this was friends and peers *seeing* it take place and, thus, *'that men were interested in me'*. To perform the role of a desired woman in whom men were *'interested'* is to embody the highly gendered role of the seductress – a role far removed the usual trope of disabled womanhood as inherently failing, undesirable and abject. While Rhona's *performances* of sexuality specifically to/for her peers (a practice also carried out by other informants) is likely carried out by many teenagers, regardless of disability, the emphasis for Rhona was upon affirming that a sexual identity is *possible* and that, as a disabled woman, she could both desire others and be desired. I interpreted these actions as Rhona (re)claiming a sexual self presumed by others to be non-existent; thus she sought to resist her desexualisation by managing her public sexual identity in this way, which in turn aided her inclusion into the sexual cultures of youth.

Thus, exclusion from the sexual cultures of youth was described as a very difficult experience, as has been found in other research (see DeLoach *et al.* 1983; Morris 1993). Some informants – particularly those with what would be considered to be a greater level of impairment – did not experience sexual relations in any form during their youth. Sally, a 21-year-old student, felt desperately frustrated about having not yet lost her virginity:

SALLY: Up until recently I never doubted I'd someday have sex, but now, I'm really not so sure. It depresses me that I might never have that experience. I really want to experience sex, I am 21 after all! Some of my friends have been doing it since they were 13! But, as I say, I just don't know how to make it happen, and I doubt it will ever happen. Who would want to have sex with me when there are plenty of normal girls more than willing?! Besides the fact, I am still stuck living with my bloody parents ... wouldn't that be cosy.

Sally's account highlights her low sexual self-esteem (*'Who would have sex with me when there are plenty of normal girls more than willing?!'*) and the difficult transition many young disabled people experience between childhood and adulthood (Goodley and McLaughlin 2011). Difficulties in finding employment and organising accessible housing and personal care can often mean living with parents later than non-disabled peers – which Sally implies affects her ability to explore her sexuality. In addition, special educational needs (SEN) transition planning for disabled young people, the final transition plan of which 'should draw together information in order to plan coherently for the young person's transition to adult life' (Department for Education and Skills 2001: Para 9:51), often omits the social and sexual aspects of 'adult life' in favour of concentrating upon independent living, further education and employment. We are yet to see whether the new Education Health and Care (EHC) plans, introduced by the British Government in 2014 to replace Statements of special educational needs and Learning Difficulty Assessments, will fare any better. While such a lack of focus on intimate and personal life is perhaps not surprising, it means that issues that Sally claims were very important to her sense of personhood as an adult were routinely discounted. It also emphasises the extent to which intimate rights mark a belonging to the world of adults and adulthood (see Slater 2015).

Informants' feelings of frustration over delayed sexual experiences were often made worse by family or friends, teachers, and peers. British disability scholar Donna Reeve (2004: 91) suggests that trusted people within disabled people's own social networks, such as family members and friends, can be 'agents of psycho-emotional disablism' and that emotional suffering is actually more acute when coming from those with whom an intimacy (or proximity) is shared (Reeve 2002). For example, many informants had experienced parents, wider family and peers telling them not 'to get their hopes up' regarding sexuality and relationships. This only served to reinforce ableist cultural tropes of disabled sexual selfhood as both inappropriate and improbable (Wilkerson 2002):

KADEEM: Family members made comments like 'we pray you get better so you can get married and have kids' ... That broke my heart.

ABRAM: I remember one of them laughing at me and telling me 'ha-ha you're never going to have sex' and I was like, 'Oh I'll show you!' I still remember that ... years later I was thinking 'he was a right wally, but I don't half feel that he's right now' ... he was spot on, he was.

Kadeem and Abram's experiences were not uncommon among informants. A few other informants confirmed that verbal bullying had targeted their presumed asexuality, reinforcing the perceived lack of a sexual self and sexual ability which positions disabled people as less than human in a society that privileges sexual activity as a sign of adulthood and citizenship rights (Weeks 1998). Siebers (2008: 140) argues that ideas of disabled people as less than human are rooted in assumptions about reproductive capacity, which 'marks sexuality as a privileged index of human ability' (see also Jackson 1999; Tepper 2000). Therefore, in having a body presumed incapable of sexuality and reproduction, Abram was considered of less value, less human and thus worthy of abuse. Speaking to gender and sexual orientation, Lees (2000: 4) argues that sexual bullying 'is intricately connected to the way sexual identities are formed and maintained in the heterosexual gender order'. She gives examples of boys centralising words like 'fag' and 'poof' when bullying each other. Such words are used not to imply that a boy is gay, but that he is Other for not fitting the markers of hegemonic masculinity. Thus, bullying is *purposeful*, because it enables the majority category to assert power and thus maintain the status quo. Lees (2000) suggests that it is this preservation of the gender order that contributes to a later denial of (sexual) citizenship rights for sexual minority groups and women.

For some male informants, feelings of inadequacy and frustration were so severe that they had contemplated suicide, showing the extent to which normative temporal markers of masculine sexuality can be deeply oppressive in contexts of disability and youth:

TERRY: I didn't think I was going to have sex, so it was quite an upsetting time, and there was a major point in adolescence where I did contemplate committing suicide because I didn't think I'd ever develop into an adult where I'd have all the experiences of non-disabled people.

ABRAM: I never had any [sex] there [at university]; by the time I left university I almost topped myself.

However, other male informants who were equally concerned about losing their virginity negotiated these feelings of inadequacy by visiting a sex worker (some during their teens). Of 16 male informants, seven had used a sex worker, and for three of these it was their first experience of penetrative sex. Using a sex worker was understood by these informants as the *only* way they could gain *vital* sexual experience, and thus acted to resist their exclusion from mainstream sexual youth cultures. While men's use of sex workers is discussed in depth in Chapter 7, it is important to note here that no female informants said they had used a sex worker. However, Sally told me in her email interview that she had considered it:

SALLY: I have read about a few disabled lads in *Target MD* magazine [disability publication] (whenever I read or hear about muscular dystrophy they always seem to refer to boys with Duchenne MD – girls have MD too!!!) who have actually paid for sex because they didn't feel they'd ever get the experience otherwise. I have actually thought about doing this myself, not now because I live with my parents and if I did it's not something I'd tell ANYONE, but perhaps when I have my own place. Then again I think my self-confidence is so diminished I couldn't ever actually pay someone for sex because ... I guess I'd feel ashamed, worthless, and I want respect, I want the person I have sex with to actually like me and be attracted to me.

Sally's account affirms that paying for sex is a highly gendered activity based on conventional ideas about male and female sexualities (Sanders 2008). It also indicates how the sexual stories of young disabled men (predominantly those with progressive impairments) are often privileged over those of young disabled women. Such masculinist stories can, in turn, both normalise the use of sex workers in certain spaces within disability communities over others, at the same time as casting female sexual desire adrift (Sanders 2010). I return to the gendered relations of sex work in Chapter 7.

Lacking privacy and managing invasiveness

Tom Shakespeare (1996: 66) argues that 'disabled people face a considerable amount of curiosity and voyeurism'. Inevitably, this is not wholly exclusive to disabled people or the impaired body; 'gay, lesbian, bisexual, queer and transgendered [*sic*] people also suffer from a lack of sexual privacy' (Siebers 2008: 138; see also Abbott 2015). To contextualise this further, it's critical to note here that, in Western advanced capitalist contexts, middle to ruling class and White communities are more able to assert and be granted rights to privacy. Privacy, and the extent to which individuals and communities can claim it, is deeply political. In the context of disability, many disabled people still reside in institutions and residential care homes, or are transinstitutionalised, with a significant lack of autonomy and privacy combined with substantial surveillance (see Shue and Flores 2002). As the wonderful Miriam Kaufman, Cory Silverberg and Fran Odette (2003: 8) emphasise in the groundbreaking *Ultimate Guide to Sex and Disability: For All of Us Who Live with Disabilities, Chronic Pain and Illness*, 'the definition of privacy changes when you have no lock on the door, or when you request private time at a specific hour knowing that it will probably be written down in a log-book'. Wilkerson (2002: 34) problematises the lack of privacy within institutions, suggesting that

> Sexuality is vital pleasure, interpersonal connection, personal efficacy, and acceptance of one's body and of self more generally, all goods which might be useful to disabled persons in nursing homes. Furthermore, because one's autonomy is already compromised by residing in a nursing home, the violation of both sexual agency and personal security imposed by this loss of privacy should be recognised as a serious harm.

The routine desexualisation (and often dehumanisation) of disabled people through processes of instutionalisation constitutes a serious denial of (sexual) autonomy, agency, and control of their sexualities and intimate relationships (Garbutt 2010; Shakespeare *et al.* 1996). These factors are integral to the accessing and claiming of rights to intimate citizenship (Richardson 2000). Much of the surveillance disabled people experience is rooted in ableist assumptions around innocence, vulnerability and of protection. Even for those who live inter/dependently in the community, privacy can still be an aspiration rather than a right. Paradoxically, this is not the only space within intimate life where a lack of privacy takes root. Once again revealing the confinement of disabled sexuality to established binaries – sexual/asexual, vulnerable/dangerous, abused/abuser and protected/unprotected – this lack of privacy is further compounded through an ableist gaze and its fetishisation of disability. A gaze that propagates disabled desire as 'inherently kinky, bizarre and exotic' (Kafer 2003: 85). To explore some of these concepts, this section will examine disabled informants' experiences of lacking privacy through care, and their experiences of managing the intrusion of multiple ableist gazes in relation to a lack of rights to intimate citizenship.

While no informants in my research resided permanently in a care home, in supported living or in a residential institution (all now lived within the community), many experienced forms of institutionalisation through, for example, regular respite care, long periods of hospitalisation (particularly those in rehabilitative spaces following spinal cord injury) and residential special education, or had done so in the past. Many informants said they lacked privacy generally within community-based caring arrangements and familial caring. Therefore, access to privacy – or rather a lack of it – was a significant factor in shaping both informants' sexual self and their expression. Privacy was disrupted and denied routinely by parents, families, personal assistants, school nurses and teachers. Many readily expressed what a lack of respect for privacy had upon their sexual selves:

PETE: Because I need such personal care I have never been able to have a 'real' personal life – no real secrets.
SHAUN: Before Hannah [wife] I had live-in carers, so you're never really by yourself ... so that was really really tough.

Pete's assertion that he has never been able to have a ' *"real" personal life'* shows the sizeable extent to which the absence of privacy can impact upon feelings of (sexual) autonomy and selfhood. Shaun emphasises the impracticalities of care in relation to privacy; never having lived alone contributed significantly to his inability to sexually explore both his own body and his sexual desires. Many older informants told painful stories about the ways privacy was denied during care they received in their youth:

PETE: New carers I didn't like especially around puberty when my bits got bigger and the growth of hair, etc. I would be very uncomfortable with myself. I have always needed help washing and showering and dressing. I remember even crying as I didn't want to undress for bed in front of new helpers. I'd get in a right old state. I wouldn't even go to the toilet as I was so embarrassed. I wouldn't drink so I wouldn't need the toilet especially at night as the regular school nurses used to threaten to put you in an incontinence urinary sheath or in an incontinent pad. I wasn't incontinent but if you needed more than one wee in the night then using one of these things was discussed… At camp I'd ask for doors to be locked while I was being showered. It never was locked … the door was always wide open.

Pete's experiences show that a refutation of privacy is not only dehumanising but also harmful and frightening. Pete, now 42, reveals that he had to manage his body (not drinking to ensure he didn't need the toilet) in order to minimise the gaze and authority of the nurse. Younger informants were still living through such experiences at the time of interview, and central to young men's stories were erections, ejaculation and wet dreams. One participant, Harjit, who had moved to the UK from Africa to study, said his parents had insisted on accompanying him to continue in their role as his full-time carers. Harjit said that his parents were very overbearing and that, at 23 years old, he still shared a bedroom with them:

HARJIT: My parents must know I masturbate but they've never really asked me and it's never really come up in discussion. I have had nights when they're having sex, but obviously I'm 'asleep' and facing the other side … it's just frustrating because it's like, I understand, fair enough, they don't get any time on their own, it's fine I'm not going to say anything … you just try and sleep and occupy your mind with something else, but it's just frustrating thinking 'well, why can't I? What's different with me?'

Sleeping in the same room as one's parents is something that would rarely, if ever, happen to a non-disabled person of Harjit's age. It not only shows that disabled sexualities remain very much a product of social environment (Taleporos and McCabe 2001), but highlights how much disabled people remain infantilised and without agency and autonomy – particularly, where little state-funded care provision and high rates of poverty together with a reluctance towards non-familial (paid-for) care can mean disabled people remain infantilised within both family and wider networks. Although, it's worth noting that significant austerity over the past five years is shaping care in the UK in similar ways. Similarly, Abram, British Asian IT worker, revealed how he felt his privacy was severely compromised during early adulthood:

ABRAM: I remember being a little bit embarrassed by ... the fact my dad was doing all my caring... I used to get quite a lot of erections and ejaculate quite a lot during the night and I remember my dad mentioned it to my mum who thought it was a problem and [said] 'Should we call the GP?' and it was like, 'Mum, mum, it's ... not a medical problem!'... It got me into a bit of trouble back in [residential school] as well, 'cos I remember one of my experiences was trying to ejaculate whilst getting washed [by an assistant] and I remember I got reported to the head of house by a couple of them [assistants] and getting called in first thing in the morning by the head of house. [...] I don't think it was that I was turned on by the caring; it was I sort of felt the need to ejaculate, erm, and that was just the only way. I think the urge was that it would be washed away and done and dusted. I felt pretty bad. I think that problem contributed to the feeling that somehow ... my sexuality was not, I can't take it for granted as being a right of mine. I've carried that through all these years.

Abram's account reveals his realities of having a body that is looked after by parents or caring assistants. His account illustrates a lack of freedom to exercise his own (sexual) body and feelings – a fundamental requirement of intimate citizenship (Plummer 2003). His parents' largely desexualised view of him cast his (normative) sexual expression into the realms of abnormality and thus defined it as problematic (and, tellingly, in need of medical attention). His story shows a direct link between this lack of privacy for sexual exploration of his own body and the problematic strategy of trying to find 'relief' via means that were not under the gaze of his parents. For example, what Abram perceives as the only accessible means for relief (ejaculating while being washed by a carer at school) involved taking great risks, as well as turning something that most people have the privilege of keeping private into a 'public' matter. Notably, his strategy simultaneously shifted his sexuality into a deviant space, for which his head of house chastised him. This shows, in contexts of disability, just how readily the normative can *become* deviant. Such experiences were common for men in my research, particularly when erections and ejaculation were 'accidental' during personal care:

PETE: At physiotherapy I used to get erections for no reason except for being stripped to my boxer-shorts ... A young woman helper could see I wasn't happy. I explained to her I needed the toilet but couldn't undo my jeans. She said she would help. She pushed me in my wheelchair into the toilet, she undid my jeans. I could smell her perfume. I stood up to go wee and as I stood her hand went on my bare bottom. I thought maybe she was making sure I didn't fall over. While I was peeing she crouched down and said 'have you finished?' I don't know why but I started to get aroused. Her perfume seemed to fill the air. As she started pulling my shorts back up she brushed my leg with the back of her hand as she did I got very, very aroused. I fell back into my wheelchair embarrassed. I was expecting her to get mad or to get a nurse. But she finished fastening my jeans ... I could see my pants getting 'sticky'.

Pete's detailed account (which happened during his childhood 30 years earlier) shows the extent to which fleeting feelings of inappropriateness, embarrassment and shame can remain. While such 'accidents' could be argued to be the 'natural' product of a young man's body being touched and intimately cared for (particularly during puberty), it is significant to note that no stories of such incidences involved male carers. This is not only because of the gendered and heterosexist nature of care work (and thus the centrality of the female worker body within care relationships), but may also have been because doing so was considered as potentially disruptive to male informants' heterosexual identity and their performance of it. Similarly, no female informants talked about arousal during personal care, either because voicing such experiences risks shame or embarrassment (particularly in the context of female sexuality), or because such experiences seldom occurred (see Chapter 7; you can read more about leakiness, containment and disability in Liddiard and Slater 2017).

Additionally, many informants spoke of their privacy being violated through the invasiveness of friends, family and peers – close others – as well as via strangers. Thus, the majority of informants' sexual lives had been subjected, often in multiple modes and spaces, to the non-disabled gaze. For example, the majority had experienced being asked the question *'Can you have sex?'*

HELEN: When I was younger I remember this one guy at school said 'Can you have sex?' I was like 'Yeah!'... Getting people to see past the chair ... it's difficult.

LUCILLE: One thing that does annoy me is how people are curious about whether you have sex or not but they never actually ask (thankfully!!!). Friends of family or family ask other family but not me. Weird, I'm sure they don't ask their family or friends the same things about their non-disabled friends! I find it funny in a way.

TERRY: People have the opportunity to ask me when I teach, and probably about 50 per cent of the questions are related to sex and relationships... I find it encouraging to have young people ask me about sexual relationships and disability because it encourages me that they want to find out more, really.

Morris (1991: 29) argues that it is disabled people's physical differences that make their 'bodies public property', which invites 'the total stranger or slight acquaintance coming up and asking us the most intimate things about our lives'. While the accounts above demarcate that such inquiry was received with good faith or could be a platform from which to educate people, for others it could be a point of heavy frustration and a difficult social situation to negotiate. Shaun, a spinal-cord-injured wheelchair user, and his non-disabled wife Hannah, explained their difficulty:

HANNAH: A lot of people [friends] will ask, 'Does Shaun's willy work?' and I always say 'Yes it does.' I remember in the beginning Shaun would say, 'Say it's none of their business' but I guess... I almost feel I have to prove that Shaun is a man.

SHAUN: And that really does make me angry because you wouldn't ask anybody else that, you know ... so it's like why do these people think they've got the right to ask these kinds of questions? I know it's curiosity but...

HANNAH: But I'd much rather say, 'Yes it works' rather than 'Don't ask', which is implying it doesn't.

SHAUN: But it does work... most of the time...

HANNAH: Yeah but I could also say 'people mind their own business' but I've had difficulty. If you say, 'mind your own business' I think that people are assuming that you're impotent, that's how I feel.

SHAUN: But I just think you put the ball back in their court and ask, 'Why are you asking me that question? You wouldn't ask me that question if I were going out with an able-bodied partner'...

HANNAH: Yeah...it's almost that thing, well – you have to prove, prove that Shaun is a man...

SHAUN: Just say, 'Yes! And it's enormous!' [Both laugh]

This dialogue from Shaun and Hannah, the only couple to be interviewed, shows how the management of curiosity into their sex lives (and bodies) impacts upon their identity as a couple. Both want to resist such intrusion but manage this through different means. Hannah shows resistance through wanting to *prove* Shaun's masculinity and virility to others (*'You have to prove ... that Shaun is a man'*), while Shaun shows resistance through wanting to challenge such curiosity and ignorance (*'Why are you asking me that question?'*). The account also illustrates how both the disabled person and their partner can share the burden of surveillance. Terry voiced a similar experience whereby people would ask his girlfriend, as he put it, *'what's it like having sex with a disabled person?'* As Sakellariou (2006: 104) suggests, while any couple may face difficulties with sex, 'when one or both of the partners are disabled somehow an utterly private issue is transformed into a public one'. Perhaps unsurprisingly, such surveillance displayed real ignorance of disabled sexual subjectivities. For example, Terry said that friends had enquired what type of porn he enjoyed watching, because they assumed that because he is disabled he only watched porn that featured disabled performers. For Pete, surveillance constituted a painful assault on his (as he described, already fragile) masculine identity:

PETE: Well, I have been asked if my wife was my sister. I've been asked if my kids are really mine. I have been asked if my wife and I needed IVF to get our kids. And I have been asked if I needed Viagra. All these things are very much a punch in the gut to masculinity.

Pete's account explicitly reveals the emasculating potential of such examination, but also the ways in which disabled people are seldom recognised as parents or as having the ability to parent (see Thomas 1997). The fact Pete (and many other informants) experienced strangers assuming their romantic partners were friends or siblings shows that many disabled people are denied the privilege of 'public recognition and validation' of their intimate partnerships, a primary area of sexual citizenship (Richardson 1998). While Richardson (1998) speaks of public validation more as a legal recognition of intimate partnerships within public institutions – for example, lesbian and gay people's claims to the right to marry – I suggest that, where disability is concerned, public validation can materialise far more literally. For example, as the accounts thus far in this section have shown, being recognised as a partner, lover, boyfriend, girlfriend, parent or sexual subject is often deeply important, and being seen in such ways by others can act as a validation of humanness, worthiness and esteem to the outside 'public' social world.

Invasiveness was also found to have spatial dimensions, becoming more prevalent in, specifically, adult social and sexual spaces such as pubs and nightclubs. Terry talked about having to managing the burden of the non-disabled gaze while in nightclubs:

TERRY: Erm, it's always women. In fact, it's never been a bloke; I think they've always asked a mate, they'd never ask me… But the women, they'll ask me to my face [about sex], and we'll have a laugh about it. You do get drunk people being very heavily patronising, they'll insist on buying you drinks, etc., or they'll want to make you their best friend the whole night, erm, and that's part of them being drunk and perceiving your disability as a fate worse than death. Basically, they're either very inquisitive about sex, or they're patronising, or they're abusive, really.

Disabled people regularly face discrimination, prejudice and abuse when in adult social spaces (Reeve 2002). As Jenny Morris (1991: 25) suggests, 'going out in public so often takes courage, it is the knowledge that each entry into the public world will be dominated by stares, by condescension, by pity and by hostility'. Terry's account reinforces this and illustrates that in these particular social spaces and environments disabled people must routinely manage such reactions, either taking on the role of educator (educating non-disabled people about the lived realities of *being* disabled), resisting patronising attitudes and passive-aggressive inquiry, and surviving the objectification of *being* the spectacle for others' entertainment and fascination. However, Terry told how he perceived this to be voyeuristic, ground in sexual attraction and sexual desire for his impaired body:

TERRY: Well, I think some of them just want to know for their own benefit and then some of them will be interested in taking it further. They're either interested, or they've asked that question 'cause they want something to go on afterwards. I mean, I can imagine that some people have a fascination of having sex with a disabled person – there was one girl, for example, she said, 'well, my ambition is to try and sleep with as many different groups of people'. So I joked, 'have you had sex with lots of ethnic minorities?' she said 'yeah, I've done a Black person, a Chinese person' and I said, 'well, have you done a disabled person?' and she went 'no, but they're on my list'. So it's almost like, there are people who want that kind of experience that's very different – so, it's curiosity, you know, you do get a few people who just find you attractive.

Terry's account shows how he understands curiosity in this context, at least partially, as a source of titillation for non-disabled people regarding the ways in which his (impaired) body *performs* sexually. Thus rather than 'curiosity' and voyeurism maintaining the impaired body purely as a spectacle of abjection (see Adams 2001), the presence of an impaired body – as *the* challenge to the heteronormative 'compulsory able body' (McRuer 2006a: 2) – invites non-disabled people to consider it as a site of sexual potentiality. As Terry's experiences demonstrate, this can be a transformative social interaction and a means of accessing sex where his impaired body becomes 'a locus of power' (Solvang 2007: 56) rather than just a 'fetishized object' (Shakespeare *et al.* 1996: 3; see also Hahn 1988; Solvang 2007; Waxman Fiduccia 1999).

The relationality of sex talk: 'can you have sex?'

Talking about sex (I colloquially call it 'sex talk' in this section) within wider social networks was something many informants found uncomfortable. This discomfort was said to increase when in medical spaces and contexts and, namely, when interacting with health professionals. As discussed in previous chapters, the pervasive medicalisation of the impaired body within an ableist cultural imaginary posits it only as a site for cure and intervention. Defining disability only through deficit models (Milligan and Neufeldt 2001; Tepper 1999, 2000), Wilkerson (2002: 34) acknowledges that medical discourse is 'insidious in its ability to shape not merely our sexual options but a sense of ourselves as sexual beings, and ultimately our very identities for ourselves and others'. In this section of the chapter I conceptualise the conversation as a public and relational space that, for some informants, required extensive management in order to present, claim or maintain a preferred sexual identity. Exploring informants' experiences of sex talk with medical professionals and, later, the materialisation of sex talk in wider social networks, I show how their right to choose how they organise their personal lives and claim identities – the very essence of intimate citizenship – was routinely denied.

Informants received variable responses from health professionals when attempting to talk about sex, sexuality and sexual and reproductive health. Often these matters were ignored within doctor–patient relationships, despite informants raising and speaking out about particular issues of concern to them (see Nancy Mairs 1996 for a personal account of such interactions). When informants did ask questions relating to sex, help and advice was not forthcoming. For example, Gemma told a story of a time when she had raised the issue of sexual pleasure (she had recently had trouble orgasming because of an associated nerve condition) with a consultant:

GEMMA: And, he [consultant] was just totally embarrassed. I thought 'how bizarre', he just didn't want to tackle it at all. He was totally … aghast … didn't comment and carried on [laughs] … I think having a couple of lesbians discussing their orgasms was not what he had in mind […] I just think that's quite telling, really.

Such an unsupportive reaction emphasises that impaired bodies that experience sexual dysfunction are seldom seen as problematic (Tepper 1999). It also affirms, as Kafer (2003: 82) argues, that 'the sexuality of people with disabilities is understood as always already deviant' that 'when queer desires and practices are recognized as such, they merely magnify or exacerbate that experience'. By seeking advice from her consultant, Gemma was presenting a sexual identity that was then disavowed. Other informants avoided talking to medical professionals about such issues, either due to doubts of the help they could offer or because they'd had bad experiences of doing so in the past. Helen, a 20-year-old mother with a progressive muscle condition, told how doctors were particularly brutal when she unexpectedly fell pregnant. The reproductive activities of disabled people are shrouded in biomedical dominance which positions them, should they choose to reproduce, as (socially and personally) irresponsible, incapable and as dangerous risk-takers. Thomas (1997: 640) suggests that having children is particularly difficult for disabled women, whose 'reproductive journeys are strewn with social barriers of an attitudinal, ideological and material kind'. Helen said that reactions to her decision to keep her baby were shocking, and that her team of doctors consistently warned throughout her pregnancy that carrying a baby to full term meant she was '*going to die*':

HELEN: They [doctors] were awful, the lung doctor just told me … 'You're going to die', which was just gruesome. I went back to see him a few months after I'd had him [her baby] and I was like 'ha!!'

While Helen could resist the medical dominance and control that blighted her pregnancy (a form of psycho-emotional disablism), she experienced doctors voicing concerns in this way as incredibly frightening. It indicates, as Thomas (1997: 636) notes, that while many women 'experience a sense of loss of control over their bodies during pregnancy and childbirth as doctors and other health professionals "take over", this experience of loss of control can be intensified when "disability" is an additional factor in the lay–professional encounter'.

However, a few informants said they had found '*helpful doctors*'. These views were usually expressed within stories about 'one special doctor' who had offered productive help and advice around sexuality, sexual health and relationships, suggesting that there are pockets of, and potentialities for, empowering sexual support within medical contexts. For example, Kadeem said that his GP gave him time to talk through his worries about sexuality, had researched sex surrogacy services for him and had even applied to his local primary care trust for funding of a sex surrogate (which was later rejected). Jenny, one of the few disabled mothers in the research (just three of the disabled women in the research were mothers), said that during her time in a spinal injury ward (where she resided from the ages of 11–14), and throughout her life, her consultant had been very supportive regarding sexual reproductive health and, in particular, her own pregnancy. She credits this support for her being able, as a woman with a spinal injury, to have a baby at all, particularly in the context of 1970s Britain, a time when civil rights for disabled people were only just emerging.

Engaging in sex talk within wider social networks could be equally challenging. Some informants said that they could talk about sex and their sexuality with ease (both within the research interview and in wider social networks), and such talk was positioned as important in the construction of (and projection of) a sexual identity. However, for others, even talking about sexuality and intimate relationships within the interview space was difficult and upsetting – this was often because they'd never talked about such topics with another person before. For the most part, informants were mindful of the asexual identities cast upon them: either they spoke of it generally ('*I'm not seen as a sexual object. I guess the perception is, disabled person, oh we're going to be on the bottom of the heap, not gonna have sexual relationships, end of story*'), or it was revealed when talking about with whom they felt comfortable discussing sex. For example, many said that they would keep quiet in sex talk with non-disabled friends (for fear of inviting an unwanted curiosity) and felt more comfortable discussing sexual matters with disabled friends, where their experiences were assumed to be better understood:

SALLY: I feel really uncomfortable and unable to join in conversations about sexual partners [with non-disabled friends] because I've never had one. I don't want anyone to know that, but at the same time I don't like lying, so I try to just say nothing either way.

PHILLIP: There's something about a disabled person who's in the same situation knowing what you've gone through, so you're more comfortable with it [talking to a disabled friend].

HANNAH: I wouldn't be too honest ... especially if they're non-disabled ... I just think it would freak them out ...

PETE: I laugh, I nod, I agree like I'm in the conversations about sex but as I said before I don't want to hear them [non-disabled friends] talking about things I can't do.

Sally and Hannah's accounts show the skill involved in knowing what to 'reveal' to whom and when. Staying silent, as Sally does, is a purposeful strategy towards managing rejection during sex talk. She is aware that her relative lack of (sexual) experience marks her as an outsider and that, in the context of youth, confessing this risks refusal. However, for Hannah, revealing too much (to non-disabled friends) was considered a very risky project towards offending or 'freaking' people out – a strategy that she explained as requiring careful management amongst different groups of friends.

Conclusion

This chapter has laid the foundations for the analyses that follow in the remainder of this book. More than this, the stories in this chapter, I suggest, emphasise the extent to which disabled people in my research routinely lacked many of the essential ingredients of intimate citizenship. For example, individual and collective narratives revealed that most were frequently short of 'control (or not) over one's body, feelings, relationships', 'access (or not) to representations, relationships, public spaces, etc.', and the ability to make 'socially grounded choices (or not) about identities, gender experiences, erotic experiences' (Plummer 2003: 14). This chapter has, then, made a modest attempt to demarcate and explore the spaces, environments and contexts in which these aspects of intimate citizenship were denied, regulated or, at best, mediated by informants. Disabled informants have spoken of (i) being asexualised – considered/presumed asexual or lacking the capacity and desire for sexual and intimate life; (ii) being desexualised, that is, being actively denied a sexual self through caring regimes, sex talk, and sex education; and (iii) being fetishised through a range of social processes and spaces. For example, young disabled people experienced significant asexualisation through their teenage years, through their own selves and embodiments being rendered incompatible with the normative areas, spaces and cultures of youth, most notably where sexuality and gender are concerned. Disabled informants' experienced desexualisation through their routine experiences of lacking privacy in a variety of forms of care, which they said negated opportunities for sexual expression, and also autonomy and agency within intimate life – all of which are central to intimate citizenship (Plummer 2003). Last, the relational disablism inherent to sex talk with a series of others revealed the extent to which the disabled sexual body and subject can be readily reproduced as an object of fetish. Therefore, I suggest that disabled people's lack of intimate citizenship and lack of a *claim for rights* to intimate citizenship is embedded in these spaces and processes of asexualisation, desexualisation and fetishisation.

What's also important to consider is the ways in which informants were conscious of their ascribed a/sexual identities and, in order to (re)form a (public) sexual self, made attempts to manage identity in various ways. However, such management and negotiation seldom turned into sexual empowerment or emancipation from dis/ableist discourse. For example, methods to resist exclusion and asexualisation within the sexual cultures of youth seemed to lead to very little sexual empowerment in informants' stories, and was negotiated primarily through becoming a sexual object, either in one's own eyes or in the eyes of the (non-disabled) Other. Furthermore, it is clear that much of this resistance remained within conventional notions of sexual life (e.g. having sex/being seen to be sexual), and thus served to (inadvertently) reproduce the very sexual norms that desexualise disabled people (amongst others). Additionally, there was little negotiation of the boundaries of privacy where informants made attempts to (re) claim a sexual self within forms of 'institutional' care (e.g. boarding schools, summer camps and respite care), particularly in ways that do not constitute deviancy, or where sexual pleasures are not shrouded in guilt and shame. Therefore, the inherent paternalism of the institution not only served to inhibit bodily exploration conducive to sexual expression, but also further reinforced disabled people's exclusion from intimate citizenship and their inability to claim for rights to intimate citizenship.

Furthermore, another consideration to keep in view is the significant psycho-emotional impacts of being desexualised, Othered and fetishised. In this chapter we have seen feelings of failure, inadequacy, and sexual shame; to use Abram's words, *'the feeling that somehow ... my sexuality was not, I can't take it for granted as being a right of mine'*. A heteronormative sex education and dominant discourses of youth and sexuality served to exclude and Other disabled young people at a time where they were – as young people – trying to forge a sexual identity and develop feelings of sexual self-worth and body confidence. Practical issues such as inaccessible social spaces, peers' attitudes, and an ineffectual transition planning process exacerbated exclusion and feelings of inadequacy and were experienced as forms of psycho-emotional disablism (Reeve 2002). Equally, the management of a voyeuristic non-disabled gaze from a range of actors and close others – family, friends, support workers and health professionals – involved mediating complex social interactions that often meant significant psycho-emotional labour to negotiate or resist.

The psycho-emotional is where I now turn in the following chapter, where I explore informants' intimate relationships as a site of multiple forms of gendered and emotional work. I critically question the work carried out by informants and consider the ways in which it was shaped by their lived experiences of gender, sexuality, impairment and disability. I do so because knowledges of psycho-emotional disablism, particularly its potential impact within the personal, intimate and sexual spaces of disabled people's lives, are both under-researched and under-theorised (see Liddiard 2014c).

5 'I need to stick with this because I might not find anybody else'

The labour of love

Accessible summary

- This chapter considers disabled people's experiences of 'love' relationships.
- The research found that both disabled men and women carried out 'work' within these relationships.
- Usually, this work was shaped by the ways in which they felt about, or experienced, their gender, sexuality, impairment and disability.
- I question what this work means for disabled people, and argue that it is a form of disablism.

While social model orthodoxy holds the psychological as problematic (Watermeyer 2009), feminist authors – markedly Thomas (1999) and, later, Reeve (2002) – have argued for the inclusion of the psychological and emotional dimensions of disability and impairment within disability studies (see also Goodley 2011). For example, in her social relational model of disability, Thomas (1999: 60; emphasis added) redefines disability as 'a form of social oppression involving the social imposition of restrictions of activity on people with impairments *and* the socially engendered undermining of their psycho-emotional well-being'. Thus, 'disability' is reimagined to have political, material, economic, structural, emotional, intimate, and personal dimensions. Redefining disability along these lines contextualises that 'the oppression disabled people can experience operates on the "inside" as well as on the "outside"' (Thomas 2004: 40); or, as Reeve (2004: 84; original emphasis) articulates, 'operates at both the public and personal levels, affecting what people can do, as well as what they can be'.

As stated above, psycho-emotional disablism is 'the socially engendered undermining of emotional well-being' (Thomas 1999: 60). Reeve (2004: 86) proposes that this form of social oppression occurs through 'the experience of being excluded from physical environments' (which, she argues, instigates a feeling of not belonging); through the routine objectification and voyeurism perpetrated by (but not exclusive to) non-disabled others; and through internalised oppression, which she defines as when 'individuals in a marginalised group in society internalise the prejudices held by the dominant group' (Reeve 2004: 91).

Thus, psycho-emotional disablism is a relational form of disablism embodied through experiences of 'hostility or pitying stares, dismissive rejection, infantilisation, patronising attitudes, altruism, help and care on the part of non-disabled people' (Goodley 2011a: 96), which 'frequently results in disabled people being made to feel worthless, useless, of lesser value, unattractive, a burden' (Thomas 2006: 182).

Building upon existing knowledges of psycho-emotional disablism, particularly its impacts within the personal, intimate and sexual spaces of disabled people's lives, in this chapter I present findings that speak to disabled informants' experiences of their intimate relationships with others. To clarify, my use of the term 'intimate relationship' refers to a (non-commercial) shared intimacy with another person, which my informants identified as significant and a source of sexual, physical and/or emotional intimacy. In doing so, this chapter details people's own accounts of intimate relationships, which reveal the – often routine – carrying out of considerable emotional work (Hochschild 1983), as well as other forms of (gendered) work, such as sex work (Cacchioni 2007). By making visible their work of 'telling, hiding, keeping up, waiting, teaching, networking and negotiating' (Church *et al.* 2007: 10), I explore the ways in which informants' work was shaped by their lived and embodied experiences of gender, sexuality, impairment and disability. Crucially, I critically question such work, suggesting that, while it was often strategically and consciously employed to manage competing intimate oppressions, for the most part the requirement of informants to carry out forms of work within their sexual and intimate lives constituted a form of psycho-emotional disablism (Thomas 1999).

Learning to labour: emotional work and disability performance

Church *et al.* (2007: 1) state that 'complex invisible work is performed by disabled people in every day/night life'. In their research on disabled employees' experiences of corporate settings, Church *et al.* (2007: 1) uncovered multiple kinds of work that employees routinely utilised within the workplace in order to 'stay corporately viable'. Types of work included hiding impairment and its effects; being extra productive to counter employers' negative assumptions about disabled employees; and carrying out informal teaching around disability issues for co-workers and managers (Church *et al.* 2007). Similarly, the brilliant Alice Wong (2000: 303) has documented the multiple forms of (emotional and other) work employed by disabled women in reproductive and sexual health care, stating that 'work has become an umbrella code that encompasses both the barriers women face and the agency they exercise in dealing with them'. Likewise, Goodley (2011a: 92) has identified the performances disabled people are expected to give as routine: 'disabled people learn to respond to the expectations of non-disabled culture – the demanding public – in ways that range from acting the passive disabled bystander, the grateful recipient of others' support, the non-problematic receiver of others' disabling attitudes'.

However, while the psycho-emotional dimensions (Reeve 2002; Thomas 1999) and 'work' and 'performances' of the disabled identity have been explored within disability studies (Church *et al.* 2007; Goodley 2011a), the concepts of 'emotional work' and 'emotional labour' have seldom been applied to disabled people's experiences (Wilton 2008). The little empirical work that has taken place has related to work settings and public spaces and systems (see Bolton and Boyd 2003; Church *et al.* 2007; Wilton 2008; Wong 2000). To clarify, 'emotional work' and 'emotional labour' are terms coined by Arlie Hochschild (1983: 7) to represent the 'labour [which] one is required to induce or suppress feeling in order to sustain the outward countenance that produces the proper state of mind to others'. Emotional labour is mostly required within employment settings and refers to the 'management of feeling to create a publicly observable facial and bodily display that is sold for a wage and therefore has an exchange value' (Hochschild 1983: 7). In contrast, 'emotional work' or 'management' are forms of work that are required in private settings, such as the family or home, and which have '*use value*' (Hochschild 1983: 7; original emphasis). 'Emotional work', then, is a better-fitting conceptual framework for explorations of disabled people's lived experiences of their intimate relationships. My definition of the term follows that of Exley and Letherby (2001: 115) and refers to the 'effort and skill required to deal with one's own feelings and those of others within the private sphere'.

Emotional work takes many forms and serves a variety of functions; for example, work can be on or for the self (Hochschild 1983); on or for others (Exley and Letherby 2001); have both positive and negative consequences (Wilton 2008); and be both a collective and individual labour (see Korczynski 2003). Predominantly, women, 'as traditionally more accomplished managers of feeling' (Hochschild 1983: 11), have been found to carry out the majority of emotional work in the private sphere (Strazdins 2000) – largely because they take prime responsibility for the emotional well-being of other family members (DeVault 1999). Identifying this work serves important functions. Early work by Blumer (1969: 148) argues that identifying the 'invisible' work carried out as part of our daily lives can act as a 'sensitising concept', in that it can thrust previously neglected activities (e.g. childcare, caring for relatives) onto the public agenda. Furthermore, DeVault (1999: 62) suggests that identifying the customary emotional work that takes place within family life is invaluable towards providing 'fuller, more accurate accounts of how family members work at sustaining themselves as individuals and collectivities', an understanding that, she argues, provides 'an essential foundation for equitable policy aimed at enhancing the well-being of all citizens'.

I must stress, however, that by utilising the concept of emotional work (Hochschild 1983), I am not individualising, pathologising or psychologising disabled informants' emotional experiences. The psycho-emotional, psychological and now psychoanalytic (see Goodley 2011) aspects of disability remain contentious within disability studies for fear that they encompass a return to early 'individual, medical, bio-psychological, traditional, charity and moral models of disability' (Goodley 2011: 716), which 'locate social problems in the head and bodies – the psyches – of disabled people' (Goodley 2011: 716). On the contrary, through deconstructing informants' work I highlight the very social, cultural, political and material processes through which their work is produced. As Bolton and Boyd (2003: 291; emphasis added) say of Hochschild's attention to the feeling rules implicit to emotional labour, these serve to 'wrest the study of emotion *away* from "its traditional guardians", the psychologists'. In the first part of this chapter I speak broadly to informants' experiences of their intimate relationships, before later exploring the various forms of work and labour these required.

Affirmation and devaluation

In keeping with Western conceptualisations of coupledom, all informants who had been in an intimate relationship before reported it as having considerable benefits. In terms of relationship histories, 21 informants reported that they had been in an intimate relationship with a partner before, with just 12 of 26 being in a relationship with a partner at the time of taking part in the research. This latter figure echoes statistics reported in research by Clarke and McKay (2008: 3), which states that for working-age disabled people there are 'a higher proportion remaining single; a lower proportion being in their first marriage or being married at all: a slightly lower proportion cohabiting; a higher proportion of disabled people being divorced or separated from marriage' (Clarke and McKay 2008: 3). Thus, informants' relationship histories were largely reflective of these trends. Often, the intimate relationship was narrated as a 'safe space' from a range of oppressions, discrimination and prejudices experienced in the 'outside world', and as a powerful means through which to challenge ableist discourses of disabled people as sexless and as not being 'prospective' partners (Gillespie-Sells *et al.* 1998). It was further described as a space where gender and sexual selves could be affirmed and, for some, re/built. For example, Rhona, a 21-year-old recently single woman with a congenital impairment, said: '*It's nice to adore and be adored. Being in a relationship is a constant reassurance in my worth as a person and a woman.*' Being '*adored*' by a man (which reassures Rhona that she is a woman) fits with conventional heterosexual scripts whereby women are valued by the extent to which they elicit erotic and romantic desire in a man. For Rhona, then, an intimate relationship offered space to feel like 'a woman' in an ableist culture that routinely denies her feminine selfhood.

For others, intimate relationships generated confidence, esteem and feelings of self-worth. For example, following the end of her marriage to a sexually and physically violent partner (discussed later), Grace used a series of short-term casual relationships to heal what she described as the emotional damage inflicted by her ex-husband. In particular, to get over the lack of esteem that experiencing disablist verbal abuse had caused, and to regain sexual confidence:

GRACE: I started a flirtation with a colleague. It was lovely. We kissed and flirted and sometimes ended up in bed. He liked me because I was Deaf, because it made me who I was. He was disabled, wore callipers. To me, his legs were sexy because they helped make him who he was. [The relationship] totally was not threatening ... I felt attractive and wanted.

Thus, this relationship restored Grace's broken sense of self-worth, particularly in relation to her sexuality, which she asserted was taken from her during her abusive marriage. Therefore, Rhona and Grace's accounts emphasise the intimate relationship as a space to embody (gendered) desirability, contradicting dominant cultural representations of disability and the impaired body as lacking, deficient and monstrous (Shildrick 2002).

The relationship was also typically experienced as a space where informants could gain new roles and be appreciated for their abilities. Rhona spoke of how she and her non-disabled partner, who had depression, were useful to each other in the roles that they respectively took in their relationship:

RHONA: I could be strong for him emotionally, and he was strong for me physically.

Rhona sets out clear roles here. In doing so she acknowledges her inability to be the physically strong partner, but casts herself in the role as the emotionally strong partner, offering a very typical gendered division of labour. This was not only limited to relationships with non-disabled partners, but also extended to disabled partners. For example, Jenny reported a similar situation with her disabled ex-husband, to which she attributes to their ability to travel the world, work together and care for their son:

JENNY: We didn't stop at anything, if we wanted to do things we would find a way. If we didn't come across a disabled toilet – although he had really bad balance he was very strong – he used to manage to lean against a wall, lift me and put me onto [non-accessible] toilets and things. He could get me up steps ... I think the disabilities complemented each other, what I couldn't do ... In that way we were sort of one person because what I couldn't do he'd do and what he couldn't do, I could do.

Jenny's experience challenges the common idea that both partners being disabled is too difficult and can be unpractical, cited by many other informants as a key reason why they wouldn't or hadn't entered into a relationship with another disabled person. However, informants who *had* been in relationships with other disabled people reported partners having impairments as a benefit. For example, Jenny made reference to the fact that, because she and her husband had both experienced a spinal cord injury, they had a meaningful understanding of each other's bodily experiences and capabilities, over which they had bonded deeply. Similarly, Grace saw her relationship with her current disabled partner as a more trusting experience than her previous relationships with non-disabled people: '*I think there was a degree of trust that we had not yet felt previously with other, non-disabled partners.*'

For informants who had acquired impairment in adulthood, relationships could act as a crucial comforting and supportive space that eased the transition from non-disabled to a disabled identity:

LUCILLE: After I had my accident, intimacy was a problem for me. In many respects I think I was fortunate to already be in a relationship as I am not sure I would have had the confidence to engage in anything physical with someone new, even now over a decade on … It changed everything, the enjoyment of sex, confidence, the ability to be happy. My poor partner was so bloody good about it all.

PHILLIP: Well, the good thing about being in a relationship [at the point of injury] is that you can experiment [sexually] early on because you've already got a sexual relationship […] I think that was one of the biggest benefits of already being in a relationship is that … as soon as we were able to have sex for the first time it was kind of done relatively comfortably and we kind of got on […] the emotional part of it, the psychological part of it, the kind of … the undressing for the first time part … when you're disabled.

For both Lucille, who became a tetraplegic during her marriage, and Phillip, who became a wheelchair user after a motorcycle accident at the age of 35, already being in relationships at the time of acquiring impairment was crucial towards exploring sexual ability after injury, particularly in terms of learning how to manage an altered embodiment and its impact upon sexual and intimate subjectivities.

While the relationship could be an affirming space – a space of comfort, confidence, a place where the disabled partner could feel sexually and romantically desirable – most informants positioned themselves as of lesser value than their (non-disabled) partner. Many said they felt not 'good enough' to be with their (non-disabled) partner, and terms such 'grateful' and 'undeserving' were littered throughout informants' narratives in order to express how they felt about their partner choosing to be with them:

RHONA: Although I knew that he adored me, I also always felt slightly as though I didn't deserve him. I am a logical person, and I know that disability puts you further down the relationship league table.

SHAUN: I'm very grateful to be in a relationship full stop.

PETE: To be honest Kirsty, I never feel I'm good enough for my wife. I truly am a lucky bloke. I'm not just saying this for the sake of saying something kind, I REALLY mean it. I don't feel like a 'man' as I'm not very confident – I'm not very good at taking control of life situations like 'real men' do. I get tired very quickly – other 'real men' don't. I haven't got a very high opinion of myself. If something 'manly' needs doing around the house, my kids go to my wife.

Here, Pete, a 42-year-old wheelchair user who had been married to his wife for 20 years, questions his role as a man, husband and father. Unsurprisingly he draws on dominant hegemonic constructions of these masculine roles and makes the case for why he 'doesn't fit'. Not feeling 'good enough' was often compounded by outsider perceptions of the non-disabled partner: many informants made reference to the fact that outsiders considered their non-disabled partner to be 'angelic' and 'good for taking them on' (see Asch and Fine 1997). Another related common thread running through informants' stories was that their partners 'deserved better' – *the* word 'better' was explained to mean a non-disabled partner. For example, Helen, a 20-year-old student engaged to a non-disabled man, made regular references to her partner 'deserving better' – '*I always think he'd be happier with somebody who could walk*' – while male informants stated their partners 'deserved better' because they couldn't carry out what they defined as 'manly' duties and roles (as Pete does above). This feeling of inadequacy was also narrated when talking about sex, particularly for male informants (see Chapter 6), even though both men and women compared themselves to what a (hypothetical) non-disabled person 'could offer' sexually. For example, Kadeem, a single 28-year-old man interviewed via instant messaging, felt 'sexually inadequate' and said: '*I wasn't gonna be enough for her coz I wasn't able to have sex properly and that she would find someone better [non-disabled] than me.*' This was echoed by Pete, who said that he regularly seeks his wife's approval following sex, showing that it is a source of considerable worry and anxiety, even when in long-term, committed relationships:

PETE: Even after 20 years of being together I still seek my wife's approval after intercourse. Even though she approves, it's not what I've already told myself ... I am afraid my wife will get bored of me and wonder what it's like to have sex with an able-bodied man.

The strategic work of staying

For many, informants' stories revealed how they had resided in intimate relationships for reasons beyond (romantic) feelings for a partner, and exacerbated by a disabled identity within an ableist heteronormative sexual culture. For example, Robert, a 26-year-old wheelchair user with congenital impairment, said that 'having' or 'being with' an intimate partner was an important symbol to others:

ROBERT: I've discussed with my [disabled] best friend, how we need a girlfriend to show 'Look a [non-disabled] real girl likes me, I have sex with her and we are in love – I must be OK, world'.

Robert's strategy of relationships with non-disabled ('*real*') women openly claims a sexual identity and thus, he feels, 'puts right' the dominant ableist assumptions of asexuality and sexual inadequacy cast upon impaired male bodies (Shakespeare *et al.* 1996). However, this identity work, which takes place both for the public and the self, is at the same time exploitative and objectifying for the non-disabled women who are utilised for such public displays.

However, for others, residing in intimate relationships, even where informants had expressed they were often unfulfilled and/or unhappy, was a means through which to avoid oppressive dimensions of dominant sexual cultures – for example, 'being single' once again (and thus losing many of the benefits listed above), being rejected on the 'dating scene' (because of disability and impairment) and negotiating the (often risky) disclosure of disability and impairment to prospective partners. Notably, this strategy required the employment of considerable emotional work (Hochschild 1983):

ROBERT: I wasn't in love for the last three months but was scared of being single, especially out of uni and knowing how hard it is to really get someone to see thru everything [his disability].

SHAUN: Because of my disability I thought 'oh well, I need to stick with this because I might not find anybody else'.

TOM: Because I am disabled, it gives you the worry about getting a girlfriend, you hold onto it for dear life, until it's like flogging a dead horse and that's no good for anybody.

The accounts of Robert, Shaun and Tom (all men with physical impairments) show how their choices to stay in (former) unfulfilling intimate relationships were shaped by the potential difficulties of finding a partner as disabled men within a gendered sexual culture that privileges hegemonic masculinities – affirming the ways in which emotions are simultaneously felt and performed as 'relations between self and world' (Laurier and Parr 1999: 98). Further, phrases like '*sticking with it*' and '*flogging a dead horse*' emphasise their emotional efforts. For example, Shaun said that in previous intimate relationships with (non-disabled) women he had painfully and silently worked past partners' infidelities because he desperately 'wanted to be in a relationship and wanted to have a partner'. Therefore, Shaun had to employ an acute form of what Hochschild (1983: 33) calls (emotional) 'mental work', whereby he not only had to perform the appropriate 'display work' of a contented partner (Hochschild 1983: 10), but carry out significant 'mental work' on his emotional self to really feel like – or become – a contented partner (Hochschild 1983: 6).

Another common chapter in informants' stories related to the ways in which they felt that a relationship, love and sex were 'out of reach' as a disabled person – a form of sexual oppression internalised through everyday tropes of disabled people as lacking sexual agency and opportunity (Siebers 2008). For those with congenital impairments, such thoughts were reported as having been internalised from a young age and had often been confirmed by (usually, well-meaning) family members; for example, telling them 'not to get their hopes up'. This was narrated to have substantial impact upon sexual self-confidence and esteem (and thus constituted significant sexual oppression) and supports the notion that psycho-emotional disablism can be at its most acute when carried out by known agents (Reeve 2002). Graham, a 52-year-old single male who acquired physical impairment at age 20, told of how he had been in intimate relationships with women to whom he was not attracted and did not like, because he saw them as the 'only opportunity' to have a relationship, but also because these relationships provided an (albeit, temporary) solution to his isolation and loneliness:

GRAHAM: I didn't like her, she was very fat … my attitude was entirely 'I've got no choice … she likes me for some reason and it's her or nothing' … I never liked her, never fancied her; I didn't like her touching me.

KIRSTY: How does it feel to be with people you don't feel … you don't actually like?

GRAHAM: It's horrible. Well it's horrible but that's it, there's no other option. You either just spend your life entirely alone or try and be with someone who's willing to be with you for whatever reason. Erm, it's horrible.

Graham spoke at length of the multiple emotional performances that such relationships required. For example, he talked about performing emotional displays of sincerity, honesty and authenticity when 'pretending' to like these intimate partners. The abhorrence Graham reveals in the above account shows that these situations required routine surface acting (Hochschild 1983). Rather than becoming an intimate partner through what Hochschild (1983: 33) defines as 'deep acting' or 'mental work', the emphasis for Graham was upon imitating the 'correct' emotional behaviours synonymous with love, intimacy and affection. To add context, Graham reported experiencing significant marginalisation and isolation, which many disabled people experience: he lived alone, said he had no real friends or family, and rarely went out. Using Thomas's (1999) social relational model of disability, Graham's marginalisation and feelings of loneliness sit at the nexus of structural, psycho-emotional and material dimensions of disability: he dropped out of university upon acquiring impairment because, he said, his institution could not cater adequately for a disabled student. A lack of qualifications combined with having to negotiate a disabled identity within an ableist labour market and capitalist economy led to both long-term underemployment and unemployment, which has in turn impacted upon his social mobility and his access to material resources (see Oliver 1990). Graham described these structural oppressions, then, as having significant impact upon his self-esteem and confidence (especially with women), denoting to him the feeling that he did not belong in, or did not have the attributes to attain, a meaningful intimate relationship (see Reeve 2004).

Survival work: the emotionality of abuse

For some informants, relationships with others entailed living through some deeply harmful situations, being subject to a range of abuses either perpetrated by a partner and/or a partner's family. This included sexual violence, physical violence and/or emotional abuse, throughout either their current or past relationships. According to Women's Aid (2011b), sexual violence includes situations whereby 'partners and former partners may use force, threats or intimidation to engage in sexual activity; taunt or use degrading treatment related to sexuality; force the use of pornography, or force their partners to have sex with other people'. Physical abuse relates to any harm of the physical body (Women's Aid 2011b). Disabled women experience an overwhelming lack of access and support in leaving situations of violence – often because the majority of women's services and refuges rarely cater to the needs of disabled women (Thiara *et al.* 2011). This is despite the fact that disabled women, in comparison to non-disabled women, are more likely to experience sexual and physical violence in their lifetime by people close to them (parents, intimate partners and carers) (Balderston 2014; Sobsey and Varnhagen 1989). While such statistics have been deemed as unhelpful by some disabled feminists because they reinforce discourses of vulnerability and victim-hood (see Morris 1991; Waxman 1991), it *is* the case that disabled people experi-ence less privacy in their lives, have increased reliance on others and institutions for care (see Cockram 2003), and experience increased access to their bodies by non-disabled people – all of which increase their chances of experiencing abuse and violence, in myriad forms (see Shah *et al.* 2016). I want to tentatively suggest in this section that being routinely humiliated, frightened, hurt, intimidated, scared, degraded, isolated and abused as part of one's daily life, as well as the labour involved in hiding it from the outside world, takes significant emotional work to survive, as well as other forms of self-advocacy labour to leave situations of viol-ence. I explicate this further, later.

While sexual violence remained the preserve of women informants (at least in terms of what stories were *able* to be told), many informants spoke about how they had been belittled, verbally abused, lied to, denigrated, manipulated, treated badly and humiliated in previous relationships. According to Women's Aid (2011b), emotional abuse includes:

> destructive criticism, name calling, sulking, pressure tactics, lying to you, or to your friends and family about you, persistently putting you down in front of other people, never listening or responding when you talk, isolating you from friends and family, monitoring your phone calls, emails, texts and letters, checking up on you, following you, and/or not letting you go out alone.

Informants spoke about such abuse in a variety of ways and did not refer to their experiences using such terminology: none identified their experiences explicitly as 'abusive' but most were aware that such situations were both 'not right' and 'harmful'. I suggest that this is because emotional abuse can often be more sur-reptitious or covert, and thus more complex to identify, classify and describe. It is also likely that, as Goodley (2011a) suggests, disablism ensures that disabled people experience discrimination and prejudice as part of their daily lives and so such experiences are relatively normalised in the context of the disability experi-ence (see also Quarmby 2011).

Much of the verbal abuse informants reported centred on disability, impair-ment and/or their sexual ability and/or performance. For example, Graham, a physically disabled man who was very insecure about being what he defined as 'sexually inexperienced', said that one partner would comment on his '*ugly*' legs and another partner would call him '*lousy*' and an '*idiot*' during sex in response to him asking her what to do sexually. Similarly, Bob, a man with physical and sensory impairment, spoke of the way in which two female partners had '*wasted very little time circulating the news of my [sexual] non-performance*' after breaking up, and said that his former partner had regularly made reference to his inability to '*sexually fulfil*' her. Helen, aged 20, told how one boyfriend used to call her '*square*' in relation to the '*wideness*' of her body shape, which she says is caused by using a wheelchair: '*obviously I'm sitting down so I'm fatter*'. Another boyfriend, the father of her baby, would taunt her about the '*boring sex*' she 'gave' and, she admitted, '*he goaded me and called me names*' about the shape of her arms, which are thin because of muscle degeneration. Helen said that these incidents '*will always stay with her*' and cites her disability as the reason for taking '*a lot of crap from people*'.

Some informants reported emotional abuse perpetrated by their non-disabled partner's family; for example, this included managing ignorance and prejudicial behaviour, being excluded from family events, being publicly humiliated and, for their non-disabled partners, being cut out of the family. Most common was verbal abuse:

JENNY: His father, he told me to f-off; he came out to my car and told me to fuck off. He [partner] didn't have any disability … Yeah … 'fuck off you cripple and leave my son alone'.

Jenny said that she experienced this kind of reaction more than once, across different partners. Tom told how he was actively 'hidden', and kept from meeting his partner's family and friends, for fear of embarrassment:

TOM: I think maybe she was ashamed of me being disabled. Looking back on it now, it's a pretty kind of – like it wasn't a very healthy relationship to be in, erm … It really, really, really, really had a big impact, it was horrible.

While a situation like Tom's *could* have been a non-disabled partner's attempt to save a disabled partner from the kinds of verbal abuse that Jenny describes above (although there are arguably far better ways to manage it), this was not how 'being hidden' was experienced or narrated by informants for whom it had been a reality, as Tom's words attest.

For others, abuse from partners could come in the form of exploitation, manipulation and humiliation. For example, a couple of informants talked about the ways in which their self-esteem was (deliberately) lessened by partners reflecting and focusing on the things they couldn't do and making a point of it to humiliate them. Others said that ex-partners had been unfaithful and that they had been cheated on multiple times in the same relationship. Some noted that ex-partners had controlled and exploited them. Jane, a 21-year-old student, talked about the difficulties with her current (non-disabled) partner, and implied that she relies on him a lot for help:

KIRSTY: In what ways does he help you?

JANE: …Makes me wear my splints, walks in front of me on the stairs so I don't fall, checks my feet for cuts as I can't feel them, comes to appointments with me…

KIRSTY: How does it feel that he does those things for you?

JANE: Loved. That most of the time he understands. It's just the odd times that he doesn't and he gets angry. Like, I'm not doing something right. I always blame myself even though I'm not wrong. And I generally just cry. I don't know any other way to react.

Jane said that these situations make her feel like '*the weaker one in the relationship*'. She also talked about how her boyfriend can be 'insensitive'; for instance, he bought her a pair of high heels that she can't walk in, because of her impairment, for Christmas. Not being able to wear heels (and thus wear feminine dress in the way she perceived it) was something Jane raised many times throughout the telling of her story. She talked about wanting to be able to walk in high heels '*more than anything*' and her boyfriend buying her some as a gift in full knowledge of this, '*felt like an insult*'. She said, '*I had to put on a front when I opened my Christmas present because he just hadn't thought about how much it would actually hurt me.*' '*Putting on a front*' once again emphasises the requirement to carry out the appropriate 'display work' required to meet expectations of the 'feeling rules' in receiving a gift (Hochschild 1983: 10). Jane went on to describe how she kept this sadness quiet for three months, at which point it broke out into an argument whereby her boyfriend called her ungrateful and threatened to leave her.

Notably, only women narrated sexual or physical violence alongside other abuses. When it comes to intimate partner violence – also known as domestic violence – disabled women (and others) suffer in myriad ways. For many disabled people, intimate partner violence goes unnoticed because their desexualisation means that they are assumed not to be in intimate, sexual and loving relationships at all (Zavirsek 2002). Additionally, the forms that violence takes can be unrecognisable within conventional understandings of 'domestic violence'. A denial of care; withholding medication and food (see Curry *et al.* 2001); encouraging self-harm; and exploiting and exacerbating incidences of psychosis, mania and depression are forms of violence unique to mental and physical impairment and illness (see Shah *et al.* 2016). In my research, Grace, a 58-year-old Deaf woman, had suffered multiple violences at the hands of her husband:

GRACE: He wanted (and got) sex at least twice a day every day. Sometimes we had sex more than twice a day – even up to five times a day. It didn't matter if I had my period or if I felt unwell or was pregnant. He wanted sex. If I was physically unable to bear penetration, I had to give him a hand job or a blow job. If I refused, he made my life a misery, sulking and getting angry and taunting me. It was easier to do as he wanted. I seldom ever enjoyed it. Over the years he became very abusive. I was treated like meat, raped, sodomised. He told me I was boring and useless, only good for a fuck. I started to almost believe it. My confidence was at rock bottom. In my heart I knew that what he was saying was wrong but I felt helpless. And there was my deafness. I had left school with no qualifications, no career. A dead-end job and an early marriage and children meant I had hardly any skills outside the home. He isolated me from my friends. Having said all this, he was not a monster and there were good times. But the abuse was always there. He could not cope with me being Deaf; as my deafness increased, he found it harder. He did not want a Deaf wife. He hit me a few times.

Grace's harrowing account shows the ways in which disability (and disability hatred) can be imbricated within disabled women's experiences of violence (Quarmby 2011). Importantly, Zavirsek (2002: 270) calls for the de-individualisation of sexual violence experienced by disabled women in order to look at what he calls 'the institutional arrangement of domination and subjugation' which determine disabled people's bodies as sites of violence. Shah *et al.* (2016: pagination unknown) summarise the cultural production of violence for disabled women adeptly:

> It is clear that continuation of violence of disabled women often stems from the inequalities associated with being disabled and female in a patriarchal society constructed around the non-disabled majority. The intersectionality of disablism and sexism helps to materially locate disabled women on the axis of power and disadvantage, and therefore provides a tool for understanding the complexity of disabled women's experiences of abuse and disadvantage.

Grace's account, I suggest, reveals the survival work she had to carry out in order to maintain a 'relationship' with her husband, which she said was for the sake of her child; the emotional ruptures caused by this extensive abuse cannot be underestimated. Further, Grace was clear that any slippage between her performance of the 'good wife' and the expectations of her husband could act as a catalyst for further violence (see Huang and Yeoh 2007). The emotional performances generated through Grace's experience of abuse, then, once again demonstrate how '"emotions" refer to something that is not only felt, but practised' (Huang and Yeoh 2007: 196).

Similarly, Jenny, a college-educated, spinal-cord-injured woman, experienced a physically violent episode at the hands of her disabled husband, to which she attributed the end of her marriage. Jenny left the marriage directly after this incident despite being told by police, whom she called for help, to go back home because it was 'just an argument'. Upon leaving, Jenny had to organise a room at her mother's sheltered accommodation because it was the only accessible venue she could find. This form of self-advocacy – another form of survival work – was necessary to be able to escape, to locate accessible and available accommodation and to seek further, longer-term support. The disabled women interviewed in Shah *et al.*'s (2016) study all stressed the labour involved in seeking support and leaving situations of violence: finding informal support close by; accessing formal support organisations and services (which, for some, responded merely by removing women's children from the family home); endlessly communicating with police, social workers and other agencies (that seldom listened to women); as well as work women had to do on their selves to bolster the agency and self-confidence required to negotiate their own escape routes.

These women's experiences inevitably support calls for better accessibility of women's domestic violence services (Chang *et al.* 2003; Thiara *et al.* 2010). Mainstream domestic abuse organisations, services and refuges can be inaccessible in a range of ways and the pragmatics of disability and care are pertinent here: the ability to leave a situation of violence, or move out of the family home (often quickly, quietly and without raising unwanted attention), can be far more difficult if the support of another person is needed, or if your home has been specifically adapted to meet your needs – as Jenny describes above. The stories of disabled survivors of domestic violence in other research have highlighted a reluctance to leave care packages that have been fought long and hard for, and that care provision is currently not flexible enough to move with women in ways that would protect them (Shah *et al.* 2016; see Thiara *et al.* 2011). This is, of course, exacerbated by recent significant governmental and local authority cuts to existing care provision across the UK. Thus, for many disabled women, leaving situations of violence often means entering into a new, often traumatic, emotional journey, through ineffective multi-agency responses to violence and an inaccessible criminal justice system. As an example, even when seeking justice, disabled women face further barriers, particularly women with labels of learning disability and/or mental illness, who are seldom supported appropriately to report violence and give evidence in court. Quite often, women's testimonies are doubted or disbelieved because of their mental health diagnosis. This is even more likely if women are institutionalised, detained (for example, under a mental health section) or are deemed to lack capacity (see Humphreys and Thiara 2003).

'Women's work'

The carrying out of emotional work could also be couched within particular forms of gendered work, most notably 'sex work' (Cacchioni 2007: 299). In her exploration of heterosexual women's perceptions of their sexual problems, Cacchioni (2007: 301) found that women carried out 'sex work', which she defines as 'the unacknowledged effort and the continuing monitoring which women are expected to devote to managing theirs and their partners' sexual desires and activities'. Of my informants, while it was not uncommon for both men and women to openly question their role as a sexual partner, particularly their ability to sexually 'fulfil' partners (in ways fitting with heteronormative sexual practices), three women (of 10 in total) in the sample took it further and were explicit about the ways in which they consciously (sex) 'worked' to 'compensate' non-disabled male partners in order to 'make up' for having an impaired body.

For example, Jenny, aged 64, who acquired spinal injury at the age of 11, talked about how she would '*get involved in every aspect of sex you could think of, any way that was pleasurable to him* [her ex-husband]'. She said: '*I would put myself out to give him that pleasure even if I wasn't getting any that particular time*'. Jenny carried out this sex work in order to not be perceived as 'sexually inadequate' by her husband in comparison with his non-disabled ex-wife. The sacrificing of her own sexual pleasure shows the 'entwined nature of embodied and emotional performance work' (Wilton 2008: 367). Similarly, Lucille, 36, who became tetraplegic at age 23 (when she was already married), told how following her injury she had offered her non-disabled husband multiple chances to be unfaithful: '*I felt so bad about not wanting sex that I kept telling him to have an affair.*' To return to Jane and her heels, when talking about the aspects of sex she doesn't enjoy, Jane reported that her boyfriend requests she wear the very same high heels mentioned in the previous section during sex for his sexual pleasure. This, she says, makes her feel frustrated: '*because I don't want to just wear them during sex. I want to wear them out*'. Putting on a front, feeling sad, keeping quiet and being frustrated are forms of emotional work that Jane had to carry out in order to manage this situation. At the same time, being reminded of this emotional pain (and feeling of inadequacy around not being able to walk in heels) was something she had to endure during sex, for the sake of her partner's pleasure. Lucille's, Jenny's and Jane's actions cannot be separated from their identities as disabled women; their sex work is indicative of the low sexual self-esteem that is widespread among disabled women generally (Gillespie-Sells *et al.* 1998) and is more likely to occur in women with greater impairment who 'tend to be furthest away from cultural constructions of ideal feminine beauty' (Hassouneh-Phillips and McNeff 2005: 228).

However, while Jenny and Lucille were explicit about their sex work, acknowledging that their labour was conscious towards embodying desirability for their non-disabled male partners, most women in the sample spoke about hiding bodily difference during sexual encounters – but seldom questioned such practices. Hiding was described by women to take place through a complex (yet remarkably routine) organisation of duvets, bed sheets, clothing and lighting in a bid to both perform and embody the highly gendered role of the seductress. I suggest that this hiding can be seen as a *private* form of 'aesthetic labour', which Wolkowitz (2006: 86) defines as 'employers' attempts to make the body more visible in customer service work through a focus on the body's aesthetic qualities'. Carrying out some form of aesthetic labour, whether private or public, is, undoubtedly, a likely reality for all women due to the ways in which heterosexist and patriarchal constructions of femininity instil an 'infatuation with an inferiorised body' (Bartky 1990: 40). However, for the disabled women in my research this was undoubtedly compounded by (impaired) bodily difference being wholly intolerable within the rubric of the normative body. Actively hiding the body in this way affirms that disabled informants fear that their departure from bodily normalcy can be a basis for rejection (even from intimate partners), and thus the need to 'pass' (and all of the work that goes with this) remains.

The emotional work of the care receiver

Emotional work through surface acting (Hochschild 1983) took place most explicitly when informants received care from partners within intimate relationships. Of 10 informants who said they regularly received care and assistance from a partner, all said that this arrangement could be a site of tension that required emotional management (see Morris 1989). Many narrated care from partners as something they had to 'put up with', in that partners did not carry out tasks correctly or in preferred ways. Even though this could be a central source of frustration – and often anger – it was a situation where the disabled partner had to show incredible tolerance and grace, and be grateful through surface acting (Hochschild 1983), often when they fervently felt the opposite. Thus, in order to manage the 'feeling rules' present within the caring relationship (Hochschild 1979: 552), rules that 'govern how people try or try not to feel in ways appropriate to the situation', disabled informants had to show emotions that were 'appropriate' for those receiving care (see Morris 1989). Importantly, this extensive emotional work was crucial towards simultaneously maintaining functioning care relationships alongside intimate partnerships.

For example, Helen, who is 20 years old and has a congenital and progressive impairment, emphasised the extensive emotional work required in having to 'teach' her new partner how to care, which involved 'smiling through' what she called 'bad care' while he learned her preferred way of doing particular caring tasks. Having been cared for by her mother all her life, Helen was reluctant to change this arrangement until she eventually moved out of the family home. However, her fiancé, who she saw at weekends (because he was a university student), had shown great willingness to take over this role from her mother. This was not a change that Helen welcomed for many reasons, but one that she felt she had to accommodate because of his willingness to care. She was clear that, while her partner learned how to care, this meant her putting up with care that is '*a damn sight worse*' than from her mother, and for which she had to be '*tolerant*' and '*grateful*' because '*he could just tell me to get stuffed!*' She said that it often dictated what she could wear, as she would pick garments that she knew her partner could cope with, regardless of whether she wanted to wear it or not. To add emphasis, she offered a story of a situation where this was not possible, and the impact it had:

HELEN: We went to London for this thing … [I had to wear] like an evening dress … Oh. My. God. [Laughs] I was gonna travel down in the dress and thought 'don't be silly, he can put a dress on' but oh my god we had an absolute fight over this dress, we couldn't get it on. It wasn't that difficult but it had a lace overlay thing and he couldn't figure out how to put my arm in it, so I was absolutely bawling my eyes out, stressed, because we were late as well and you just think [sighs] 'how much easier would it be?' you know, you just get depressed, you just get upset... But you blame yourself because you think 'if I'd have just got Mum to put it on me before I'd left or' ... but then obviously he gets stressed as well and I'm bawling and shouting and you reach a point where ... you can't, you lose the tolerance in a way because you think 'for god's sake, how thick are you being? Just put my arm through the hole!' And it just leads into a major heated argument.

In this account, Helen talks a lot about being upset, distressed and blaming herself. The interview often became a space for people to vent such feelings regarding the standard and quality of care from their partner – presumably because such feelings would make them appear ungrateful or unappreciative if voiced in other spaces. Shaun's non-disabled partner Hannah offered a chance to see the perspective of the non-disabled partner. Hannah talked about times when Shaun's personal assistant was unavailable:

HANNAH: I may be less respectful of Shaun's body as a carer because... and Shaun is less likely to say something to me than he is to the carer [PA]. Like if I'm in a mood or I'm in a rush, like this week, I know that I've probably not done things exactly how Shaun would like it but I know he won't say anything because he doesn't wanna piss me off and I won't necessarily offer because I'm in a rush. I do see it as a job, in that sense and... That's something that I struggle most with is the kind of resentment because I've often said to Shaun, 'I wonder if you're with the right person? You know, someone who's more caring than me!' Because if I do a lot of stuff for Shaun I get backache and then feel resentment towards Shaun, and that's something we've talked about haven't we? [To Shaun] About those feelings ... and Shaun feels a lot of guilt generally to me and towards anybody erm ... so that's something that we really had to look at, and most of the times when I have to help Shaun out, like a holiday, or like this week, I can mentally prepare myself and I am ok with it. The things I find difficult is the middle of the night or, you know, then I might not be so nice... [Laughs] And, you know, spur of the moment things or if [PA] is late or ... it's the things that I haven't expected, that's when I find it quite difficult and I really feel like Shaun owes me a favour even though in my mind I can say 'he doesn't owe me a favour, he needs this' but somehow I am keeping score when things like that happen.

Hannah is incredibly honest about how she feels when having to take on a caring role for Shaun. Her account shows an awareness of the emotional work Shaun carries out: his keeping quiet, having tasks carried out in ways that aren't preferable, feeling guilty and being resented. It also shows the considerable emotional work that many carers undertake. Importantly, though, the (emotional) work of those in caring professions (and unpaid carers) is well documented, for example, nurses (Frogatt 1998; Henderson 2001; Millward 1995; Smith 1992) and personal assistants and care workers (Earle 1999; Treweek *et al.* 1996), while the emotional work of the cared for is much less so (Hughes *et al.* 2005; James 1992; Morris 1997). Moreover, Hannah's account shows the problematic changes that caring can bring to a relationship that they both recognise as loving, intimate and valued.

Often these difficult dynamics increased when the disabled partner had an increasing level of need; for example, on becoming ill or through impairment progression. Pete told a story of when he was admitted to hospital and then discharged with a catheter inserted, which caused him intense pain and anxiety about cleanliness. He explained this as a point of conflict in his relationship with his wife:

PETE: I developed an obsession with cleanliness with myself. I used to seek assurance from my wife. I got obsessed, which caused a few problems around caring ... I never thought the catheter site was clean enough – I was scared of infection. So I'd ask my wife to clean it over and over. We'd sometimes argue, which I hate – my wife is so good to me. I'd nearly always have infections and I didn't how or why, I was clean. When the catheter needed changing I'd drink lots of alcohol, beer, or whisky to help with the pain and spasms. This resulted in vomiting. My wife would get annoyed.

Likewise, Gemma, a 42-year-old lesbian who has immunity impairment, told how a cancer diagnosis meant she had to be cared for full-time by her then-partner. Gemma spoke of the ways in which she had to manage her partner's anxiety around her cancer, when she was the one who had it. Notably, this emotional work had to be carried out at a time of significant personal emotional anxiety that is coming to terms with a cancer diagnosis, emphasising the ways that emotional work is often on or for others (Exley and Letherby 2001). Gemma said that the relationship ended when her partner got '*too into the role*', causing her to feel, as she described, like she had lost power, and therefore control, autonomy and agency.

Some informants said that receiving care from a partner affected the way in which they dealt with conflict within their intimate relationship. Thus, caring was often conceptualised as something a non-disabled partner could offer, rather than a requirement. As such, it was also something that could be denied: for example, Helen chooses to take on a 'passive' role generally in her relationships (with her fiancé and mother as carers), to ensure her care needs are met:

HELEN: The trying-to-be-nice if you're having an argument, that definitely ... because you've kind of lower your boundaries ... Like, just go along with things that you really don't want to do.
KIRSTY: Do you do that consciously?

HELEN: Yeah... Consciously, a lot. I know I do things just 'cos it's easier, definitely. Just to not cause trouble, really.

Helen's work to be passive is *functional* and her performance of gratitude must appear genuine in order to not disturb her care arrangement. The fact she does this work consciously, I suggest, shows that she experiences this power imbalance in a very real way. Specifically, some informants said that their need to receive care from partners affected their power in the relationship, with arguments being positioned by many to increase this imbalance of power. For example, Robert, age 26, and Terry, age 20, who both have a congenital physical impairment, said that they avoided conflict or arguments with a partner, as a strategy to ensure continued care:

ROBERT: If an argument arose, could I really defend my point even if I'm right, but then ask for help knowing they're annoyed with me?
TERRY: With a girlfriend, I know that I can't be easily irritated by things they do, because I've got to rely on them to help. In the past I haven't had an argument with a girlfriend unless it's been at a time where I don't need them for any help.

Like Helen, Robert and Terry's actions to purposefully avoid conflict are evidence that receiving care from an intimate partner can mean having to consciously mediate and manage these complex relationships through very careful strategies. Such strategies undeniably required various forms of emotional work, management and performance – notably, tolerance, 'submission', graciousness, the assessment of when and when not to assert oneself, and the general management of a very problematic set of power relations, in order to continue to receive the required care or assistance from intimate partners.

Drawing some conclusions

The stories (re)told throughout this chapter have uncovered the work and labours of disabled men and women within multiple locations of their intimate relationships. Throughout their stories, informants cast themselves as active subjects, revealing their diverse roles as teacher, survivor, sex worker, negotiator, manager, mediator, performer and educator. Paradoxically, much of the skilled emotional work disabled informants carried out is highly valued within Western labour markets (Hochschild 1983), from which they are largely excluded. Notwithstanding, recognising and labelling the work of disabled people within their sexual and intimate lives is important. First, doing so provides fuller, more accurate and inclusive descriptions of the complex ways that disability, impairment, gender and sexuality interact within sexual and intimate life – as well as of the potential psycho-emotional dimensions of such interactions. Second, by identifying informants as skilful managers of their intimate and sexual lives – regardless of the outcome or efficacy of their work – their labour challenges dominant constructions of the disabled sexual identity and subjectivity as passive and lacking agency (Siebers 2008).

However, clearly evident within informants' stories and in the analysis of their feelings was the extent to which they devalued their (sexual) selves, revealing the ways in which low sexual self-esteem and self-worth, feelings of inadequacy (in relation to heteronormative discourse) and low body confidence can be common parts of the disabled (sexual) psyche in ableist sexual cultures. Despite exercising a form of sexual agency as active 'emotional workers', then, the requirement of informants to carry out forms of work within their sexual and intimate lives, I argue, constituted a form of psycho-emotional disablism (Thomas 1999). For example, rather than overt transgressive resistance, much of the (invisible) work uncovered was carried out largely through necessity – in order to survive, to be loved, to be human, to be included, to be 'normal', to be sexual and to be valued. Thus, it is crucial not to underestimate the sizeable extent to which work was rooted in, and thus indicative of, the oppressive and inherent inequalities of ableist culture.

Furthermore, analysis has shown that informants' work was both located and produced at the intersections of disability, sexuality and gender, emphasising the value of appreciating relational and psycho-emotional dimensions of disability (Reeve 2002, 2004; Thomas 1999) when exploring intimacies in the lives of disabled people. The fact that much of informants' work was routinely employed for the benefit of others supports Goodley's (2010: 92) notion of disability performances that fit with 'expectations of non-disabled culture'. Significantly, where emotional and other work did take place on or for the self, it extended only to emotional and/or bodily management; typically, through a conscious and rigid policing (or hiding) of emotional responses or bodily difference – forms of work that seldom bought informants pleasure or personal fulfilment. For example, surface and 'deep' acting within intimate relationships, engaging in forms of sex work and providing 'appropriate' performances of gratitude and gratefulness when receiving care were markedly detrimental to a positive sense of (sexual) self in most cases and constituted a distinct form of psycho-emotional disablism that operated at a level which required informants' complicity.

In certain spaces, typically gendered performances that affirmed dominant constructions of masculinity and femininity were offered – notably seen within the different strategies men and women employed to sexualise themselves, either in their own eyes or in the eyes of others. Thus, disabled male informants' employment of forms of emotional work within intimate spaces challenges the idea of the male identity as privileged within emotional working (Hochschild 1983) and sheds light on the ways in which alternative (non-hegemonic) masculinities interact with emotional work and labours. Moreover, women's employment of normatively gendered labours such as sex work (Cacchioni 2007) and 'private' aesthetic labour (Wolkowitz 2006) reveals how emotional work is rooted in their social and political positioning as disabled people and – as with the motivations of non-disabled heterosexual women – by normative notions of womanhood, femininity and (hetero)sexuality. This emphasises the similarities between the experiences of disabled and non-disabled women, who occupy analogous subordinate positions within heteronormativity and heterosexuality. It also illustrates – as other disabled feminists already have (Morris 1989; Thomas 1999; Wendell 1996) – the need for mainstream hegemonic feminism to be more inclusive of all types of women and thus broaden its contextualisation of the female experience that, while diverse, is unified by women's suppression under patriarchy and male (sexual) power (see Chapter 2).

The analysis detailed in this chapter supports, then, feminist contributions to disability studies – particularly those that have called for inclusion of the gendered and psycho-emotional dimensions of disability (Reeve 2004; Thomas 1999). Crudely, a 'pure' social model barrier-focused analysis would simply not have bared the intimate, personal and affective oppressions central to informants' lived experiences. As Thomas (1999: 74) points out, rather than psychologising disabled people's emotions, applying a (feminist) disability studies or social relational lens to disabled people's emotional lives removes these from being ' "open season" to psychologists and others who would not hesitate to apply the individualistic/personal tragedy model to these issues'. In this vein, then, revealing the connections between structural and psycho-emotional forms of disablism can actually serve to depathologise disabled people's experiences in ways advocated by social modellist politics, at the same time as theorising and reframing disability in ways that best attend – most importantly – to the emotional well-being of disabled people.

6 'If I ever wanted an affair I'd have to send my lover to lifting and handling classes first!'

Sexual normativity and othered bodies

Accessible summary

- In this chapter, I consider the lived and material realities of impairment that were most prevalent in informants' sexual stories.
- I explore the meaning of such bodily difference in informants' understandings and experiences of (hetero)sex, gender, pleasure and eroticism.
- I identify heteronormative sexuality and its prescriptive rules, rather than bodily impairment/disability, as the *problem*.
- Disabled people routinely spoke of feeling a 'failure', 'inadequate', 'disgusting' and 'abnormal', despite the fact that their own bodies often expanded what we know about sex and pleasure.
- Gender was a key factor in determining how informants experienced sexual and intimate relations with self and other.

Bodies labelled impaired pose a powerful challenge to heteronormative sexuality; especially those that experience the 'hard physical realities' (Wendell 1996: 45) of pain, spasms, leakiness, scarring, a 'loss' of sensation, immobility and weakness. This is because the *natural*, moral, and compulsory sexual desires, pleasures and practices required of heteronormativity and heterosexuality marginalise all other sexual modes, bodies and desires. I follow Holland *et al.* (1998: 171) to define heteronormativity as 'the asymmetry, institutionalisation and regulatory power of heterosexual relations' (see also Lancaster 2003; Richardson 1996). As a form of socio-sexual order, heteronormativity eclipses difference and diversity and reifies sameness and structure. To explicitly draw disability *in*, as McRuer (2006a: 9) suggests, heterosexuality and able-bodiedness are intimately related:

> they are linked in their mutual impossibility and in their mutual incomprehensibility – they are incomprehensible in that each is an identity that is simultaneously the ground on which all identities supposedly rest and an impressive achievement that is always deferred and thus never really guaranteed.

McRuer's concept of 'ability trouble', in essence, demarcates that, although compulsory, desired and endlessly laboured for, able-bodiedness (and by association heterosexuality) is always an 'inevitable impossibility' (McRuer 2006a: 10). Thus, disabled sexualities exist at these thorny intersections of disability, ability, heterosexuality and ableism.

In short, this 'fucking ideology' (Shakespeare *et al.* 1996: 97) – the focus of this chapter – ensures that *successful* sexual interactions become characterised as necessary, spontaneous, mutually satisfying, always orgasmic, and genitally focused, taking place primarily through (heterosexual) penetration. To move from the psyche and psycho-emotional in the last chapter to the body and the embodied in this, in this chapter I situate the body, gender, embodiment, sexual pleasure and heteronormativity as central themes. While both the 'messy possibilities' of sex and the 'hard' lived realities of impairment have often been omitted from existing literature on disabled sexualities (although there are good exceptions, see Liddiard and Slater 2017), this chapter explores how the sexual pleasures, practices and interactions of disabled people in my research are shaped by both their 'anomalous embodiment' (Shildrick 2009) and dominant discourses of heteronormative sexuality. Pardon the pun, but these rub up against one another routinely, as the sexual stories in this chapter will show. Therefore, I problematise heteronormative sexuality, specifically with reference to (impaired) bodies, taking account of how the bodily realities of impairment interact with the conventionally gendered sexual identities and practices required within hegemonic masculinity and femininity.

Importantly, disabled people in my research were dynamic and vibrant in their mediation of the requirements of heteronormativity, accepting, resisting and negotiating discourse through a variety of means. While the reality of the impaired body was largely interpreted as a barrier towards *achieving* normative gendered sexual practices, impairment simultaneously was a site where 'creative sexual agency' (Shuttleworth 2010: 3) could be exercised to produce new possibilities and pleasures (specific to the impaired body) to, in part, redefine and expand conventional notions of sex, gender and the normative body. Thus, for some, impairment could expand heterosex in locales where, for non-impaired bodies, the scope for transformation is limited (Jackson 1999; Shakespeare 2000; Shildrick 2009). Crucially, however, this was rarely how such sexual experiences were understood by informants, many of who customarily positioned their alternative sexual practices as Other, inadequate and even grotesque (see Goodley *et al.* 2015). This reveals the ways in which, as Wilkerson (2002: 46) proposes, ableism and disablism ensure that even disabled people can come to render 'their sexualities incoherent, unrecognizable to others or perhaps even to themselves' and that this constitutes 'a clear instance of cultural attitudes profoundly diminishing sexual agency'.

.Sexual pleasure and desire

This section explores informants' experiences and celebrations of sexual pleasure, considered by Tepper (2000: 283) as 'the missing discourse' within disabled sexual dialectics. I focus initially on informants' 'pleasure talk', before moving on to explore the ways in which the impaired body could resist and expand heteronormative sexual pleasure. To add some context, before sex was supposedly liberated[1] in the 1960s through cultural, legal and policy changes, its purpose was situated intransigently within the realms of reproduction. However, modern discursive constructions of sex have shifted our focus far more towards pleasure as the central aspect of sex. Sexological works, as stated in Chapter 2, have quantified, measured and charted the key stages of pleasure within the human sexual experience (see also Chesser 1950; Kinsey 1953; Kinsey *et al.* 1948; Masters and Johnson 1966). Such reductionist views locate sexual pleasure and desire firmly *within* the (normative) body, meaning that an absence of these integral elements of 'successful' normative sexuality come to be pathologised and medicalised (Cacchioni 2007; Nicolson and Burr 2003), creating dysfunctional bodies and sexualities (Bullough 1994; Hawkes 1996; Tiefer 2001). Mainstream sexological discourses therefore render the impaired body (and other bodies which do not fit its criteria) as abnormal and defective if they fall short of embodying sexual pleasure in mapped ways.

To experience sexual pleasure in the form of orgasm is, according to Masters and Johnson (1974), 'authentic, abiding satisfaction that makes us feel like complete human beings'. According to this troubled (and ableist) logic, then, to orgasm is to be human: our humanness is reified by our ability to orgasm, rendering the myriad bodies and people that can't, won't or don't orgasm as less than human. In these neoliberal times, where biopedagogies – 'instructions for living ubiquitous in our individualising, biomedicalising, homogenising culture' (Rice *et al.* 2016) – dictate relentless labouring on our bodies as *products*, the orgasm has become necessary for life, self and health. For example, via the 'healthicisation of sex' (Cacchioni 2007) 'healthy' bodies, which orgasm in the right way (and at the right time), are rewarded with multiple believed health benefits: protection from heart disease and (prostate) cancer; the relief of depression, stress, anxiety and headaches; and an increase cardiovascular health (Komisaruk *et al.* 2006). Impaired bodies, however, are not viewed as 'acceptable candidates' for sexual pleasure (Tepper 2000: 285), largely because they are presumed to be physiologically incapable, to self and others. Much of this belief stems from the acute medicalisation of the impaired body: 'impairment per se is of central concern – its detection, avoidance, elimination, treatment and classification' (Thomas 2002: 40; original emphasis). This, as Tepper (2000: 285) suggests, combined with 'a biologically determinate viewpoint of sex as solely the province of reproduction, and 'reproduction solely the province of the fittest', has resulted in the sexual encounters and pleasures of disabled people being 'largely ignored, vilified, or exploited' (Tepper 2000: 284) (see Chapter 1).

Pleasure talk

In my research, all informants stated that they experienced what they identified as sexual pleasure, and, for the most part, talked about sexual pleasures and desires relatively freely and without the sexual shame that Wilkerson (2002) suggests is inherent to the erotophobia experienced by disenfranchised groups and sexual minorities. Younger women (e.g. under 30 years) were considerably reserved about pleasure, choosing 'safe' statements such as '*sex was great*' and '*I enjoy it*' but rarely elaborated on why and how. Older women showed more willingness to talk about the embodied pleasure they experienced:

RHONA: Sex was brilliant, and we both enjoyed each other immensely: intimacy, proximity, sensations, comedy, lack of control, feeling desired, being treated roughly and not as though I might break. It is also one of the few examples of when my body allows me a 'time-out', and I feel liberated. Done right, it is all pleasure and no pain.

For some men, talk about pleasure often tied into hegemonic masculine sexual identities and ideas of performance:

ROBERT: [favourite part of sex] When we both climax – plus I do love boobs.
MICHAEL: Well it's the greatest endorphin rush ever [sex]. It's a masculine role I can achieve.
TOM: I'm quite cave-mannish – [laughs] – especially when it's somebody I don't know; it's purely a hedonistic experience.
ABRAM: Um ... I loved touching her, I loved getting a blow job, I loved – I'd read various opinions on how it felt to get your balls sucked and I decided I – [laughs] – very much did like getting mine sucked. I'll always have that visual of [name of girl] there with my come [ejaculate] on her lips, which is a porn fantasy.

While these statements are undeniably couched in hegemonic masculine performances, other men talked about enjoying typically 'feminised' sexual activities, such as foreplay, closeness and sensuality, without embarrassment:

OLIVER: I definitely enjoyed sex but it wasn't the be-all and end-all, I enjoyed the foreplay more and the intimacy of being together.
TERRY: Well, I mean I most enjoy ... well, one, actually looking – I mean, especially this is in terms of loving the person – is looking into their eyes when you reach a climax. The second one is really the after-bit of just lying with the person and just that sense of them – you know – when you can just lie together and feel that everything's stopped. They're the most enjoyable bits.
PETE: I enjoy being together, alone without the kids or anyone else. I enjoy being without clothes alone with my wife. I enjoy getting undressed before having sex. The anticipation. I enjoy kissing. I enjoy being softly touched. I enjoy touching my wife. And just holding her afterwards, smelling her hair and kissing her neck or ear. I enjoy not trying to be someone I'm not. I enjoy oral sex. I enjoy mutual masturbation. I enjoy the obvious release it gives. I enjoy the tension then the release of my muscles.

While non-disabled men also talk about pleasure in such 'feminised' ways (see Seidler 1992), and can equally experience hegemonic masculinity as highly oppressive, these alternative male accounts of pleasure suggest that disabled men's *exclusion* from hegemonic masculine sexual identities might offer emancipation from, and an opportunity to negotiate, the domineering gender binaries created and maintained through both heteronormativity and heterosexuality (see Gerschick and Miller 1995; Phillips 2010; Shakespeare 1999b). As Shakespeare (1999b: 63) contends, 'non-disabled men have things to learn from disabled men, and could profitably share insights into gender relations, sexuality and particularly issues of physicality and the body'. Appreciating intimacy, kissing, looking into a lover's eyes and enjoying soft touch – and talking about it openly – shows resistance to hegemonic male sexuality. Noam Ostrander (2009: 15) suggests that impairment and masculine sex roles as 'in conflict' can mean that, for disabled men, 'orgasms become less important than pleasing their sexual partner' (see also Vahldieck 1999). Therefore, as Siebers (2008: 150) contends, 'disabled sexuality not only challenges the erotics of the body, but transforms the temporality of love making, leaving behind many myths found in normative sexuality'. However, Guldin (2000: 236) suggests that such 'feminised' activities actually bolster conventional masculinities:

> For a man to be a patient, sensitive lover who is willing to go slowly and focus on the woman's entire body and on her pleasure may be seen as a more feminine model of sexuality. But if our cultural definition of being a 'masculine man' is somewhat contingent on being able to sexually pleasure women, then this 'feminine model' of sexuality actually increases masculinity.

Being able to pleasure a woman is a vital part of the rubric of modern hetero-masculinities (Seidler 1992). Thus, as Guldin (2000) proposes, learning methods of 'doing sex' which are less focused on male pleasure, at the same time, offer men an equally central role in sex whereby they remain the pleasure provider. Thus, taking part in 'feminised' activities reinforces this alternative, but still desirable, male sexual performance (see Holland *et al.* 1998).

The construction of the orgasm within heteronormative scripts is 'the natural outcome of sex – the only option for successful sex' (Cacchioni 2007: 306). Most informants (both men and women) with spinal cord injuries (SCI) said that they no longer experienced orgasm in the way they had prior to injury. *Lacking* the ability to orgasm, something sexologists Masters and Johnson (1986) defined as a 'disease' called 'Anorgasmia', reinforces the primacy of orgasm for sexual pleasure (Hawkes 1996). As happens so often, the condition of anorgasmia has developed over time; it is now considered to have physical and psychological causes. It is now known as Coughlan's Syndrome, female orgasm disorder (FOD) or male orgasm disorder (MOD), and has its own typology: you can have anorgasmia that is lifelong, acquired, or generalised. According to NHS Direct, it affects over 50 per cent of women, but just 10 per cent of men (and if that's not the social and cultural production of impairment, I don't know what is... See

Chapter 2). Although informants described *not* orgasming as a 'loss' (see Sakellariou 2006; Tepper 1999), they did talk about alternative forms of sexual pleasure, feeling and embodiment. For example, Lucille expressed her experiences of no longer being able to orgasm in the conventional way:

LUCILLE: Why would you want to have sex if you couldn't feel anything other than a weird nerve pain and why would someone want sex with a girl who couldn't orgasm? I can't feel any sensation that one would normally have but the way I feel does change in a way I can't describe. Teamed with my imagination it can be very pleasant, makes me feel sexy I guess, but I almost feel wrong for using it, like I shouldn't.

Feeling like 'she shouldn't' emphasises the ways that people with acquired impairment can feel desexualised following the transition to a disabled identity, but also that her newly queered body (which no longer achieves pleasure in normative ways)[2] is uncomfortable, because it challenges culturally dominant preconceptions of what (and where) pleasure and erogenous sensation should take place. Jenny, a 64-year-old woman, who experienced a SCI at the age of 11, had a similar experience and said she seldom masturbated because she did not have the *ability* to orgasm. Thus, in conjunction with dominant discourses of pleasure, she had decided that without the obligatory orgasm masturbation was rendered meaningless. Phillip, who became disabled through a motorbike accident at age 35 (just three years before our interview took place), also said his sensations had changed:

PHILLIP: It's very hard to describe actually, but you get … obviously you've lost outer sensation and the ability to climax, but it's amazing how strong the mind is and the enjoyment you get from, you 'know, the act, if you will, of sex. So … that has diminished … it's diminished the kind of … I guess the, it's not enjoyment as such because I love having sex, but it's the … there's … I could say there's something missing in it, actually. I mean you get … the best way of describing it is you get this sort of sensation; you don't ejaculate but you kind of get sensations of orgasm but it's not a full-on orgasm so you get sensations and those sensations are great so there is a … erm, you know … erm, you get a sensation of climaxing but you don't … but it's not as strong as it was before.

Phillip's assertion of something being '*missing*' supports Tepper's (2000: 289) research with men with SCI, which found that most described post-injury pleasure as '*not the same*'. While Phillip did report *increased* sensation outside of standardised erogenous zones (e.g. his arms), and said that this made him more sensitive to touch '*in a nice way*', he felt it wasn't a replacement for the loss of genital sensation. Tepper suggests (2000: 289) that such feelings originate from 'the absence of quality sexuality education combined with learning about sex primarily from having genital intercourse' (see Chapter 4), which leads 'to sexuality embodied in the genitals and cognitively focused on perfect perform-ance with the goal of orgasm'. This can be difficult to work past. Phillip's account also shows the way in which informants (particularly those with acquired impairment) often found sexual pleasures difficult to describe, suggest-ing that there is little alternative language or lexicon through which to verbalise sexual pleasure outside of 'climax' and 'orgasm'. Even these can be hard to define, as 'climax' and 'orgasm' are, in a sense, descriptions of 'events' rather than feelings. As Jackson suggests (1999: 171), heterosexual language is 'restricted to very predictable conventions such as terminology from *Mills and Boon* novels and pornography'.

Cripping pleasure: resisting and expanding normative pleasures

One man with SCI, Shaun, a 33-year-old who became a wheelchair user in an accident at the age of 10, *could* orgasm through stimulation of conventional erogenous zones, but took advantage of the ways in which his revised body facil-itated new forms of pleasure. He said his shoulders (just below the point of injury) were incredibly sensitive to touch and that he and his wife Hannah had incorporated these sensations into their sex life. Below, they discuss the won-drousness of this displaced erogenous zone – a product of Shaun's impaired body – and the ways in which this reinscribes their heterosexual sex with new meanings for them:

SHAUN: I have very sensitive areas on my shoulders and ... 'cos that's where I was injured so that's kind of a natural thing ... so it's nice just for the touch-ing side of things, really.

HANNAH: Yeah, I remember the first time, because I didn't know that about spinal injury and I was stroking Shaun's shoulder and he was like 'wow!' [Collective laughs] I was like, 'What?!' I think I must have stroked it for an hour!

SHAUN: She gets bored after a couple of minutes now! [Laughs]

HANNAH: So that was an eye opener, that wow, so ... I think you could get to the stage of having an orgasm through touching above the injury, which is amazing really.

The ability to orgasm through one's shoulder undoubtedly crips the sexually embodied norms of the conventional erotic body that dictates that orgasms are bound to genitals (Ostrander 2009). Shaun and Hannah's experiences show the *possibilities* of pleasure, through exploration, that impairment can produce (Parker and Yau 2012). Similarly, Pete, who lives with congenital impairment, reported his muscle spasms as very pleasurable, which added to his overall enjoyment:

PETE: My legs, stomach, bottom, feet, toes and (arms not so much) have spasms (muscles get real hard) when I'm in the throws making love, increasing the more excited/aroused I get. Once I've climaxed/ejaculated these muscles and joints quite quickly relax – I like that feeling of tiredness and relaxedness whilst in the knowledge I've pleased my wife. I can't walk for a while after.

Pete's *extra* fulfilment from his palsied muscles forcefully challenges conceptualisations of the impaired body as an inadequate site for pleasure (see Overboe 2007). Instead, it speaks to a deeply erotic body; a body whereby pleasure is not merely an activity of the genitals, but where 'every surface of the body is available for polymorphous excitation' (Cohen 2015: 156). Pete's pleasure isn't bound to mapped convention; the non-normativity of his body offers emancipation from such rubrics. Such experiences affirm crip and queer approaches to the (impaired) body (see Chapter 2), which define it as a space of vivacity and production (Overboe 2007), and that which can 'expand and envelope in exciting ways' (Goodley 2011a: 158).

Normative sexual practices and pleasures are positioned in sexological accounts to occur in sequence, 'building' up to the 'end goals' of climax and orgasm. In addition to the different *forms* of pleasure impairment could bring, for some informants impairment meant that the orgasmic body could be unpredictable and unruly. Gemma, a 42-year-old lesbian cancer survivor with an immunity disorder, talked about the way her impairment episodically affected her ability to orgasm and how she labelled her body '*dysfunctional*' at such times. Her experiences show that the *necessity* for goal-orientated orgasm-focused pleasure, which is rooted in heteronormativity or heterosexual desire, can be internalised by all people, regardless of sexual orientation or whom it is we desire. This is in much the same way that ableism is not the preserve of disabled people, but subsists as a far broader form of control where all bodies are concerned. Other informants had similar experiences. However, a strategy to manage an unruly sexual body was to displace, decentre or demote the orgasm within the sexual experience. Hannah and Shaun told a story of how they'd struggled extensively regarding the 'need' to orgasm as a marker of '*good sex*'. The couple's narrative was rooted in the ways in which they had successfully dealt with this pressure, which could impact upon Shaun's ability to sustain an erection. Shaun said they were trying to expand their views around sexuality, and that this brought them less pressure and more pleasure:

SHAUN: Stereotypical views of how sex should be. This is something we found quite … you're very goal orientated, sex is like 'well she's got to come and he's gotta come or the other way around or … you 'know, you've got to have intercourse and that's part of sex, you 'know, there's a set … wham bam thank you maam kind of steps […] I think that was just adding to it [the pressure] and we were getting to a point where, at the end of this period of an hour of trying, there was disappointment because it wasn't what we expected it to be … But over the last 5 or 6 months it's kind of, yeah, if you lose that goal orientation kind of thing and there's no pressure … […] we have a very strong relationship and good sex would be the icing on the cake, if you like ... but we get as much out of cuddling and being close to each other as we do out of sex, I think. It's ... I guess some people may look at that and go 'you're just a couple of freaks' but the sex is nice and it's good and it does make you feel that ... that close, that little bit more intimate, it's not the be-all and end-all. [An orgasm] it's nice, obviously, but I get as much enjoyment from other things ... from just being close to Hannah and just maybe being touched and being stroked... In fact, I probably get as much satisfaction out of seeing Hannah have pleasure than I do from actually getting it myself, which you know, [to Hannah] you should be whooping about surely?! [Collective laughs] That's just the way I seem to have developed in this relationship, it just seems to be that way and I don't necessarily need to have an orgasm or whatever to, to enjoy that intimate time together.

Thus for Hannah and Shaun, resisting heteronormativity and its narrow prescriptions, particularly in relation to the orgasm, was the route to *regaining* pleasure (in various ways) and renewing the enjoyment of their sexual life. The assertion of the *'freak'* nature of their enjoyment of cuddling and intimacy expands phallocentric sexuality to become that, which, as Sakellariou (2006: 102) states, can be 'closely connected with emotional closeness and pleasure, which can be achieved through any range of practices'. In a similar vein, Tom Shakespeare (2000: 164) questions whether disabled people should strive to be included within mainstream sexual cultures that propagate the 'Cosmo conspiracy of great sex' – the (false) idea that most people are having great sex, all of the time. Thus, as Shaun and Helen's experiences above illustrate, not only can the pressure of such *conspiracies* be so overwhelming that they end up being counterproductive and, in their case, resisted, but the very inability of Shaun's body to meet such a *conspiracy* simultaneously offers him a means through which to defy it. Thus, in this sense, impairment opens up possibilities and makes space for working the edges of heterosexual hegemony and the rules of heteronormative sexual practice.

Other means through which normative pleasures were expanded were through the acts of sexual *fantasy* and obtaining pleasure through *visual* means – shifting pleasures away from the flesh, and radically decentring touch, proximity and corporeality. For Lucille, a 36-year-old married woman with acquired SCI, fantasy offered freedom from the way she felt about her physical body:

LUCILLE: I think of scenarios in my head when I am in bed, things I wished could happen, I suppose what I am saying is I fantasise, usually about a particular man I like. I like it that I get some me time when I am in bed and I can let my imagination run free and I can be who I want to be... I think for someone in my situation imagination has a big role to play, the mind is the most erotic organ as far as I am concerned [...] Sometimes the thought is better than the doing. That's a terrible thing to think.

Similarly, Hayley, 32, said that '*a good imagination*' was an alternative means to embodied pleasure because she couldn't physically masturbate in the conventional way. Sally, a 21-year-old self-identified virgin, also said she enjoyed sexual fantasy as pleasure, but expressed that she was worried this was '*all she would ever have*'. While women were coy about fantasising (never revealing the content of fantasies), one man who said he used fantasy regularly was more forthcoming with detail, showing once again the typically gendered nature of sex talk, Bob said: '*My mind drifts in fantasy. I've had an interest in women's buttocks and often imagine a girl bending over my knee, pulling her skirt up, slowly pulling her knickers down and fondling her buttocks and thighs.*' Such accounts show that, in times of desire, informants could disassociate with their fleshy bodies in order to affirm the imagination as an erogenous zone in and of itself although this was contoured by gender. The ability to arouse oneself and, for some, orgasm *through* imagination and fantasy alone undoubtedly emphasises the ways in which disabled sexualities expand sexual normalcy's privileging of the fleshy.

Pleasure was also reinscribed as *visual*. Despite the fact that Graham *could* experience masturbation, orgasm and ejaculation alone in private, for a variety of reasons he never experienced these pleasures with another person (see Liddiard 2016). He also said that this pleasure was deeply lonely, and thus wasn't particularly desired by him, and that masturbation was merely 'necessity'. Most of his narrative was centred on his inability to 'consummate' any of his relationships and he defined sex as '*sex for me isn't touching a woman, it's looking at her*'. In order to satiate his desire to look at women (as a form of sexual pleasure), Graham had started posing as a professional glamour photographer, inviting (unknowing) prospective models into his home to photograph them. He would invite wannabe glamour models – young women – over to his flat for photo shoots. Graham was not a photographer and never printed the photographs. He didn't even keep them. Sometimes he wouldn't even put film in the camera. This act – duping women – manipulating them to expose themselves is, of course, deeply problematic and demarcated by the inherent sexual power of masculinity; as Plummer (2015: 199) states, men are much more likely to be consumers of sex, they are 'much more likely to feel they can assert themselves to "take sex" … they are more likely than women to have a specific turn on – a little out of the ordinary – which must be met'. Yet Graham's disgust at touch, warm breath, fluids and bodily warmth, which were rooted in his early disability experience of illness, meant that looking was his only route to pleasure with another person. Looking was safe: Graham was not, as he saw it, at risk of infection or illness. Looking, without the other person knowing the context of the look, offered power over passivity and pleasure over pain. Graham's engagement with pleasure again offers us the transformative potential of crip – the cripping of pleasure through decentring touch, and affirming eroticism though visual modes – once again shifting pleasure beyond the flesh.

On the other had, however, Graham's experiences also centre the ambivalence of this shift – the ways in which crip and queer pleasures can be precarious to self and other, and are always at risk of being rendered perverse, and thus can enter people into the realm of deviancy (see McRuer 2006a). Not only were fantasy-based and visual pleasures experienced and defined by informants as 'not the same' (despite the ways in which they unsettled predictable corporeal notions of pleasure) but, for Graham, went much further towards categories of deviance. For example, Graham's 'abnormal' pleasures first led to him having several traumatic encounters with sex workers where he forced himself to try and have 'sex' in 'normal' ways (see Chapter 7). As this wasn't possible, his feelings of failure caused him to pathologise his own behaviour. He spent thousands of pounds on sex surrogacy and sex therapy, which put him into considerable debt. Upon seeing his GP, Graham was subjected to '*two years of referrals through the health service*' and was even referred to what he identified as a well-known clinic for '*weirdos ... paedophiles, serious, serious criminals*'. Graham's experiences not only show, then, how non-normative pleasures come to be further pathologised through medical discourse, but that his *self*-regulation of his *own* sexuality was 'complicit' in such pathologisation (Foucault 1976).

The impaired body

In this section, I move beyond pleasure to explore in greater detail the aesthetics and function of the impaired body as 'a sexually challenging idea' (Goodley 2011a: 41). In doing so, I counter disability studies' somatophobia to draw in and upon the corporeal body. I do so to understand how the lived and material realities of bodily impairment interacted with disabled informants' sexual selves. I begin by examining accounts of body image and the shoring up of bodily hatred, which was narrated as deeply impactful, particularly for disabled women. Later, I discover what informants said about bodily *function*, as well as their negotiation of impairment where it troubled the performance of the sexy body, considering the intimate politics of striving to embody heteronormativity.

Body image

Body image or, rather, bodily hatred, was a routine chapter in informants' sexual stories: the (impaired) body's exclusion from the idealised and hegemonic Euro-American beauty aesthetics required of women, and more increasingly men, affirms its status as wretched and abject (Liddiard 2014a). Some informants' self-hate was fuelled by the way their bodies deviated from embodied norms: scarring, muscle wastage, 'deformity', and weight gain (due to inactivity) firmly underscored the dogma of the 'monstrous' impaired body (Shildrick 2002). Disabled men compared their bodies to the (male) body beautiful, which is muscular (informants talked frequently about 'six packs'), strong, perfected and achieved. For some men, not meeting such bodily expectations caused feelings of disgust and self-hate, but for most others it was an area of their sexual story where talk became pragmatic, practical and matter-of-fact:

ROBERT: My body is not Arnold Schwarz thingies but I can live with that!
TOM: I'm no Brad Pitt yeah, but I'm no Quasimodo!

Such pragmatism likely results from 'body talk' being an activity culturally less available to men than women: 'confessing' body insecurities may have been avoided because it would be seen to disrupt masculine performance. Tom's use of metaphor (Quasimodo) reveals a desire to create distance between himself and discussion of body image, possibly to preserve a crafted performance. Other men told longer, *success* stories of 'coming to terms' with body image, explaining their bodily acceptance as a journey and, once again, an *achievement*; that working to change the perception of their own bodies enabled the reclamation of a positive body image:

TOM: We live in a society where we're constantly projecting the idea of a perfect self, erm [sighs] and sometimes it's very difficult to reject that and create your own identity and your own self ... but of course I do, like, you look at people like David Beckham and you look at how he's idealised in terms of his sporting and physical prowess and then you realise that you can't do any of those things that society perceives as being sexually good or sexy or beautiful, and then it, it kind of triggers a thought process that in the end that – what you do is work through that, and come to terms with that you are who you are and that you are beautiful.

Men like Tom show what Ostrander (2009: 16) suggests disabled women experience: the development of body competence, which 'provides women with more confidence to engage in sexual activities'. Or, as Guldin (2000: 234) suggests, disabled people can 'negate, displace, or supersede' their feelings about non-normative embodiment to *achieve* 'what is constructed – if not a sexy body – is nonetheless a sexy being'.

Importantly, women seldom spoke of equivalent journeys through which they could occupy or exhibit the power to reject normative bodily aesthetics and narrow prescriptions of cultural attractiveness. Bartky (1990: 40) suggests that women are made to feel shame within femininity; that femininity constitutes an established 'infatuation with an inferiorised body' against which women will always feel inadequate. Thus, as Wilkerson (2002: 46) suggests, 'heterosexual women are made, and make themselves, complicit in hierarchies that systematically disadvantage them'. My findings here illustrate that disabled women are, of course, not an exception to this *rule*. Perhaps not surprisingly, body worries *did* surface in men's stories when speaking about sexual identity, and many expressed great concern that prospective sexual partners would make comparisons between normative 'perfect' and impaired 'different' bodies, and thus would feel 'cheated' at this bodily divergence. Thus '*not looking the same*' (as the normative body) and feeling '*unsexy*' featured continuously in the majority of informants' stories. Some women said that the times they felt sexiest were when consuming alcohol or when sexiness was affirmed by a male partner; and while both men and women spoke about their 'relationship' with '*the mirror*' when talking about body image, it was women who talked of hiding or deflecting bodily difference through the use of clothing and other means. In addition, women tended to describe their bodies carefully and in great detail, often 'listing' the bodily difference that brought them the most displeasure:

LUCILLE: My body – hideous, unattractive, untoned, feeling – loss of any sensation.

SALLY: I hate, hate, HATE my body!! My lower spine is curved, so I'm really short in the body and asymmetrical … which means clothes (the few that fit) actually look really awkward and don't hang well which makes me look even worse. Because my condition is muscle wasting, the tops of my legs are like jelly and from the knee down – really skinny so I never wear skirts/dresses – usually trousers with long boots. Equally, the tops of my arms are jelly like and my wrists are really skinny, bony and as I'll always remember one lad at school saying – spider like! Horrible! I have a horrible serpent like, skinny neck and no shoulder muscle. My right foot turns in and looks like a club-foot (despite two very painful operations) erm … the list goes on. I'm currently paying privately for fixed braces and am hopefully having a boob job in the summer as I literally have no boobs – 12-year-old boys have bigger boobs than me! I'm trying to fix the things I can – like teeth, to try and improve whatever I can.

Sally's talk of committing to 'body projects' to 'fix' and 'make the best of the body' through clothes or more permanent bodily work are cultural practices shared by non-disabled women. This is no truer than in current times where cosmetic surgery has become a global industry that routinely dictates and normalises a perfected 'new normal' where our aesthetic and sexual bodies are concerned. As an example, Barbara *et al.* (2015) draw attention to the increased numbers of women and girls now seeking female genital cosmetic surgery, both for aesthetic reasons and to enhance sexual 'functioning', the latter often after childbirth. They argue that 'this phenomenon is associated with the development of a new vulvovaginal standard due to Internet pornography and the increased exposure of female genitalia' (Barbara *et al.* 2015: 1). Such practices not only reveal the ways in which *all* women remain defined and valued through their material (and now erotic) body, but are symptomatic of neoliberal individualist discourses prevalent in the West where the body comes to have exchange value and hence subsists as a project upon which to work (Rose 1998). Negative feelings about the material body were also found, for some, to impact pleasure and performance:

PETE: This inability to relax enough to climax was becoming an issue. My wife would finish her orgasm and would have to stop before I climaxed as she was so tired, I still couldn't ejaculate. We'd be at it for hours. It was so frustrating and I was worried she was going to run a mile. She went to the newsagent and bought some porn magazines. I asked her why she'd bought them (feeling a little threatened). She said 'I want you to relax about sex, it's nothing to be scared of, we're learning together. We'll take our time together'. We talked about the [porn] photos and I discovered that I may move differently to an able-bodied man but I looked the same naked (have all the same things/shapes/sizes in all the same places). There were photos of men with full erections – my wife said 'there see, you are no different to any other man!'

Pete's experience shows how crucial bodily appearance – and proximity to the normative body – can be towards the acquirement of heteronormative sexual practices. In this account we see Pete experience the opposite to what Barbara *et al.* (2015) describe above – he discovered, through porn, that his body did indeed meet the erotic *norms* propagated (and I would say, reified) through porn. This is likely because the pornified male body is not as perfected as that for women porn performers, at least in terms of genitals; the cock, while having to be sizeable enough for the hyper-phallocentrism of porn, can remain relatively untouched from (surgical and other) intervention (see Potts 2000). Likewise, other informants said that in order to 'manage' their proximity to the normative body, they tried to hide non-normative ('deformed') parts of their body from sexual partners and even themselves during sexual encounters. For example, Jane said that she doesn't enjoy sex as much when she can see her feet, which are a non-normative shape and scarred due to her impairment (and subsequent surgery). Although she says that her partner likes her feet, Jane said she only has sex in positions where her feet are out of her eye line; alternatively she will keep her eyes closed. Similarly, Oliver told how he routinely wears long sleeves during sex so as not to expose his *'thin arms'* (due to muscle degeneration). Helen told how she had gone to great lengths to hide a part of her body of which she felt very self-conscious. These attempts at hiding meant she couldn't *'let myself go during sex'*, she said, *'I've always got to worry'*. However, her partner later 'discovered' what she had been hiding:

HELEN: My bum's kind of got this, like, indent on it … it sounds really gross. Erm and I always try and hide it and I always think I do and then the other week he said to me, 'Do you know you've got an indent on your bum?' I was like [looks exasperated]. I don't even know, like, what I said … I was like, 'How do you know?!' I was gutted, I thought I'd hidden it, but obviously I hadn't, obviously he'd seen it one day when the light was on or something.

Helen considers her *'indent'* unacceptable within the rubric of the normative body: 'the body from which all other bodies are judged' (Davy 2010: 186). Helen's and others' experiences of hiding suggests that, both for themselves and for others (their intimate partners), disabled people fear that their departure from bodily normalcy can be a basis for rejection, and thus the need to 'pass' (and all of the work which goes with this) remains (see Chapter 5).

Function and practicality

For many informants, tiredness, fatigue and pain had significant impact upon the ability to engage in sexual encounters. For example, Gemma, a lesbian with an immunity disorder that causes extreme fatigue, said that both humour and a negotiation of reciprocal pleasure were fundamental at times where she was exhausted:

GEMMA: I mean it's something we negotiate, you know, I'm quite comfortable just saying 'Oh look, I'm really knackered' you know 'How about a quick orgasm, help me go to sleep' and she'll go 'Alright then'. I mean, we sort of laugh about it, she goes 'Oh you'll owe me, I'll expect one in the morning' sort of, you know … I mean I think it's just sort of about being grownups really, it's … and having a sense of humour about it.

Gemma and her partner's willingness to negotiate equitable pleasurable exchanges reinforces that some lesbian women may be liberated from hetero-normative gender norms and oppressive heterosexual hegemonies which situate pleasure as a necessarily simultaneous and 'mutual' exchange (though one where the terms of the exchange are usually mediated by male sex discourses). However, for others, tiredness was very frustrating and could encroach upon per-formance of sexuality:

LUCILLE: Despite my suggestive comments to [husband] in the morning, I fell asleep almost immediately. In my head I've got so much energy but the sad truth is I just get so tired sometimes that my body can't keep up with my head.

In this account, Lucille positions her sexual mind and body as separate entities – thus her rational (sexual) mind is functional, while her unruly physical body is unmanageable. Such Cartesian thought, the mind and body as divided (Descartes 1974), was a common theme in informants' stories, in which the impaired body was positioned as disruptive to an otherwise 'normal' sexual psyche and self. For my informants, pain impacted negatively upon sexual life and often affected whether sexual activity took place at all, as found in other research on pain and sexuality (see McCormick 1999). Helen said that severe and progressive hip pain now means she can no longer simply be lifted on to the bed by her partner and that transferring from her wheelchair to the bed is now a more complex process which takes considerable time (thus affecting how she feels when reaching bed). Lucille had a similar situation and found humour a useful strategy for dealing with this situation; in her journal she wrote: '*Must be fab to get into bed and out of bed yourself … If I ever wanted an affair I'd have to send my lover to lifting and handling classes first!*' Pete said that despite the pain in his legs and hips affecting his enjoyment of sex, it is his wife's fear of hurting *him* that has the most negative influence. Therefore, even if the disabled person can 'work through pain' a partner's fear of worsening pain and causing harm might be distracting for both partners. This contradicts Scarry's (1985) positioning of pain as that which can't be shared nor confirmed by others and suggests that effective pain management is integral towards maintaining sexual life for *both* partners. Kolárová's (2010: 50) writings add emphasis to this; she argues that 'pain is not located solely in/on the individual body, but, in contrast, involves interaction between those who are in pain and out of pain'. Other research has explored the intersections of pain, disability and sexuality through BDSM practices – bondage and discipline, domination and submission, sadism and masochism (Sheppard 2017) – of those who live with chronic pain (see Patsavas 2014; Sheppard 2017). Such research makes space for considering pain as more than just 'as an unwanted, aversive, sensation' (Sheppard 2017: 11).

Speaking about leakage (otherwise known as 'incontinence') in the context of sexual and intimate life was very difficult for most informants, even though many had impairments that made them 'singly or doubly incontinent' (to make use medical language for a moment). This mirrors the lack of attention paid to leakiness within literatures on disabled sexualities – despite it being, according to Morris (1989: 91), 'one of, if not the most, inhibiting things about paralysis when it comes to having a sexual relationship'. Morris (1989) found that for many of the disabled women in her research, leakiness was enough to stop women looking for or having a sexual relationship at all. Culturally, 'incontinence' is associated with babies, infants and older people (Lupton 1996) and thus is seldom acknowledged within disability studies for fear of reaffirming discourses of infantilisation. As Liddiard and Slater (2017: pagination unknown) suggest, the bodily containment of urine:

is an expectation of normative adulthood, which results in the oppressive infantilisation of those not meeting up to the (contained and containable) raced, cis-gendered, heteronormative and dis/ableist expectations of what it is to be adult. *Becoming adult* is not a natural progression or development, then, but socio-cultural, used to serve a particular function of a particular time and place.

In other research, Leibowitz (2005: 92), who also carried out research with disabled women, found that her informants' fear of leakage 'affected the ability to enjoy sexual encounters, their conceptualizations of themselves as sexual beings, and their willingness to meet new men and/or resume sexual activity after injury'. Another of my informants, Lucille, said she was conscious of her non-urethral catheter during sex – that she knew it was there – and that she worried about keeping it out of the way so it wouldn't interfere during intercourse (a convoluted process which involved a lot of tape).

However, other women in the research felt differently. For example, Jenny and Gemma said that they had (accidentally) urinated on sexual partners during sex, and that, while this wasn't ideal (and could be particularly awkward with new partners), humour was a key strategy in managing this issue:

JENNY: Like, pissing yourself is not a particularly attractive quality, let's be honest [laughs].

While pragmatic, Jenny is clear that her body 'spilling the boundaries of the proper containment required of feminine bodies risks not meeting the narrow prescriptions of cultural attractiveness' (Liddiard and Slater 2017). To protect this, Jenny – as I have said elsewhere (Liddiard and Slater 2017):

> went on to explain an intricately embodied strategy through which she avoided urinating and defecating during sex. In short, this strategy involved completely emptying her bladder and bowels as much as possible prior to sex (which minimised the chances of 'accidents'). This everyday practice ensured that her body fitted into the appropriate gendered and sexed categories required of heteronormativity. While Jenny reported this strategy as largely 'successful', she was dismayed that it compromised her ability to engage in spontaneous sex – an eroticised form of sex and pleasure whereby she wanted to be taken by her male lover at any moment (Shakespeare, 2000) and thus embody the highly gendered role of the sexually available female body.

For other people, the need to stay contained was more troublesome and painful, and many considered catheters a hindrance to sexual activity. Pete found having a (temporary) catheter an excruciating experience and said that this pain became more intense when he had an erection. He changed to a supra-pubic catheter (a catheter inserted via the abdominal wall rather than through the urethra), but sex was still painful and so he and his wife refrained from sex during this time. Likewise, a sheath, a body-worn device resembling a condom which fits over the penis and allows for urine to be collected in a bag, added considerably to the preparation that needed to take place before sex. Thus, impairment could impact upon the unspoken practicalities of having (normative) sex: preparing the body for sex, establishing the *correct* environment for romantic sexual scripts, and the carrying out of post-sex bodily work (e.g. 'cleaning up'). Characteristically, for those in an intimate relationship, a partner carried out much of this work. For Hannah and Shaun, the need to prepare Shaun for sex was a key feature of the couple's sexual story and the level of extra-caring labour required of Hannah could be a point of tension in their relationship:

HANNAH: Because Shaun wears, like a sheath [for urine], I often feel like I'm too tired to prepare to have sex and it's something that we really … Well, usually I have to take the condom off [urine sheath], give it a wash… Have a shower; maybe brush your teeth … I'm a bit anal about that [Laughs] … erm, that's probably about it.

SHAUN: But then it's no different really because you'd expect that of an able-bodied partner.

HANNAH: You would, but the difference being that I have to help you do that ... whereas...

SHAUN: You have to help me do it, yeah.

HANNAH: An able-bodied person would do it themselves, erm...

Here, Hannah talks about having to suddenly switch roles from carer (providing preparation for sex) to lover, and said that this impacted significantly on her arousal ('*I found I wasn't getting wet* [aroused]') and that this had a major bearing on the sex which followed. However, the couple expressed that such barriers were not insurmountable and that they were trying to find ways around them:

HANNAH: But we're trying to find ways ... sometimes I think 'oh, I must be lazy that I don't want to take off the condom' [urine sheath], give it a wash and then put it back on, but we're trying to find ways ... that maybe the carer comes in and helps Shaun have a shower to kind of ... so that I only have to put it on afterwards or just stuff ... the killjoy stuff, to kind of reduce that, or we do it [sex] on shower days, that we have a shower together and kind of do it [sex] as part and parcel of that so it's not, not so much of a focus.

Showing that strategies can be put in place to deal with the leaky body, Hannah cites the couple's PA as having a role to play in preparing Shaun's body for sex; as Liddiard and Slater (2017; see also Ogden 2013) argue, leakiness often ensures that one's body be actively contained by others: parents, peers, carers, siblings, personal assistant and nurses. Yet, at the same time, solving the *issue* this way means relying on a third person, which can restrict sex to certain times, contexts and spaces. Ultimately, such intimate labour was deemed purposeful towards ensuring that leakiness – and all of the humiliation, embarrassment and shame that this could evoke – didn't encroach upon the (re)claiming of an eroticised, embodied and gendered sexual self (Liddiard, 2014c). As Liddiard and Slater (2017) maintain:

Such emphasis upon control shows the extent to which leakiness is unacceptable within the rubric of the bounded, knowable, normative, sexual, and adult body. It can purposefully expel urine in clean and controlled (normative) ways, but never leak. To leak waste is to lack self-control, bodily discipline and integrity – neoliberal values which circulate the politics of our (gendered) embodiment.

In addition to leaking *waste* (urine/faecal matter), expressions of other types of fluid (cum/semen/vaginal discharge/female ejaculate) were also deemed to be insufferable and had the potential to rupture the (risky) performance of the self-governing sexual body. 'Cleaning up' after sex could be difficult to manage, and particularly awkward, embarrassing or – as one participant stated – '*traumatic*':

LUCILLE: It's not the greatest way to do things is it, for a man – to have sex and then wash your partner as she is unable to do it herself. Then the incidental things like not messing the sheets because a PA is in to help transfer the next day, not getting messy yourself because you can't just hop in the shower – that's a two person job as well.

Lucille's account emphasises two important points. The first – 'messing the sheets' – echoes the impact of PA involvement in her sexual intimacy with her husband. For Lucille, PAs coming in to assist with washing and dressing in the morning also meant dealing with the embarrassment of them knowing she'd had sex the night before. This explicitly shows the (often) uncomfortable rub of sex and care and, for Lucille, the shame and humiliation it often engendered. The second noteworthy point is the way in which she *genders* both the bodily mess and the act of cleaning. As I have suggested elsewhere (Liddiard and Slater 2017: pagination unknown):

> not being able to clean herself after sex (a messy activity for anyone) – or rather, the fact that this intimate labour was a task for her husband – is interpreted by Lucille as failure in her self-conceptualisation of her feminine identity. In order to both desire and be desired, not only is she – as a sexual woman – expected to be bound, controlled and orderly in the face of the sexual, but be the solo labourer in control of cleaning the mess.

Thus, the act of her husband carrying out a typically feminised task disrupted 'the (active) male and (passive) female' (Jackson 1999: 171) demanded within heteronormative sexual interactions. However, Terry's strategy was to incorporate such bodily 'duties' into the sexual experience itself:

TERRY: Yeah, I think probably the bit I don't like is the fact that because I have to rely on someone else to assist, it means that they have to clean up everything afterwards. It's like, at first that was the most traumatic thing. But then with girlfriends it kind of ... you were able to incorporate that into the experience. So for example, afterwards, if you had the time, you could then take a bath or whatever together, and it'd be nice to experience that as well. It can become part of something that isn't just a practicality ... [but] part of the romance as well.

Terry's experience of both embodying and being creative with the practical duties required of the impaired body during sexual intimacy is a positive route towards shifting such assistance (which he first defined as '*traumatic*') to '*part of the romance*'. However, as Terry points out, this strategy is likely to be restricted to intimate relationships and romantic contexts (rather than casual ones) and requires a supportive partner. Speaking more abstractly, needing another person to assist in the maintenance of the singular, discrete and bound sexual body – whether PA, partner or, for some, parent – once again expands sexual norms and reveals disability as a space of (embodied) relationality and interconnectedness, often in the most intimate of ways. Speaking specifically of the cared for/carer relationship, Kelly Fritsch (2010: 1) suggests that such a proximity between disabled people and their PAs means 'a leaking of (their) identities, a mingling of (their) sexualities, and multiple intimate slippages of selves' (see Chapter 7). This level of intimacy emphasises the incompossibility of the human subject that is bolstered by humanism and ableism, and recasts sexual bodies as always co-constituted and blended, as well as corporeally interwoven with other bodies and selves in multiple and creative assemblages.

'Meeting' the requirements of heteronormative sexuality

'I can't move – who is going to want sex with a girl who can't move?' *(Lucille)*

In this final section, my analysis reveals informants' attempts to 'meet' the very physical, gendered, penetrative and spontaneous requirements of normative heterosex. Heterosex was understood by most to be a highly physical activity that required particular bodily capabilities: strength, movement, control and flexibility. Lucille, who acquired disability through an SCI, said that the sheer physicality of penetrative sex made her feel '*completely asexual*':

LUCILLE: That I can't move is a problem and so many other things that affect my ability to enjoy sex as it should be enjoyed.

Similarly, Helen and Rhona, both wheelchair users, said they worried about what they physically couldn't *do* within sex. For example, Helen said: '*I can't do the things a walking person can do ... you obviously can't do things that, there's always a few lacking things ... you can't do what a normal person would do*'. Thus, these (and other) women's accounts show a readiness to define oneself as *lacking* for not meeting the physical expectations of heterosex (which non-disabled women are assumed to unquestionably meet), and thus relate to sex primarily as it *should* be enjoyed. Other informants made frequent references to not being able to 'do' certain sexual positions, or feeling limited in what they could offer because of issues of bodily flexibility and strength. Informants continuously used the (always non-disabled) 'sexually able' body as a marker of normalcy regarding sexual practices, and through their stories made the case for how their bodies 'deviated' from these norms. However, some men recognised that many non-disabled people may not reach such expectations; as Michael said, '*I couldn't perform certain sexual acts, the crazy ones in the karma sutra, but I don't think anyone does*'. Nevertheless, Michael also said that his high degree of '*manoeuvrability*' (meaning his relatively 'mild' impairment) means he is '*fully functional*' and thus a '*proper full man*' showing that, as with other male informants, disabled men, despite being routinely rejected from its confines, often continue to define themselves through – and enact – hegemonic masculinities. Existing research shows that people with what are considered to be 'severe' impairments have lower sexual self-esteem than those with 'milder' impairments (Hassouneh-Phillips and McNeff; McCabe and Taleporos 2003). Yet, as the deeply gendered sexual stories in this chapter thus far have stressed, gender was far more likely to emerge as a key determinant of sexual self-esteem than any other factor. Michael's assertions highlight, then, the competing demands of disability and masculinity as 'complex phenomena that are negotiated and renegotiated, day to day, in diverse social, political, and interpersonal contexts' (Phillips 2010: 120).

For all informants, movement heavily related to the gendered roles adopted during sexual interactions: the majority felt they had to adopt a different role during sex to the one they wanted. For example, many men wanted to adopt the customary (gendered) practice of taking a 'dominant' role (e.g. being on top of a woman during intercourse), but found it difficult because of their impairment. For some, again, this was met with pragmatism, and, others with humour – Tom joked that he was a '*lie-back-and-think-of-England type of man*'. However, for most others not being able to exert dominance through physicality was felt to seriously undermine masculine sexual identity:

PETE: I'm not the one who's in control as, I feel, a man ought to be during intercourse. Maybe if I was the female in the relationship I wouldn't feel such a
failure as I do in my role as a man.

Pete's account reveals the prevailing gendered sexual roles in typical heterosexist scripts: as a man who cannot take what he defines as an active role in sex, he has failed. His assertion that if he were a disabled woman he wouldn't '*feel such a failure*' further upholds such scripts, which dictate that a woman's role during intercourse is one defined by its passivity and submissiveness. Notably, this wasn't at all the way that the majority of disabled women felt; most were made to feel deeply inadequate by the physicalities of gendered heterosex. Male informants were also concerned that a woman being on top during sex was 'unmasculine' and that it impacted negatively on their sexual partners. Most male informants routinely referred to the *type* of sex they could offer partners:

KADEEM: Like she would have to be on top … girls like guy on top and getting
banged, like hard sex … I would love to be on top of a girl and fuck her
hard … I used to talk to that girl about this and she said we can try things,
but I knew it would be too difficult.
PETE: She's never asked me but what if she'd like to make love differently?
What if she'd like it rough sometimes?

'*Getting banged*', '*fuck her hard*' and '*liking it rough*' are descriptions of sex embedded in hegemonic masculinities and normative heterosexist scripts. Such expressions of masculinity denote heterosexual prowess and sexual boasting

(Allen 2006), at the same time as revealing the desire for a masculine subject-ivity that is 'heterosexual, virile, competitive, and predatory', and re-produced and reified through pornography and popular culture (Allen 2006: 74). Fittingly, many men expressed great frustration at their impairment causing a reliance on (female) partners for the pace and control of intercourse. Some positioned this 'lack of control' as problematic to their (male) sexual autonomy and agency:

ROBERT: I can kiss, caress, but not thrust – girlfriend one got lazy and reverted to doing 'stuff' rather than the effort at times, like hands on each other to climax but not intercourse, girlfriend two was awesome with it [penetrative sex], girlfriend three was just not that sexual I think so it was less disability and more lower sex drive.

Robert's (somewhat sexist) accounts of his previous girlfriends shows how the disabled person can lose agency within sexual interactions and is, as in other areas of their life, reliant on someone else for assistance. However, Terry said that a lover had suggested his inability to control the pace of penetration made sex 'better':

TERRY: I found out for certain girls, they've enjoyed it more because they've always wanted to go on top and their [previous non-disabled] partners haven't wanted them to go on top [...] I remember one girl said to me she actually felt it was better to have sex with a disabled person than a non-disabled person; she just said because your positions are limited and because you can't move around as much as a non-disabled person it means that she can get the optimal position for her and the most enjoyable for her. So that was kind of – that was kind of a boost, really [...] But, as I said, you know – there was a time when I thought 'oh, I can only do it on a bed' and then, you know, through experimenting, the wheelchair became a viable option as well. So ... you find new experiences ... new ways of exploring.

Terry's partner's assertion that sex with a disabled man is 'better' because it gave her more control regarding position and pace (and thus more pleasure) emphasises once again the ways in which impairment defies the conventions of heteronormativity – in this case, through challenging the naturalised gendered hierarchies of active/passive within heterosex (Jackson 1999) Consequently, some informants said that the 'natural' strategy to not being able to move one's body is to verbalise needs and wants during sexual interactions. Informants talked about this verbalisation in different ways – for some it bought pleasure, but for others it was frustrating, tiresome and a burden to the sexual role they wanted to perform. In addition, the act of verbalising was found to have different meanings for men and women.

ROBERT: I have to verbalise a lot if I want her to move me or her to come closer ... Then I verbalise how I feel and [can] initiate positions I flourish in.

TOM: Erm, it's like negotiating a different role, if you want to move in a certain way you have to ask the other person to move [you].

LUCILLE: I'd love to be able to start things without verbally communicating that that's what I want! I'd really like to experiment a lot more as well but I don't know, it's hard to communicate that, discussing everything first makes things seem dirty sometimes and it ends up that I don't say a thing, I just have all these thoughts circulating in my head.

RHONA: It just isn't the same when you have to talk everything through.

These accounts suggest that the act of verbalising what one needs or wants as part of the sexual encounter is obstructive; that doing so *interrupts* desire. They also suggest that verbalising is an act culturally more available to and acceptable for men than women. Lucille's assertion that speaking aloud about '*what she wants*' makes her feel '*dirty*' encapsulates the discourses of inappropriateness that constrict female desire. More importantly, Lucille shows that the risk of disrupting a suitable gendered performance causes her to say nothing at all. Rhona's assertion that verbalising 'just isn't the same' once again shows how deviating from heteronormative scripts *too much* is largely interpreted as failure. Thus, the inadequacy of verbalisation as an alternative to movement (something that is readily assumed by informants to equate to a sexual freedom to act on desire) simultaneously fortifies that heterosex is ultimately always 'of the flesh' (Tiefer 2001).

Many women said that their impairment impacted upon the more active role they would like to have within sexual relations, countering their ascribed passivity. As Ostrander (2009: 16) found, 'women shared the concerns [of disabled males] about role of disabling perspectives on their sexual pursuits'. For example, Lucille felt that her acquired disability meant that she could no longer be an instigator of sex with her husband in the way she had been before her accident. She said her attempts to instigate '*a fumble*' result in '*me clumsily hitting him somewhere he'd rather not be hit! It's not always like that, but sometimes it's incredibly frustrating*'. Lucille also said that her acquired impairment made her less sexually '*assertive*'. She told a story of how she'd bought a vibrator for her husband to use on her during sex, but as it '*did nothing for him*' they stopped using it and she felt she couldn't '*press the issue*'. Rhona had similar feelings:

RHONA: Yes, I would love to be able to initiate, and take control more. It is incredibly frustrating not being able to do things for your partner that you know he would enjoy. It's also annoying that he has to do all the work, although he seemed to think it was more than worth it … It means I am much less actively involved than I would like to be.

Concerns about partners doing '*all the work*', as Rhona puts it, was related to general anxiety around a partner's sexual enjoyment and pleasure, affirming once again the privileged status that mutual pleasure holds. Helen also said she wished she could do '*more things*' for her fiancé during sex, and that her inability to carry out certain sexual practices made her feel '*bad for him, I feel bad for him rather than me*'. Hannah, Shaun's non-disabled wife, talked in detail about gender and dominance, saying that she had had '*negative sexual experiences with previous partners*' and did not feel comfortable taking the 'dominant' role (of being on top of Shaun) during intercourse:

SHAUN: I think you come into it and you think, how is this going to work? It's gonna be Hannah on top all the time ... but again that's something that with the Intimate Rider, it's something that there are ways and means, you just have to be much more imaginative really.

HANNAH: Yeah, I think that was something that I was worried about, about having to be in charge, because of my bad experiences I really wanted Shaun to be [in charge] and I think that, with the Intimate Rider and the electric bed, that Shaun can sit up and erm ... be more in control...

Hannah and Shaun's strategy was to use technology in the form of an electric bed and a piece of specialist equipment called the Intimate Rider. The Intimate Rider enables men with paralysis to enhance their mobility during intercourse. It is advertised as equipment 'designed for people who REFUSE to let physical challenges get in the way' (Intimaterider.com, 2011). Its advertisements typically feature happy and attractive couples (including male models with 'hypermasculine' physiques), with its marketing aimed at disabled men who wish to *reclaim* the physicality synonymous with a masculine sex role. The application of technologies to the sexual body serves to reaffirm its blurred boundaries. For example, the Intimate Rider, as a sexual tool, positions such technologies as extensions of the erotic body; the body becomes hybridised, a mix of flesh and machine, thus constituting a form of sexual cyborg (Haraway 1991). Through using this product the couple could negotiate their difficulties with the physicality of intercourse (albeit in normative ways). No other informants mentioned the Intimate Rider, nor any other sex toys specifically designed for disabled people. Importantly, Hannah made reference to the absence of the Intimate Rider from the sex and disability advice and information offered by SCI charity literature, in which, she said, '*there was nothing [featured] about the chairs out there, products, straps, swings and things to do. I just thought it was very narrow-minded*'. While Hannah and Shaun both advocate using such products, the Intimate Rider (which was designed by a male paraplegic) proposes and promotes assimilation into normative categories of sex and gender. Much of the literature for the product features a reclamation discourse based on 'natural' and 'normal' ways of 'doing' (importantly, only) heterosex, thus upholding sexual normalcy rather than challenging it. Such (normalising) products may disrupt and hamper intimate experimentation, and the discovery of novel pleasures and practices that may be available to the (newly) impaired body.

Penetration and spontaneity: what to do with 'harder!' and 'now!'

Wilkerson (2002) suggests that the cultural compulsion to have intercourse obscures more creative polymorphous forms of sexuality. As Cacchioni (2007: 304; emphasis added) states, within heteronormative sexuality 'kissing, touching, and oral sex are relegated or demoted to "foreplay" and not "real sex", they are the *other* to the ideal of coitus ending in orgasm'. Thus penetration has 'the privileged place as the essential heterosexual act' (Jackson 1999: 171). For male informants who *couldn't* maintain an erection and therefore have penetrative sex in expected ways, it remained central to their masculine identity. Bob, an older man with physical and sensory impairment, understood his inability to have penetrative sex with his late partner as reason for her untimely death:

BOB: On Sunday 14th April she lay on her bed nude, saying she felt sexually unfulfilled[...] On 24th April she told me she was going out for a packet of cigarettes just before 19.30. The nearest shop is at the end of the road and, as she was a Coronation Street viewer, I expected her back within five minutes but as she hadn't returned by 20.15 I became slightly anxious. A few minutes later she rang saying: 'Hi darling, I'm just having a coffee in Hammersmith, I'll see you later.' I was slightly relieved, feeling she may have needed some time to herself but, two hours later, I had a phone-call from a guy who'd found her handbag on the wall by a small slipway near [name] Bridge. Her body was discovered, a couple of miles down-river, 11 days later [...] I feel that if full-scale intercourse had been a regular part of the relationship and if I'd sexually fulfilled her on that Sunday afternoon things could have been radically different.

In this deeply distressing account, it is clear that Bob understands his inability to penetrate and sexually fulfil his partner as justified reasoning for her death, illustrating the normalising power of phallocentric discourse. As Annie Potts (2000: 87) suggests, 'the "sexed" male body corresponds to the erect penis – the "hard on" is the essence of male sexuality'. Without an erect penis that can sustain penetration, Bob's sexuality becomes non-existent and he has failed both himself and his partner. This is a stark reminder of how phallocentrism serves to castrate and emasculate disabled men (and others) who don't meet its demands (Drench 1992; Murphy 1990; Shakespeare 1996). Or, in the words of Leonore Tiefer (2001: 90), 'If it's wet and hard and "works", it's normal; if it's not, it's not'. Such emphasis upon the body-that-functions reduces impairment to that which 'removes people's ability to engage in "normal" sexual practices and/or their capacity to incite "normal" sexual desire in others' (Galvin 2006: 502), rather than a site that enables new possibilities for sex and gender.

However, other informants were able to resist phallocentrism and *decentre* penetration from their sexual and intimate relations. Thus, the providing of sex and pleasure were, in essence, removed from the penis and displaced to other body parts (e.g. tongue, fingers) – a finding that has been echoed in other studies of disability and sexuality (Ostrander 2009; Sakellariou and Sawada 2006). For example, Abram, a 35-year-old man who employed a sex worker to lose his virginity, said that his tongue was central to pleasure giving. Others spoke of fingers, arms, necks and backs. Thus a (necessary) decentring of the penis was cause for some men to learn to 'specialise' and excel in the sexual practices their embodiments enabled, such as foreplay, oral sex and mutual masturbation. For example, Robert said that he tries '*to show passion in other [non-penetrative] ways*' and that he '*wants to please in any way I physically can*'. Tom felt similarly and said that he '*has to be the best you can possibly be at what you can do*'. However, such pressure to excel at performing *alternative* practices – as seen in the first section of this chapter – mirrors and replicates conventional notions of the male body as the primary source of pleasure and thus remains grounded in hegemonies of gendered bodies and eroticism (Guldin 2000). It also reinforces the essential *reciprocity* of heterosex – the necessity of a mutual exchange of pleasure in order for sex to be deemed successful. However, it was acknowledged that 'alternative' practices could be 'more' pleasurable and beneficial to female sex partners:

GRACE: His physical limitations meant that he used fingers and tongue to very best effect. Also, he took time, lots and lots of time. One hour was minimum, more often two or more. Foreplay was everything and he always, always made sure I came first – more than once.

In this account, Grace shows how such sexual practices, combined with the more time her disabled partner needed, made sex more pleasurable for her (see Vahldieck 1999). Thus the very presence of her partner's impairment displaced routine phallocentrism and inscribed foreplay with new meanings. Rembis suggests (2010: 54) that some disabled people 'see disability as a vehicle for learning about and exploring their own sexuality, as well as that of their lover or partner, which they claim makes them a more sensitive and responsive, or in some cases, creative and courageous lover'. Guldin (2000: 236) labels this is an 'inversion of ability/disability' whereby

physically non-disabled men become sexually disabled by their lack of sexual skill and sexual introspection. This 'sexual disabling' of bodies that are – according to cultural definitions – functional, challenges notions not only of the 'sexual body' and 'sexuality' but also of what it means to be 'disabled'.

As with penetration, normative expectations of spontaneity were prevalent within informants' sexual stories. Literary, media and pornographic portrayals of sex have long created an impossible sexuality whereby 'great sex' is adventurous but spontaneous – spur-of-the-moment, unstructured and *free* – as well as mutually satisfying with orgasms seemingly on demand, ready and waiting. Dune and Shuttleworth (2009) call this the 'myth of spontaneity' and argue that it not only is unrealistic for all people, but also undoubtedly excludes people with impairment, and also others such as women with the label of 'female sexual dysfunction' and people who live with HIV/AIDS. According to Dune and Shuttleworth (2009: 106), 'people attribute these "sexual difficulties" to a personal inability to act as prescribed in terms of this internalized sexual script'. Thus, the impossibility of the spontaneous script is seldom interrogated; rather, the marker of failure is once again inscribed on the material body. Informants consistently drew upon the myth of spontaneity throughout the telling of their sexual stories and many articulated that not being able to participate in spontaneity was to the detriment of their sex life. As Robert said, '*If they [women] like spontaneity then I'm buggered*'. Spontaneity was felt to be compromised by a range of factors related to impairment, for example, using a hoist to get into bed; unavailable sexual support and care; the management of catheters; or fatigue and pain.

Informants' stories inferred that the act of 'being spontaneous' (even though many had never experienced it) was sexier, more passionate and gratifying, emphasising the extent to which internalised knowledges of sex are learned through (popular) culture, media and pornography (see Allen 2014). Once again, gender typically impacted feelings around spontaneity. For example, two women said they felt frustrated that their immobility meant they couldn't spontaneously 'prepare' for sex by taking part in the feminine practices of 'throwing on sexy underwear' and 'seducing' their male partners and the majority of men, as I've shown, deem spontaneity a symbol of masculinity and virility: for example, Pete lamented that '*sometimes I'd like to be able whisk my wife in my arms, spread her on the kitchen-table or on the floor, and make love. Be in total control*'. Shaun and his non-disabled wife Hannah said that they had, originally, struggled considerably with feelings about spontaneity:

SHAUN: Obviously it's the spontaneity you lose, which we're having to learn at the moment … we're being taught by different people that, you know, just because sex isn't spontaneous it's not that it's any worse… In fact, they say the better sexual encounters are the planned ones, so that's something that we've both got quite stereotypical views about how sex should be from watching pornographic films, not that we've done it recently, but when you grow up and watch that kind of thing, it gives you a very fake view of what sex is actually about.

The learning Shaun refers to in his account occurred within a sex and disability workshop run by the organisation Outsiders, the (self-proclaimed) only sex and disability organisation in the UK. Outsiders is an organisation which, despite being publicly celebrated within particular spaces of the disability movement, has attracted scholarly criticism, namely because 'the concept of a club especially for disabled people feeds traditional ideas about segregated provision, even in relation to socialising and sex' (Shakespeare at al 1996: 127). Some of my informants who had made use of Outsiders narrated negative experiences. Much of Outsiders' own literature affirms it as an organisation underpinned by heterosexist and essentialist perspectives of sexuality, which promote individualist discourses of sexuality. Ironically – for me – it is a deeply disablist organisation, and actively excludes people with a range of impairments: 'When somebody applies who we feel ill-equipped to cope with, e.g. people who cannot manage their own affairs because of learning disability, mental health problems or brain damage, they are signposted on to more suitable clubs' (Outsiders 2011). However, Hannah and Shaun found the Outsiders workshop they attended very useful, because it offered a chance to hear the sexual experiences of fellow attendees, which gave them comfort that others are in similar situations.

For those informants who acquired impairment in adulthood, and who had experienced spontaneous sex prior, the transition to post-injury positive sexual adjustment (Parker and Yau 2012) was difficult. Lucille's acquired SCI wholly transformed her sexual self:

LUCILLE: Sometimes I think about stuff from the past and it really makes my heart skip a beat and I wish I could do those things all again, be spontaneous... Lack of spontaneity – having intercourse [has] become like a military operation – no coming in the door after work and getting amorous on the kitchen table! No ... sliding board, un-creased sheet, catheter tube out of the way, a roll ... hardly the stuff of a great sex life! And of course the harking back to what was how it was and how it wasn't ever going to be that way again. It changed everything, the enjoyment of sex, confidence, the ability to be happy.

Lucille's experiences echo existing research findings that have documented the catastrophic effects of sudden disability upon sexuality (Parker and Yau 2012; Tepper 1999, 2000). Spontaneous sexuality, for Lucille, has been replaced with a form of sex that she likens to a '*military operation*' – she lists equipment, affirms order and structure, and draws upon the routinisation that she feels intercourse now requires. Lucille, like most other informants, problematically relates ideas of spontaneity to sexual freedom and liberation, and thus her inability to perform spontaneously is perceived as a failure that '*changed everything*'. The satiation of spontaneous desire and pleasure, affirmed by the 'Cosmo conspiracy' (Shakespeare 2000), remains an ever-present sexual narrative despite the fact that most of us seldom have spontaneous sex (particularly the '*kitchen table sex*' type Lucille cites above) – for a wide range of reasons: tiredness, children, working too much, embarrassment and mess! However, informants' attribution of an inability to perform spontaneously to impairment is confirmed and maintained through wider discursive constructions of the impaired body as insufficient, incapable and asexual and through governing heteronormative narratives of what it means to be erotic and sexual with the self and others.

Conclusion

To conclude, the impaired body – as that which can deviate from conventional forms and methods of sexual desire, pleasure and practice – challenges the very essence of heteronormative sexual pleasure and disrupts and shifts sexual embodied norms (Ostrander 2009). Where the impaired body posed a challenge to mapped sexual pleasures (e.g. arousal, climax, orgasm) through conventional means (e.g. penetration, intercourse), informants developed *strategies* for the acquisition of pleasure that expanded conformist notions of heteronormative pleasure. Strategies included, for example, expanding views on what counts as 'sex', decentring the orgasm and participating in sexual exploration that, for some, facilitated discovery of alternative pleasures. Such experiences reveal the possibilities of pleasure that the materiality of impairment can open up, to expand heterosex. However, these alternative pleasures were often considered by informants as inadequate, 'not the same' and 'unfinished', and thus unnatural and abnormal within the rubric of sexual normativity. Therefore, to informants the ability to recognise their bodies and impairments as rousing sites of sexual potentiality was firmly undermined by prevailing heteronormative discourse, meaning any erotic possibilities were not readily realised, acknowledged and celebrated.

Moreover, while disabled informants' feelings of bodily inadequacy were quite typically gendered along normative lines – with men's concerns revolving around meeting a hegemonically masculine and sexual body and women's centred on meeting a feminine aesthetic – for people of all genders it was clear that *proximity* to the normative body was crucial, and that deviation could affect the ability to experience sexual pleasures (see Liddiard and Slater 2017). In terms of bodily function and the practicalities of impairment, analysis suggests that, despite the significant impact of the 'hard' realities of the impaired body (Wendell 1996) (such as tiredness, fatigue and pain), informants could adapt through devising strategies to deal with bodily difficulties, once again illustrating sexual agency. Therefore, although impairment can be problematic within the confines of conventional notions of what constitutes a 'sexual body', informants' management and strategic work ensured that their bodies could be sites of sexual pleasure and enjoyment.

Finally, the very physicality of heteronormative sexual activity was central to the majority of informants, most of who felt that their impaired bodies 'restricted' the normative gendered sexual role they wanted to perform and enact with and for intimate others. Likewise, spontaneous and penetrative sex remained the fixed norm from which other sexual modes were judged. Findings show that for those disabled men who could resist and reject the oppressive requirements of hegemonic sexualities (such as phallocentrism and dominance), a more empowering sexual project was available whereby they excelled in non-penetrative practices, thus inverting ability/disability (Guldin 2000) to become defined as 'better lovers'. Men's exclusion from traditional gender identities (with regard to sexuality) could serve as an opportunity to play with, and negotiate, gender – revealing the emancipatory possibilities that disability and impairment can mean for disabled men in the context of hegemonic gender binaries preserved through heteronormativity and heterosexuality.

However, while disabled men *could* negotiate gendered sexual identities and performances, the scope for disabled women was limited. Women were found to seldom have the manoeuvrability and agency of men when defining – or at least narrating – their sexual selves, lives and bodies. Instead, findings have shown that disabled women had little alternative sexuality to claim, and thus remained feeling 'not enough' for, and not adequately meeting the (assumed) needs of, sexual partners. For example, while many women desired a more active role within their sex, this was rarely achieved. Women's accounts of their sexual selves and relationships suggest that this is as much because of the restrictive boundaries of normative female sexuality (which is characterised by docility and asexuality) as the embodied realities of impairment. Thus, (disabled) men's increased social and sexual power offered more scope – either through acceptance or rejection of hegemonic masculinity – to negotiate a more empowering alternative sexual role.

Notes

1 It's important to note here that only heterosexual sex was 'liberated'.
2 This chapter treats crip and queer as fluid categories that merge and converge in relation to body and self (see Chapter 2).

7 '...They finish off with a blow job'
Politics, power and the precarity of pleasure

Accessible summary

- In this chapter I explore 'sex work', 'sexual surrogacy' and 'sexual support' through men's stories and women's silences.
- Disabled men gave lots of different reasons for paying for sex.
- Choosing to pay for sex and accessing sexual support were mediated by experiences of gender, disability and sexuality.
- Therefore, this chapter argues that these forms of sexuality, intimacy and support can be exclusory, particularly to disabled women and marginalised others.
- I question what this means for disabled people's claims for sexual and intimate citizenship.

This chapter focuses on informants' experiences of commercial sex and to a lesser extent their experiences of sexual support, otherwise known as 'facilitated sex' (Earle 1999, 2001). Sexual support is an intimate labour that is usually carried out by a personal assistant, carer and/or partner. It can encompass a range of practices; for example, to assist social or sexual life, to support procuring and/ or paying for sex or, as Earle (1999: 312) proposes, 'a person [PA] might be required to facilitate sexual intercourse between two or more individuals, to undress them for such a purpose, or to masturbate them when no other form of sexual relief is available'. I use the all-encompassing term 'sexual support' in this book in recognition that it is a broad category of support (as shown in Chapter 1). At the same time, I acknowledge that labelling it in this way poten- tially proffers certain risks. For example, some people might view it as unhelpful to seemingly *lump* all forms of sexual support together; that such terminology lacks the distinction and nuance to recognise, for example, that there are marked differences between styling a person's hair before a date and masturbating someone, as the latter half of this chapter will show. Further, assuming all sup- ports are the 'same', in part, risks alienating the many people who find sexual support already difficult to request, or who believe that such intimate supports are outside of, or extraneous to, one's rights to good quality care and support. Thus, I propose thinking of sexual support as being on a continuum. This acknowledges that it is, inevitably, a varied set of supportive practices, but more importantly that it is a continuum upon which all people (regardless of disability) can be located – that, in reality, we all make use of supports within our sexual and intimate relations with ourselves and others, and depend upon a range of knowledges, services and technologies that both make and determine our sexual and intimate selves, lives and bodies in neoliberal capitalist times. I return to these debates in the latter half of this chapter, where the distinctions between different forms of sexual support become clearer.

It is, then, perhaps not surprising that both commercial sex – paying for sex via a sex worker – and sexual support as a practice can be sites of contention that encompass moral, social, practical, financial, legal and emotional issues (Earle 1999, 2001; Mona 2003; Shuttleworth 2010). Such debates take place both inside and outside of the Academy and reach the very heart of disabled people's sexual politics and their (emerging) campaigns for sexual citizenship (Plummer 2003; Sanders 2008). Information about commercial sex and sexual support are seriously under-represented within disability and sexuality research (Sanders 2007; Shuttleworth 2010), possibly because of their assumed deviant disposition. But such silences routinely further risk contaminating (particularly) disabled male sexualities with connotations of deviancy and ethical ambiguity, reinforcing ableist constructions of disabled sexualities as Other, oversexed and unruly. The commercial sex industry includes a range of workers, but I speak primarily about sex workers and sex surrogates in this chapter. The roles of sex worker and sex surrogate, despite having different intentions and aims, are often conflated and misunderstood, with sex surrogates sometimes labelled as 'elitist prostitutes' (Roberts 1981). This originates from the fact that both are paid-for, commercial services that involve sexual bodily contact (Shapiro 2002; see also Noonan 1984). For clarity, a sex worker sells sexual services and a sex surrogate is a worker who provides, according to Shapiro (2002: 72; emphasis added), 'a therapeutic process which attempts to have the *patient* begin a dialogue with their own body in an attempt to, in a meaningful way, transcend simple gratification' (see also Davies 2000; Shuttleworth 2010). The shifting meanings of these roles are unpacked through this chapter.

As such, then, this chapter builds on my critique of heteronormativity. I explore the experiences of informants who engaged in commercial sex and particular forms of sexual support (such as assisted masturbation) and those who did not in order to capture the range of lived experiences regarding these forms of sexuality. In the first half of the chapter I look at the motivations of disabled informants who purchased sex – all men – and locate them in dominant constructions of disability and masculinity. I then explore the complex power relationships between disabled men and non-disabled female sex workers within commercial sex work exchanges. In the second half of the chapter I examine informants' experiences of sexual support, focusing predominantly on the integral role of the personal assistant (PA) within men's commercial sex purchases, and, for some others, their experiences of assisted masturbation from paid-for support workers and carers. I conclude that both of these forms of sexuality are intimate practices embedded within conventional gendered ideologies of power, heteronormativity and masculinity. This not only serves to further marginalise the sexual desires of (heterosexual) disabled women and LGBTQ-2SIA disabled people, but serves to reify discourses of heteronormative sexuality which, as I have argued throughout this book, oppress and exclude disabled people (amongst many others).

'Rights' to sexual pleasure?

International discourses of sexual rights are increasingly recognising sexual pleasure 'as a human right' (Oriel 2005: 392; see also Petchesky 2000). For example, the World Health Organization's (2002: 3) definition of sexual rights lists, among other sexual health-related rights, the right to 'pursue a satisfying, safe and pleasurable sexual life'. It is the lexicon of 'satisfying' and 'pleasurable' that makes the WHO's definition distinct from other rights documents. Such rights have been problematised by some feminists on grounds of their gender-neutral language (Jeffreys 2008; Oriel 2005) and their failure to 'explain how the right to sexual pleasure, or any sexual right, may affect women and men differently' (Oriel 2005: 392). As Kanguade (2010: 197) reminds us, however, the very concept of sexual rights is a 'powerful tool to expose the relationship between human rights and the sexuality of persons with disabilities [*sic*]'.

In order to become 'full sexual subjects' (Kanguade 2010: 197), some disabled people have begun campaigning for their sexual citizenship within a rights-based framework that, Sanders (2010: 151) argues, has offered activists 'a means to speak out about sexual oppression'. A rights-based framework is argued to legitimise disabled people's sexual and intimate desires by placing them firmly on the agendas of disability rights movements (see Tepper 2000), and that doing so has ended the historical absence of sexual life from a disability rights agenda (see Chapter 2). This framing of sexuality follows on from disabled people's campaigns for rights within public life; as Davies (2000: 188) protests, 'we've fought for equality in terms of access to the built environment, to education and employment and now we want our rights to love, form relationships, and have sex with ourselves and with other people'. Thus, notions of rights to pleasure are becoming increasingly normalised within certain disability activist spaces (e.g. Sexual Freedom Coalition; TLC Trust; Outsiders' Free Speech Campaign; Sexual Health and Disability Alliance) and this has been used to advocate for disabled people's purchasing of (specifically, hetero) sexual services from sex workers and sex surrogates (Liddiard 2014a; Sanders 2007).

Disability publication *Disability Now*'s 'Time to talk sex' survey of 1,115 disabled people conducted in 2005 revealed that 22 per cent of disabled male respondents reported having paid for sexual services, in comparison to just 1 per cent of disabled women (Disability Now 2005). Similarly, just 16.2 per cent of disabled women had *considered* paying for sex, in comparison to 37.6 per cent of disabled men. Interestingly, there are no comparative statistics for non-disabled men and women (Sanders 2005; see also Wellings *et al.* 1994). This marked lack of women's experiences not only emphasises the highly gendered nature of commercial sex work, but further mirrors the widespread absence in both academic and non-academic fields of women as sex purchasers, although there are some exceptions (Browne and Russell 2005). Reflecting these findings, out of a total of 16 disabled men who participated in my research, seven had purchased sex from a sex worker (one had additionally purchased sexual surrogacy); all disabled women who participated said they had never purchased sex, though one said she had considered it (see Chapter 4).

Responses to initial questions regarding commercial sex were varied – reactions ranged from disgust to indifference. Many women responded with laughter and shock; likely, because the very notion of purchasing pleasure counters the inert sexualities extended to women in heteronormative sexual cultures. Past this initial reaction, very little was said by women, which is contradictory to existing research carried out by Browne and Russell (2005: 392) in which disabled women expressed their views, for example, about the 'lack of opportunities for them to engage in commercial sex', 'the idea of a [paid-for] fuck buddy' and their feelings about cost implications. As such, the voices and experiences of women informants are in relatively short supply throughout this chapter in comparison to other chapters. However, rather than see this as a lack of data, I suggest that this absence *is* data; that the exclusion of disabled female sexuality and desire from commercial sex work contexts not only reinforces the highly gendered nature of such practices but, as I go on to argue, that such practices *reproduce* a heteronormative sexuality which is predicated on a mode of sexuality that requires female passivity, meaning disabled women (and others) are unable to participate in this form of sexual access.

In contrast to women's silences, many male informants who had *not* purchased sex offered lengthy explanations as to why. As Sanders (2007: 452) argues, impairment does not make paying for sex inevitable: 'like non-disabled men, they [disabled men] visit sex workers because they have unfulfilled sexual desires for a range of reasons'. As such, men offered broad responses, locating their decisions *not* to purchase sex both inside and outside contexts of disability:

BOB: I've yet to have my first encounter. There was an occasion, about five years ago, when I was walking at King's Cross station, when a slightly bedraggled-looking girl approached me saying how much fun we could have together. I asked her how much she charged; she asked me how much I had but I'd decided by that point that I didn't want to proceed. She seemed half asleep; I assumed she was probably a drug addict. I felt sorry for her, as she seemed so potentially vulnerable, and saddened that anyone should opt for that sort of lifestyle. I felt that I'd have to be pretty desperate to agree to anything in these circumstances.

ROBERT: Now, I still maintain I wouldn't, but I have considered it more. I know only disabled people who have. That makes me feel mixed. My yardstick is an average life. If generally people don't, I won't. But then, I could be enticed... Overall it's still a no as I would feel failed, dirty and probably worse afterward as it'd have no meaning.

PETE: To be honest, I have always been frightened of catching some disease. It has never really entered my head to pay for sex. I wouldn't know where to buy sex, Kirsty, even if I wanted it. I'd probably get turned away anyway!

PHILLIP: I haven't and I wouldn't seek to. Again, however, whether you were to ask me that question again in 20 years' time... The biggest issue for me in paying for sex is that erm, about exploitation. I worry about the girls being exploited... But that isn't to mean, if they weren't exploited, I wouldn't tomorrow go and pay for it.

Thus, reasons included concern for sex workers; moral objections; fear; not knowing how or where to buy sex; and not 'needing' to (because they had access to sex in their intimate relationships with partners). Additionally, some men feared that paying for sex would confirm them as an object of disgust or pity; as O'Brien (1990: 13) states, 'hiring a prostitute implies that I cannot be loved, body and soul, just body or soul'. Notably, through such long explanations many implied that doing so was not out of their reach as heterosexual disabled men; for example, purchasing sex was routinely situated as a practice in which they had 'not yet engaged' (Bob); one to which they 'could be enticed' (Robert); especially 'if exploitation weren't involved' (Phillip). This *potentiality*, then, in comparison to women's silences, once again illustrates the gendered imperative of sex work as a heteronormative form of opportunity, underpinned by masculinist constructions of desire.

Decision-making: beyond 'need'

Back in the Academy, sex work is a hotbed of feminist debate (see LeMoncheck 1997; O'Connell-Davidson 2002). Radical feminists predominantly use terms such as 'prostituted women' (Jeffreys 2008; Raymond 2004) and 'prostitute user' (Raymond 2004) and argue for the abolition of prostitution. This is on the grounds that male purchasing of women's bodies is a form of sexual exploitation supported by and reproducing the 'male sex right' (Pateman 1988): 'the privileged expectation in male dominant societies that men should have sexual access to the bodies of women as of right' (Jeffreys 2008: 328). Moreover, 'prostitution' is positioned as deeply harmful for women sex workers because it requires 'self-estrangement' (Chapkis 1997), commodifies the female subjectivity and body, can impact upon their personal sexual subjectivity and relationships (see Høigård and Finstad 1992) and thus equates to a form of sexual violence (Jeffreys 2008). However, feminists who adopt more nuanced perspectives, using terms such as 'sexual labour' (Boris *et al.* 2010), 'sex workers' and 'clients' (Sanders 2007, 2008, 2010), 'sex surrogates' (Noonan 1984) and 'johns' (Holt and Blevins 2007), conceptualise prostitution as inevitable within capitalist structures where the sexual body becomes another commodity. As such, they argue that 'prostitution' should be recognised as a legitimate form of labour and commercial service work (see Boris *et al.* 2010) that requires survival strategies similar to conventional service work (Weinberg *et al.* 1999), and where regulation of the industry would offer sex workers legal, political and civil rights (see Chapkis 1997; Jennes 1990). While space precludes me from highlighting the gulf of debate between these two polar positions here, they are fleshed out within this chapter. I align myself far more within the latter of these two perspectives, but also follow Weatherall and Priestley (2001) in rejecting a singular and fixed definition of the meaning of sex work. I do so in order to 'highlight the multiple and contradictory meanings of sex work' (Weatherall and Priestley 2001: 324), which are, I suggest, necessary within the context of the disability experience. As such, I take a broad liberal feminist positionality, which is further grounded in critical disability studies, and thus rejects radical feminist perspectives of sex work. This is not only based on their inherent essentialism (Weitzer 2009), but also because of the routine dis/ableism that often features in such analyses (see Jeffreys 2008 for a deeply dis/ableist analysis of disabled men's sex purchasing).

Existing research has shown, then, that non-disabled men who purchase sex often have multiple reasons for doing so which extend beyond 'needing' sexual release or gratification (Campbell 1998; McCabe *et al.* 2000; Sanders 2007). In her research with (non-disabled) male customers, Campbell's (1998) male informants said that their motivations to buy sex were based on 'excitement; sexual services not provided by current partner; sexual variety; convenience; lack of emotional ties; loneliness; and an inability to form sexual relationships' (in Sanders 2007: 444). Elsewhere, motivations such as unattractiveness, poor sexual development (Atchison *et al.* 1998), and thrill (Monto 2000) have been cited. Teela Sanders' (2008: 400) research reports that men's 'commercial sexual relationships can mirror the traditional romance, courtship rituals, modes and meanings of communication, sexual familiarity, mutual satisfaction and emotional intimacies found in "ordinary" relationships', emphasising that motivations to pay for sex are more complex and multifaceted than they may at first seem.

Interestingly, disabled men's purchasing of sex has been constructed within activist, academic and practitioner discourses far more upon notions of an unmet 'need' for sexual gratification and human intimacy (Hollway 1984, 1996). Certain activist campaigns advocating commercial sex work as a legitimate form of sexual access for disabled people have positioned heterosexual disabled people as deeply sexually frustrated, wronged (in that their 'natural' needs are insatiate) and thus as sexual victims (Shakespeare *et al.* 1996). For example, the TLC Trust, a British organisation aimed at 'helping professional sex workers and other service providers cater to the needs of the sexually dispossessed [*sic*]' (TLC Trust 2011), advocates commercial sex for disabled people on the basis that sex workers 'rescue disabled people from personal anguish, sexual purgatory, and touch deprivation' (TLC Trust 2011; my emphasis). Further, this legitimation of (male) need is replicated in the scholarly works of some sex radical feminists, who conceptualise sex work as a socially valuable form of labour through which 'disabled people, folks with chronic or terminal illnesses, the elderly, and the sexually dysfunctional' (Califia 1994: 245) can benefit. As

O'Connell-Davidson (2002: 88) suggests, 'the implication is that sex work should be respected and socially honoured because it expresses a form of care or creativity'. Furthermore, within practitioner contexts access to sexual pleasure for heterosexual disabled people has been, particularly for disabled men, entwined within notions of 'quality of life' – though this has been argued for non-disabled men too (see Sanders 2008) – with access to 'sexual relief' often being considered essential to psychological, emotional, sexual and bodily well-being (see Browne and Russell 2005).

In contrast, for the most part, men in my research offered a wide variety of motivations behind their decision to purchase sex and used a much wider lexicon of explanation that extended well beyond essentialist notions of biological need (Holland *et al*. 1998). Motivations were, at the same time, rooted in the social, cultural and material disenfranchisement of disablement. However, at times these could include explicit and implicit references to men's 'need' for sex:

KADEEM: I needed sex 'cos I do get really horny.
TERRY: I just felt like I needed sex, I don't want to say it was like a fix because it wasn't like I was craving it, but it was just the fact that – for me it's a solution – it's a solution to wanting to have sex a lot.

Being '*horny*' and '*needing sex*' are enactments of a normative masculinity to which disabled men are often denied (Shakespeare 1997). Terry and Kadeem offer typically gendered performances through which they attribute their sex purchases to (male) need, thus being entrenched within a male biological sex drive discourse where ejaculation is a required bodily 'release' (Hollway 1984 1996; see also O'Connell Davidson 2002).

To give some early context as to men's sex purchases in general, all informants who had purchased sex said they were not in an intimate relationship at the time. For younger men, purchasing sex typically offered their first sexual encounter. Largely, informants sought to purchase heterosexual and heteronormative sexual services from female sex workers; no experiences of 'alternative sexual practices' (Reynolds 2007: 40) such as kink, BDSM (bondage, dominance, sadism and masochism) or fetish practices were mentioned. The potential illegality of their actions, safety and sexual health were seldom raised, despite often taking part in 'risky' activities. An absence of concern about illegality may have been because most sex purchases were made within indoor sex markets such as brothels, working premises and sex workers visiting informants at home (Sanders 2005) (meaning there was less of a requirement for the buyer to 'solicit', currently illegal in UK law). A lack of concern for sexual health might have been rooted in ideas that indoor sex workers are much less considered to be 'contaminated spreaders of disease', which is an identity more often ascribed to street workers in outdoor markets (Sanders 2008).

Most men offered extensive reasoning as to why they made the choice to purchase sex. This could have been because they felt they had to offer 'valid' and substantive reasons to 'justify' what remains considered a socially unacceptable practice. It also may have been exacerbated by the fact they were being inter-viewed by a woman (presumed feminist) researcher. A couple of informants referred to '*ardent feminists*' through their stories about sex purchasing (usually in the context of chastising their actions), and some informants were often overly apologetic and cautious about how they were being perceived while storytelling: '*I hope you don't think I'm a pervert...*' However, men's extensive explanations suggest that, although 'need' is a powerful discourse, it is not enough to 'justify' the practice (see Sanders 2008). For example, for Abram, aged 35, who required 24-hour care and purchased sex from a sex worker, and for Graham, aged 52, who purchased sexual surrogacy, doing so was narrated as a way to gain 'neces-sary' sexual experience and skills:

ABRAM: And then she sort of started kissing me ... I'd never even been kissed before [long pause] ... I think the first thought was how wet her lips were. It was new and I tried to get my lip action going a bit as well. I was able to just experiment, really. And just learn a little bit more what I'm capable of – there was one point where she was sort of sat on my face and just let me lick her and taste her. And I'd always wondered about that – I can't stick my tongue out very far so I always sort of wondered 'what could I do with my tongue in that respect?' Well, now I know. And it was probably better than I thought I would be capable of.

GRAHAM: It was the first time I realised a woman's body was warm, with no clothes on, naked, she was warm and that was a shock to me.

The erotophobic social environments extended to disabled people within dis/ ableist sexual cultures and the potential difficulty of finding sexual and/or intimate partners can mean that disabled people lack opportunities for sexual experiences (Sanders 2008; Shakespeare *et al.* 1996). This, further combined with the compulsory and persistent sexuality ascribed to male bodies, can make purchasing sex a fruitful means for disabled men to gain sexual experience. While this means of learning about sexuality is commonly conceived as an answer towards solving the 'problem' of disabled men like Abram feeling 'inad-equate' or inexperienced as lovers – in terms of heteronormative sexuality at least (see Aloni and Katz 2003) – some radical feminists argue that the commer-cial context detracts from 'genuine' learning because it offers only a 'deperson-alised, objectifying form of sexuality' rather than one that is mutual, shared, and reciprocal (Jeffreys 2008: 334).

However, disabled men in my research strongly expressed that the commer-cial context was integral towards learning even the most 'rudimentary' of intimate experiences, such as sensuous and erotic touch (e.g. how to enjoy touch which isn't medical, therapeutic or part of care). Graham's account shows this explicitly; his not knowing that a woman's body is warm emphasises not only the deprivation of sensuous feeling that can be part of the disabled experience, but how commercial contexts can be a viable means of providing such embodied learning. His experience illustrates how sexual surrogacy is understood as 'well suited to treating the lack in psychoemotional development and sexual confidence that some disabled people exhibit as a result of the sexual barriers they face and their sociosexual isolation in adolescence and young adulthood' (Shuttleworth 2010: 6). Thus, as Shapiro (2002: 72) claims, it can 'function as a real and meaningful form of erotic communication and self-realization'. However, while sex surrogacy is supposed to offer more intimate and sensual contact than paying a sex worker (Noonan 1984), Shakespeare *et al.* (1996) express caution that the therapeutic nature of surrogacy serves to once again locate disabled within a medicalised context, thus reinforcing a medical model of disability, and also rests upon assumptions that sex work cannot also be deeply intimate, as well as foster self-confidence for buyers and workers.

For other male informants, purchasing sex was positioned as crucial towards learning about their own sexual body and sexual capacity (as Abram emphasises in the above quotation) – not only for themselves, but also for the specific purpose of learning how to provide sexual pleasure both with and for others. Moreover, some men positioned learning these 'necessary' skills to pleasure a partner as a productive step towards (later) gaining a fulfilling, mutual and reciprocal (non-commercial) intimate relationship. Therefore, sex purchasing was largely seen as *purposeful*, but only ever temporary, echoing findings from research with non-disabled men who seldom positioned their sex purchasing as 'a permanent feature of their lives' (Sanders 2008: 46).

Abram also said his decision to purchase sex was centred upon concern for the well-being of his 'sexual body', and that purchasing sex was a way to invigorate his sexually 'defunct' body:

ABRAM: Up until [purchasing sex], for a couple of months I'd barely felt any stirring at all down there. I was beginning to think that, physically, my body's given up. That's one of the reasons why I was really desperate to do this … to reassure myself that my body hadn't given up. When I did used to ejaculate in my sleep and it'd be a, you know, an embarrassing, messy business; but then it kind of stopped happening. And that can be even worse. That I'm feeling nothing – I'm just feeling complete emptiness. I think this whole experience kind of woke that up in me again, in that there were days afterwards where I was feeling excited. And I felt like there were things happening down there, and it was just giving me a buzz.

Thus, for Abram, the act of *having* sexual relations sexualised both his sexual-self and his material sexual body. His lack of previous sexual excitement and ejaculation ('*stirring*'), as a man, left him feeling '*complete emptiness*'. Experiencing this through purchasing sex reaffirmed his male sexual capacity and potency. Notably, Abram was the only informant in the sample to be interviewed twice. During his first interview he talked extensively about how he had 'trained' his body and mind to '*shut down*' the desire for sex and a relationship. However, a few weeks after this interview he got in touch again to say that talking about his experiences as part of the research had been a catalyst towards making changes in his life (discussed later), and that he'd since lost his virginity to a sex worker and wanted to be re-interviewed about his experiences.

Equating *feeling* and *being* sexy to sexual *action* with a woman was a common assertion by male informants, tying in with dominant hegemonic notions of 'doing masculinity'. For example, Graham said *'there needs to some sort of proof [to feel sexy], like having girlfriends, having sex, all that, that's the proof that you are ... [sexy]'*. Tony said that as a virgin he'd never been in a situation to 'feel sexy' and Mark said that purchasing sex made him *'feel very sexy'*. Needing affirmation of one's desirability from a partner (paid or otherwise) to 'feel sexy' is also likely rooted in the discourses of undesirability that circulate disabled people. For Harjit, a 23-year-old single man with physical impairment, 'doing masculinity' included having sexual experiences to contribute to 'male talk', thus assuring his inclusion in the masculine sexual cultures of his friends:

HARJIT: Erm, I had been looking around for an escort for a while and just thought ... well, a lot of my friends go out and they talk about it [sex] and you see it happening and you hear about it [sex] and it was just like I don't see why I can't ... but to find a place [to have sex], to find a time ... again, I'm always with parents at home so there's no privacy whatsoever.

Harjit was one of two informants who required 24-hour care and came from what they identified as a restrictive ethnic and cultural background. Harjit, 23, lived with his African[1] immigrant parents, while Abram came from a British Asian background. Their stories were similar in that both felt infantilised by overbearing families who allowed them little autonomy and, as both stressed, financial control. Harjit and Abram's purchasing of sex was therefore embedded within a wider emancipatory narrative whereby both men told stories of elaborate escapades when purchasing sex, which were meticulously planned and enthusiastically retold through the interview:

HARJIT: There's lots of thing you have to consider because, erm, you've got to try and see when you can get away from home and all my money matters, all my bank statements everything like that goes to my parents and they open it. They scrutinise it [Harjit's spending]. I had to draw cash out [to pay for sex]. Erm, what would I tell them? Where am I going? 'Cos if I'm not home they'll probably go out for a walk, so what I am going to do if they find me where I'm not supposed to be? So if I'm walking around in town, what am I going to say? [...] It just so happened that they had to go to [city] last week and my grandmother was here so, again, getting in and out of the building is a lot easier when there is someone to open the door for you. I told her, 'look, I'm going to uni and I have to go for a meeting' but erm ... and I told my mum 'I'm going to be out for a couple of hours, probably, go to my meeting and then on to the library'. [Whispers] which I didn't ... but I had to think of something, Well ... I had to change my whole banking system so that I don't get any statements and it's all done online so that my parents won't see that I withdrew that much cash out... Hopefully now I won't get asked 'Why did you withdraw...?'

ABRAM: Yeah, I normally need to get cash. And every now and again my dad will look in my wallet and say 'you've got £20 – do you need some more money? How much do you want?' And I was just; I didn't want to keep, like, sneaking bits of money out, and then saying 'can I have more money?' It kind of seemed a little bit duplicitous, but I had some cash that my dad had left in a drawer for emergencies. It was about a £180 or something, but I didn't just want to use all that up because I never knew when my dad would go looking there again. I took bits out of there and I got most of – well, I got about half of the money I needed from that, thinking that 'he doesn't look in there that often – I'll just try and sneak a bit more money back in – and top it back up to what it was before'. And I started to try and pay by card for things when I went out shopping that I would normally pay for by cash [via cashback] so if my dad noticed that I was running low on money he wouldn't start to wonder why it was; he'd think 'oh yeah, he went shopping'. So eventually I got there ... I'd arranged it for Sunday night. I wanted it to be private from my parents and I managed to make it happen and managed to organise it. I managed to ensure my parents had no idea. Um ... and anyone that does know are only people that I've chosen to let know.

Such accounts were strikingly different from the sex work stories of other male informants in my research of similar ages, and were indicative of the lack of agency many disabled people can experience throughout their lives (Brown 1994; Shakespeare *et al.* 1996). From the excitable way such stories were told it appeared that a lot of the 'buzz' both men said they got from their respective sex purchases was as much from exercising agency, control and independence as it was about experiencing sexual fulfilment and pleasure.

However, for other men, sex was purchased because it was an 'easier' process than investing money and time in dating (non-sex worker) women:

TERRY: I knew that I wasn't going to be able just to walk into a – you know – so it just seemed like an easy route before university. I wanted to feel that experience because it had been a while and I can't go into a nightclub and easily pull, although I have in certain circumstances but I wouldn't – I can't do it easily. So this is really just like a short-term fix, really.

KADEEM: I didn't wanna pay, I wish I could go out and meet someone but it's not that easy.

Terry's account reflects findings from research on non-disabled men's motivations; for example, that paying for sex can mean evading 'the added burden of the "courting" rituals that are expected in heterosexual interactions' (Sanders 2008: 43). Kadeem's account affirms the general difficulties in accessing normative social and sexual spaces. These include the general inaccessibility (as well as cost) of adult meeting spaces such as pubs and clubs (Earle 1999; Shakespeare 2000), and attitudinal barriers and discrimination (particularly verbal abuse) that many of my informants experienced while visiting such places. The attitudes of prospective (sexual) partners can also pose a major problem. As Shakespeare *et al.* (1996) suggest, the difficulty of sex for many disabled people is not how to do it, but who to do it with (see also Rintala *et al.* 1997). While non-disabled men equally experience this, the social undesirability of the disabled identity within ableist cultures combined with (potential) non-normative embodiment and low self-esteem common to the disabled experience undoubtedly intensifies this issue. Other men said that they were paying for, as Tom stated, '*a different type of sex*':

TERRY: When you pay for sex you've got a sense of – you get a really different feeling from what you would get from being in a consensual relationship. You feel more – I don't want to say powerful, because you're not. You feel – you feel very – everything's directed towards you, and everything in the sex is to your standards. So it's more – when I'm in a relationship with someone probably around 90 per cent of what I'm thinking is if they're going to enjoy it; is it okay for them? Whereas with someone you're paying for you don't have that kind of stress of demand – it's quite easy for you and everything is directed towards you. So you can just relax, instead of trying to share the experience with someone else.

ABRAM: I was able to experiment without guilt, without the tension of worrying about how the other person feels; in particular how they feel about how limited I am in what pleasure I can give. By paying I didn't have to worry. In fact I think at one point I did, and she just sort of like smiled and told me, like, 'forget about it – this is for you'.

These accounts show that one of the benefits of purchasing sex from a sex worker is being able to relinquish active responsibility for producing a woman's pleasure. Non-disabled men have been found to also pay for sex for this reason (see Campbell 1998; Sanders 2008), thus potentially contradicting Califia's (1994) proposition of disabled men's sex purchases as having a higher 'social value' than those of non-disabled men. However, abandonment of the role of the male pleasure provider may be further welcomed by disabled men with physical impairments who, because of the possible restrictions that impairment and constructions of sexual normalcy place upon sexual practices, may feel more inadequate in the role of a pleasure provider (particularly in normative ways) than non-disabled men.

Making the purchase: value, fulfilment and power

Due to their exclusion from the labour market, most male informants' incomes came from statutory government benefits (Sanders 2007; see also Earle 1999). As such, many said they had to search for the cheapest prices, a logical justification given their financial precarity. Thus, for most, sex purchases were restricted by income making price a crucial factor:

TERRY: I think the rates are extortionate for what you're having [...] Erm, but you know – it's a market. And anyone can price themselves however they want in that market.

ABRAM: It was £150. Um ... yeah, it seemed a very, very unusual thing parting with that much cash. Erm ... because the weekend before, I'd gone to a gig and that cost me, like, 25 quid. And it went on for three hours. And I was thinking, this is six times as much and it's going to last one hour.

MARK: Yes, I remember exactly how much I paid, it was the cheapest I could find, £100. The rates haven't seemed to have gone up in 15 years. Which is good for the clients, but not for the ladies.

The ways in which Terry, Abram and Mark speak about the costs of purchasing sex are indicative of how being the customer can be the more powerful position within a commercial sex work exchange. While Terry's account acknowledges that as an unregulated market (thus not linked to inflation), sex workers can (in theory) charge whatever they wish (this was emphasised by another participant asserting that his sex worker sometimes had 'special offers on'), Mark's recognition of the stagnancy of pricing corresponds with academic accounts which demonstrate that sex workers have few rights or protection in the sex trade (Jeffreys 2008). Discussions of cost ('*the rates are extortionate for what you're having*'; '*six times as much*') further suggest that these informants readily conceptualise that what they were purchasing was the use of a worker's body, rather than her personhood and subjectivity. O'Connell-Davidson (2002: 86) states that within the sex work contract the purchaser doesn't *buy* the person; instead he buys the temporary 'fully alienable labour power'. Some feminists have debated whether this is an exploitative loss of self for the worker and thus emblematic of male domination (and a violation of human rights) (see Jeffreys 2008; Raymond 2004), or a productive instrument that the worker uses within the commercial transaction; thus she temporarily suspends her 'self' rather than loses it completely (see Chapkis 1997). Importantly, the above protestations regarding cost show that men based their conceptualisations of price for sex on the service as an *unembodied* exchange, and that, for the women *providing* sex, doing so costs nothing but time and body.

For most men, the value of the exchange was determined through the performance of the sex worker and most were able to distinguish what constitutes a 'good' and 'bad' sex worker. For example, a 'good' sex worker was 'chaste', in that many men preferred sex workers who were new to sex work or not very experienced, or who were selective about customers. At the same time she must be cheap, attractive, professional, punctual, accommodating to male confidence and access needs, knowledgeable about impairment and disability, available, honest, warm and genuine (not too mechanical in her work), and good at chat/ pleasantries. She must also not be too concerned about time; be someone who doesn't rob, steal or manipulate, and who is convincing in that she wants to be having sex with the client. Meanwhile, a bad sex worker (who did not offer 'value for money') was rough, mechanical, rushed or speedy (therefore too aware of time), under the influence of drugs or alcohol, unaccommodating, had too many 'rules' (e.g. no kissing), was deceitful, rejecting, unattractive, fat, and old. Thus men constructed sex workers in very particular ways through their stories which bolstered their power as male purchasers, mirroring typical castings of sex workers identified in the sex work stories of non-disabled men (Holt and Blevins 2007; Holzman and Pines 1982; Sanders 2008):

ABRAM: Erm, I was looking [online] at two [sex workers]. I first started looking at [name], but it seemed like she'd been round the block a few times, she was sort of quite well-known, I think. She seemed like she was very comfortable with just about every ailment [disability]. And – although she seemed to be very popular – and, sort of very, um, very well-known, she didn't apply partly because of her experience... And also the fact I didn't really see myself with a Black woman, if I'm honest – it's just not my – not my bag [Laughs]...

Abram's assertion that the sex worker he didn't choose had '*been round the block a few times*' and was '*very comfortable with just about every ailment*' is problematic, in that what many men also wanted was a professional service which offered the illusion that sex work was not her occupation, combined with considerable knowledge of impairment and disability; both of which arguably come with a worker with significant experience. Abram went on to say that the sex worker he did choose was attractive, the right age and was, as he puts it, '*spiritual*', showing the '*right attitude*' and thus was of good character. His attraction to a sex worker who showed the 'right attitude' of being inclusive and accommodating demonstrates disabled men's fears that sex workers can knowingly capitalise upon their social exclusion, marginalisation and desexualisation. Abram's declaration that a Black woman is not his 'bag' highlights his racialisation of sex work. Ethnicity was also a factor for Harjit:

HARJIT: It was a choice of two really, a Polish or an English ... who were working at the flat. There were more at the other building, but ... I thought English was easier to speak to and try and explain to her what needs to be done.

Harjit's account accepts a racialised hierarchy of sex workers, situating communication (or the ability to speak English) as integral to the purchase (O'Connell-Davidson 2003). His words, 'a Polish or an English', reveal the potential objectification and dehumanisation sex workers can experience. Some other male informants told of how they would intentionally break a sex worker's rules. For example, rules such as '*no kissing*' and, as Mark asserted, the '*come once rule*', whereby it is 'polite etiquette' for the client to ejaculate only once during the purchase, were routinely broken and often boasted about. Breaking the rules, in effect, refuses a worker's right to outline the contact she's willing to make, and again asserts male purchaser power. Thus, situations like this reinforce the actual power disabled men experience in these interactions: rules can be set by the worker, but a worker may have little protection or means through which to assert herself, short of not seeing a particular client again; and, if she works for an agency, this may not even be within her control.

Furthermore, male informants said it was important that the sex worker appeared to care about her work, echoing the requirements expressed by non-disabled men in existing research (see Sanders 2008). For example, Holt and Blevins (2007: 346–347) found that for male purchasers 'the quality of the sexual experience depended heavily on the attitude and demeanour of the prostitute', with sex workers 'who vigorously performed during intercourse or appeared to enjoy the sexual act' preferred. 'Good value' purchases were not just (sexually) fulfilling and enjoyable for my informants, but also believable, convincing and authentic:

ABRAM: She [sex worker] wanted to do it well and kind of make a difference to someone. Not just 'give me the cash – wham-bam out of here' … I never felt like she was just doing it for the money.

MARK: It occurred to me I guess some people just enjoy it, it's not just the sex part, it's actually making someone happy, spending time with people, they like that other aspect of it. [Enjoy it?] I think so yes. [Long pause]

In contrast, some were clear that sex purchases were 'fake', as Graham stated: '*I want it to be real. It's a fake, it's a fake, it is pretence, it's not real, but that's the only way I can get women*'. Other men said that a 'bad' sex worker rushed, or was too formulaic in her work:

KADEEM: 'Cos you're payin' them, it was rushed, and was fake for them … they go through [the] process, bit at a time, like kissin, then they let you suck their tits, and they get you hard and get on top, [then] they finish off with blow job. But they did each bit for few minutes, like tryin' to fit it all in and finishin' it off … was crap. I enjoyed waitin' for them and when they first start it's nice but then you start realisin' they rushin' and not that into it [and] then you're just goin' through process.

Kadeem believes that his sex worker did not offer enough variety or spontaneity, making him feel like it was routine for her and thus she provided a less genuine performance than he would have liked. Kadeem preferred the idea of sex surrogacy (but couldn't afford it) because it offered the '*girlfriend experience*', identified as the 'ideal' relationship with a sex worker (see Bernstein 2007; Sharpe and Earle 2003), in which 'the woman is enthusiastic about the sex act and makes the john feel special, as though they are in a non-commercial consensual relationship' (Holt and Blevins 2007: 336). Graham made similar distinctions between sex surrogates and sex workers, saying that sex surrogates made him feel '*comfortable*', '*relaxed*' and that they '*took the responsibility off*' while sex workers made him feel '*uncomfortable*', '*horrible*' and like there was '*no option – it was that or nothing*'.

Graham also said that he had got into significant debt through paying for sex surrogacy, paying £400 per weekend for a 'one level' course with the School of ICASA, a UK sexual healing centre for surrogate partner therapy (School of ICASA 2011). Graham said he completed all 15 'levels' in quick succession (around £6,000) but that it was not as helpful as he'd hoped: '*I learned a lot about love and intimacy but I learnt nothing about sexuality*'. Graham's words not only show how sexual '[surrogacy] can serve to reinforce feelings of inadequacy and difference' (Shakespeare *et al.* 1996: 133), but that men's expenditure did not always match their assessment of the value of a purchase. Thus, for many informants 'good value' was strongly related to sex and intimacy that felt *real*, was affective, embodied and sensual, and thus *not* a mere economic exchange. Men weren't solely paying for the unemotional and mechanical sex as defined through talk about '*extortionate*' pricing above, indicating a discrepancy between price and value. As Holzman and Pines (1982: 112) argue, while male purchasers pay for sex, they do 'not want to deal with someone whose demeanour constantly reminded them of that fact'.

Very much in contrast to a 'good' and 'professional' worker, a 'bad' sex worker was heavily chastised in men's stories, as has also been found in the sex work stories of non-disabled men (Holt and Blevins 2007; Holzman and Pines 1982; Sanders 2008). Some men made derogatory comments about a sex worker's appearance (see Holt and Blevins 2007); for example, a 'bad' sex worker was unattractive, old or fat. Mark said, '*What came around was a woman in her mid-fifties, not attractive at all, a bit fat. [Laughs] If I don't find her attractive, I can't come [ejaculate].*' A 'bad' sex worker also manipulated time. Some men said they had been 'short-changed' and thus not received value for money. For example, Harjit said he paid £140 for '*45 minutes of chat and 15 minutes of sex*', while Kadeem said 'you pay between £120–150 for hour but you never get the hour, it's more like 20 minutes'. Manipulating time may be a strategy of a sex worker: engaging men in talk and thus using up time means shortening physical contact. It may be that such strategies are easier to carry out with a disabled male client, some of who may be socially isolated and have little contact with women in a sexual context. Thus, sex workers may exploit a disabled client's marginalisation, and exercise more power through such encounters. Most male informants feared this strategy, and those who had experienced it, such as Kadeem, interpreted it as manipulation and dishonesty.

Despite the fact that only one man had experienced criminality within his purchase when a sex worker stole his mobile phone and money, a 'bad' sex worker was routinely positioned by many to be criminal, or as 'rejecting'. For those who had been rejected by a sex worker (based upon their disability/impairment status), it was narrated as a very painful and humiliating experience. For example, Mark (who had been rejected more than once) said that one sex worker had turned up, left upon seeing him and yet the agency he used still required him to pay a cancellation charge of £60. Equally, male informants said that accessibility was very important. Kadeem said that he went to an inaccessible massage parlour, which resulted in him having a '*hand job*' in his car because he couldn't get into the building. Not only was this not what he wanted (and meant he missed out on the included body massage), but also it meant he had to take part in a risky activity (e.g. sexual acts in public). Likewise, Harjit said that on his first (and only) visit to a sex worker he did not receive the full sexual experience he went for because the worker couldn't move him out of his wheelchair or move the chair to an adequate setting to facilitate intercourse. This meant that Harjit was fully clothed throughout the purchase (the sex worker unzipped his trousers), which significantly detracted from his experience.

Interestingly, the informants who had used what I call a 'disability-specific service' positioned their sex purchases as more fulfilling than those who made their purchases through typical sex work agencies or brothels. Internationally, in countries and states where sex work has been decriminalised or legalised, such specialist services are much more common and are often merged with sexual surrogacy services. For example, in the Netherlands, state funds have been used to provide sexual services to disabled people for over 30 years (Sanders 2010) – although Kulick and Rydström (2015) say this oft-stated fact is misleading – and in New South Wales, Australia, an organisation called Touching Base 'brings together sex workers, people with disabilities and service providers working in the disability sector' (Wotton and Isbister 2010: 155). While sexual surrogacy is available in the UK, it is far more widespread in other countries, such as the USA and Denmark (Earle 2001).

A few informants had used the TLC Trust to organise their purchases. Its website features a list of male, female, trans and BDSM service providers (sex workers and massage therapists) organised by geographic location. The website also features a forum where users can discuss a range of topics and share their experiences of purchasing sex. Sanders (2008: 68) argues that online spaces (for non-disabled and disabled purchasers) can be a 'valuable resource for decision-making' and also foster a sense of community among sex purchasers. Coincidentally, some informants knew each other's stories through reading them on the site (see Soothill and Sanders 2005). The TLC Trust website makes strong use of discourses of health and wellness and, in true heteronormative form, crudely emphasises an urgent necessity to be sexual, regardless of cost:

> Many disabled people say that they cannot afford the fees that sex workers charge. Then we find out you have been on skiing holidays, own an expensive hi-fi, or smoke 20 fags a day. Where are your priorities? Remember, sex keeps you fit, mentally and physically. And one session with a sex worker can fuel a thousand fantasies on the nights you spend alone.
>
> (TLC Trust 2011)

For the informants who used the site, however, like Abram, it had a powerful effect:

ABRAM: Um, they've got this kind of self-help thing trying to encourage people to take ownership of how they're feeling, and I was just exhausted from feeling stressed out and helpless and felt like there must be something I can do – just to change the way I feel. As soon as I started reading the website, I guess it just really legitimised the whole thing for me. I wouldn't have done it otherwise. I think I – I was more confident in contacting a sex worker from that website. I would not have known where to start my search otherwise. I mean – there's loads of agency websites but, you know, it's like a massive meat market. It certainly made me see that there were quite a few people that had used them – had come through it kind of okay – had repeated the trick. Erm, and that it didn't seem seedy or morally wrong, and I think that being able to kind of have a fairly short list [of sex workers] there was only, sort of, seven or eight. It narrowed it down and it showed each sex worker was – it wasn't going through an agency; you could contact them directly. And I just think that made it seem just more normal, as well [...] I'd be very scared about going through an agency, [pause] I think maybe [you'd] get someone who's a mechanical get-it-over-and-done-with [type]. I wouldn't get anything out of that. I'd just be too intimidated.

Thus, for Abram the TLC Trust website carried out a range of functions: it legitimised and normalised his desire to purchase sex; it facilitated his search and offered him a collection of sex workers who welcomed disabled clients; and it ensured his sex worker was a specialist (rather than from the standard '*meat market*'). Although Abram paid slightly more for purchasing from this specialist market, for this he had extensive online contact with the sex worker before and after meeting her, which was seldom experienced by other informants. He experienced this as ensuring the genuineness of her work. Abram's interview with me took place via video messaging (Skype), meaning he was able to read the sex worker's emails to me verbatim during the interview:

ABRAM: [Before] We exchanged a few emails first. And they were just really, really positive. I've got 20 messages [laughs]. I emailed her basically saying 'I'm 35, I've got [name of condition], intelligent and friendly but never had a girlfriend – never had sex; I don't even know what my sexual function is'. And, er, basically, you know 'I want you to undress me, guide my hands around your body, have a kiss or intercourse' – basically that. She replied back the day after, saying things like 'I think it's really great that you've decided to contact a sex worker. I'm really glad you contacted me. If you lived in Holland I would be free on the NHS'. [Laughs] 'Regarding disability I can see you, provide you with a very sexy, fun experience. I've only just recently started. I've not seen anyone with your same disability but I worked as a holistic therapist with disabled people' [...] [After seeing the sex worker] I emailed her after we met basically to say that I thought she was really incredible and I was really grateful... I said 'I can't honestly tell if I feel different today but yesterday was really fun. You helped me live out a few of those fantasies I never expected to experience. You're wonderfully affectionate, and I know that physically I leave an awful lot to be desired – but you made me feel pretty sexy at the time and that takes some doing. It was the most incredible privilege for me to be intimate with a human being as beautiful and sexual as you and I hope behind your professionalism you didn't find it too uncomfortable being with me. I wish you all the best in the future and I have the upmost respect for what you do, and I hope you provide lots more pleasure for many more men, especially men with needs like mine'. And, she replied back and said 'I can't tell you how much I appreciate you saying that and that I was able to make it a good experience for you. I was a bit nervous that I wouldn't live up to your expectations and I truly wanted it to be a really wonderful and comfortable experience'. She said 'I can promise you from the bottom of my heart that I didn't find you unappealing at all. Just different. You have a lovely face. You're a gentleman, lots of fun to be with physically, easy going, curious and I love that you so wanted to touch and taste me'. Um… she said it was a 'privilege to be the lady that you chose to experience sexuality with for the first time – it's an honour that will stay with me for my whole life'.

Therefore, this intimacy was integral to Abram considering his experience fulfilling rather than shameful. Potentially, 'specialist' sex workers could provide a better service for customers by obtaining special training (currently illegal within the UK), for example, which focuses on health and safety, manual handling, and an understanding of disability and impairment (Wotton and Isbister 2010). I concur with Sanders (2007), who calls for this training to be a collaboration between disabled people's organisations (DPOs) and sex worker rights organisations, after many sex workers in her research said they wanted more information and guidance about working with disabled customers, on a range of issues.

The professionalisation of sex work within a disability context could be argued to empower sex workers, relocating their work in relation to disabled people's sexual politics, therapeutic intervention and sexual enablement – casting away the prevailing discourses of social deviancy, nuisance and antisocial behaviour that plague their skilled intimate labour (see Kantola and Squires 2004; Outshoorn 2001). Moreover, sex workers and their disabled clients share common political interests. Both are minority groups that have been 'sidelined and ignored' (Wotton and Isbister 2010: 157) and which experience significant stigmatisation and marginalisation. As Sanders (2007: 453) protests, both are 'fighting for sexual rights, autonomy and freedom'. For example, Wotton and Isbister (2010: 163), two sex workers from Touching Base, state that 'coming from a community that has often been treated with disdain [the sex worker community], we have found it incredibly refreshing that our professionalism and dedication to Touching Base has always been highly regarded'.

While I support professionalisation of sex work, it's important to be cautious of what this means for both sex workers and disabled people. For example,

O'Connell-Davidson warns that elevating particular types of sex work at the same time serves to demean others, such as those 'who give blow jobs to able-bodied men out on their stag night [*sic*]' (O'Connell-Davidson 2002: 93) – affirming existing hierarchies within the commercial sex industry. The TLC Trust website follows suit (once again, crudely), educating disabled people about the difference between TLC workers, cautioning: 'be warned not to hire street walkers' (TLC Trust 2011). Furthermore, assuming that specialist sex workers and disabled men are only, as one informant put it, '*making things better for each other*', masks the complex power relationships between disabled male customers and non-disabled female sex workers. For example, Sanders (2008: 450) suggests that 'gender relationships between men and women [sex workers] when one partner is disabled may be more equal because of the marginalised status of men with impairments'. However, she also notes that that sex workers can be (physically) stronger, more sexually experienced and, as a professional person within the context of the purchase, can occupy and utilise more power over disabled men, which they may not with non-disabled customers (Sanders 2008). Furthermore, even 'specialist' forms of sex work as currently constructed, like those advocated by the TLC Trust, conveniently overlook the prevalence of male power as situating the female sexual body as a commodity to be bought and sold. As such, its advocates fail to tackle how it, in essence, places disabled men's rights over the rights of women. Additionally, on a more practical level, such services assume that disabled men want or need this kind of therapeutic sexual service; that, in a therapeutic setting, neither party can be exploited or exploitative, or violent (see McKeganey and Barnard 1996); and that this type of service is more fulfilling ('more intimate') and therefore reduces disabled men's sexual oppression. For example, while Abram narrated his experience as comparatively different to other male informants, and positioned the context of the market from which he purchased sex as integral to this fulfilment, he later said that the fulfilment he obtained was only temporary:

ABRAM: I mean in all honesty I would say maybe in the last couple of days – up until a couple of days ago – I was quite excited, quite buzzing, kind of always looking at my watch thinking, you know 'at this particular time on that date that many days ago', you know, 'this is my 10-day anniversary' or 'this is my 11-day anniversary'. For some reason though I think that as the memory is starting to fade; again I've been going through a few periods of feeling a bit, kind of, down about not really knowing what the future holds. I still desperately long for a relationship.

Therefore, despite purchasing from a specialist market, Abram's assertions about fulfilment of his desires were not dissimilar from those who purchased from standard markets who said that they were often unfulfilled or only temporarily fulfilled through sex purchases. Other informants, even those who were initially enthused and excited about their first purchases, were unsure if they would pay for sex again:

HARJIT: Would I do it again? Possibly, maybe, I mean, in time, maybe […] it was a bit of a weird feeling actually, of thinking 'was that all?'

KADEEM: Then afterwards you're left feelin' crap … 'cos it puts you up there in the bad category, relief for my cock, mind and heart feelin' shit.

MARK: It's like being gutted I suppose, you just got sex and you actually want the whole package: a relationship, sex and everything else.

These accounts are emblematic of the lack of fulfilment that can be experienced through purchasing sex. Kadeem indicates that paying for sex leaves him unfulfilled because his actual desires (along with many other male purchasers) were for intimacy, closeness and desirability, which the sex work context doesn't (for him) in reality provide, although it may provisionally feel like it. This finding suggests that sex work be considered as just one form of sexual access for disabled people amidst a range of opportunities (Griffiths 2006; Sanders 2010). It also highlights the dangers of conflating sex and intimacy, which may leave many men dissatisfied, unfulfilled and frustrated following sex purchases. As Graham stated, the context of paying for sex was largely unavoidable: *'you can't not be aware [that] there is a woman there because you're paying her money … you can't get away from that'*. As these accounts show, sex with a paid partner is often limited in what it can provide – purchasing sex for informants in my research only had a temporary effect on feelings of social isolation, marginalisation and, as they narrated, their experiences of loneliness and their longings for love, sex and intimacy. Not only does this stress the extent to which commercial sex work offers only an individual 'solution' to a lack of access to sexual pleasure (and certainly not one that is problem-free), but that disability community campaigning for access to sex and pleasure via commercial markets closes down broader, more creative, collective and equitable 'solutions', which may have greater emancipatory potential for disabled people's (individual and collective) sexual citizenship. Finally, it further affirms the inadequacy of rhetoric about sexual 'need', because, as men's own accounts have shown, satiating sexual need and/or desire does little to solve feelings of isolation and aloneness in the longer term, and offers little challenge to the very structural, institutional and systemic dis/ableist discourses that desexualise disabled people.

Sexual support – form and function

Like sex work, sexual support, regardless of form, can be 'fraught with moral complexity' (Earle 1999: 309). As informants' experiences within this half of the chapter will show, some forms of sexual support are more contentious than others and remain embedded within traditional gendered ideologies of power propagated by heteronormative discourse. While sexual support remains a significantly under-researched area of disabled people's sexual lives and an area where 'sexuality and disability researchers should shine a beacon' (Shuttleworth 2010: 4), there has been some attention to the legal, safety and intimacy issues involved (Bahner 2012, 2013; Earle 1999, 2001; Mona 2003). However, there is little research from a disability perspective which explores sexual support through the lenses of gender and sexuality, nor which reflects on the experiences of disabled people themselves. This is in comparison to the considerable literature focusing on personal assistant, carer and support workers' experiences of 'managing' (usually) male sexuality (Thompson *et al.* 1994). The absence of such inquiry from a disability perspective not only emphasises the controversial nature of certain forms of sexual support within disabled people's own communities, but also leaves it to be understood in the contexts of medico-therapeutic disciplines that fail to consider the disability politics of such practices.

As I introduced in Chapter 1, sexual support is contentious because it contradicts the fundamental norms of conventional heterosex that advocates sexual mores that are 'heterosexual, private, ideally reproductive, and above all autonomous' (Shildrick 2009: 70). As Shildrick (2009: 70) identifies, 'facilitated sex – by definition – cannot be wholly private or self-directed', thus shifting disabled sexualities further away from the heteronormative order towards dressing 'their sexual practices in deviance and perversion' (Siebers 2008: 133). Importantly, Shildrick (2009) makes the point that the UK's Sexual Offences (Amendment) Act 2000, which requires all 'homosexual' sex to take place in private, effectively criminalises gay sex between disabled men who require sexual support. She argues, 'clearly gay disabled sex is, strictly speaking, illegal if it is facilitated by a personal assistant whose physical presence is required' (Shildrick 2009: 73). Further, this same piece of legislation 'outlaws sexual activity between a disabled person and his or her personal assistant [PA]' (Hollomotz 2010: 28). This means that PAs who take part in the more embodied or *direct* forms of sexual support – for example, masturbating someone – can be prosecuted and would consequently be prevented from maintaining a clear mandatory Disclosure and Barring Service (DBS) check, which is currently required at the commencement of each new employment contract.

However, despite the legal, ethical and policy boundaries, Earle (2001: 433) argues that 'for many disabled people, facilitated sex is an important part of everyday life'. Mona (2003: 212) argues that, given the fact that 'many people with disabilities often need to structure their life plans around public and governmental supports, it becomes impossible to conceptualise their sexual life experiences outside of societal influences and socio-cultural norms' (see also Bahner 2013). Informants' stories of care often featured the role of the 'third person' – in this case, the PA. PAs played a key role for some informants in accessing sexual pleasure, as well as the general facilitation of sexual life through a range of activities (Earle 1999). For example, these included intimate labours such as pre-sex and post-sex help and support – such as preparing the disabled person for sexual activity, 'cleaning up' and providing personal care after sex had taken place (see Chapter 6; see also Liddiard and Slater 2017). None of my informants said that they had received direct support during sexual relations, such as physically assisting movement during foreplay and/or intercourse. However, for some disabled (male) informants who were not in relationships, PAs had directly facilitated masturbation and self-exploration, as well as played an integral role within purchasing sex and pleasure from sex workers.

Informants' reactions to questions about sexual support were varied. For those who had utilised PA support before and after sex with partners, this was seldom understood as sexual support. Instead, sexual support was assumed to refer only to assisted masturbation (rather than a broad range of practices). Only two male informants said they had experienced a PA assisting masturbation and were comfortable speaking about such experiences. Some informants showed awareness of assisted masturbation but said that it is not something they would morally or practically consider (as it may disturb a care arrangement, for example), while others strongly objected to the practice. This difference in reactions shows that the practice is, first, commonly known about by the majority of disabled people who receive personal assistance, but also that this embodied form of sexual support remains highly contentious.

While women's voices were largely absent from discussions on purchasing sex, they were more present during talk about assisted masturbation. The nature of this talk was largely upon advocating for the rights of PAs not to have to carry out assisted masturbation on behalf of male clients; and many women positioned disabled men who requested or participated in this as deviant and exploitative. In contrast, Browne and Russell (2005: 385) found that the disabled women in their research desired a greater awareness of their sexualities from PAs (for example, help with masturbation) and thus 'agreed that research is needed to explore gender issues, particularly in relation to the needs of women, including lesbians living with a disability'. One of my informants, Jenny, a 64-year-old wheelchair user, spoke of an online discussion forum where she works as a moderator. A male member, much to the disgust and disapproval of female members, had raised the topic of assisted masturbation:

JENNY: The response was incredible. Some of the men seem to think that they should ask [PAs to masturbate them] ... others said no. It was mostly women who said 'hang on a minute, you 'know, you're looking at almost a prostitute role aren't you?' 'Could you be that non-medical?' 'Would you just stick your gloves on and go [mimes hand job]?' I think ... what would that do for the person having it done? I mean, surely there ought to be some pleasure in it? It's violating, it's just like a medical procedure, and what would the relief be in that? I really feel for these lads that have still got all these emotional and sexual feelings and have got no way of relieving it; it must be dreadful. I do feel that. But to ask a young woman carer to come in and do it for you, I can't see that ... would you personally do it? I know I wouldn't unless I was in love with someone. I think it's too intimate a thing to ask of another person who you're not ... [in a relationship with] ... I also think it's one step beyond the boundaries of a carer and I don't think many carers, if someone said, 'Right, that's your job and you've got to go in there and wank him off', I mean, you're not going to do it are you? People [PAs] will be going, 'Right, that's the end of that job, I'm going to go and find something else... I'm going to sell things on a market or something'. I think carers are hard to come by, good carers, and starting that sort of expectation of them I don't think... but I feel the frustration of these people, men and women, it's not just men who get frustrated it's...

Jenny's account identifies the possible lack of pleasure, or sensuality, within assisted masturbation carried out by PAs, and she highlights the '*violating*' and '*medical*' context as highly problematic and both contradictory to intimacy and harmful (see Shakespeare *et al.* 1996). Her account resembles typical heterosexual romantic scripts; for example, she talks about love, intimacy and (emotional) feelings in relation to sexual pleasure, characteristic of normative femininity. Her account equally reveals empathy for the '*lads who have all these sexual feelings*', which simultaneously implies that the desires of young disabled women are less important (although she later goes on to include women when talking about desire and frustration). Most importantly to Jenny is her concern that assisted masturbation goes beyond the *appropriate* boundaries of the professional relationship, and that movements towards this being expected of individual PAs is problematic in that this may lead to the loss of good quality care (see Earle 2001).

The role of the PA in sex purchases

For many men who had purchased sex, a PA was integral to a successful purchase. Tasks included: helping a man decide whether or not to purchase sex; attending to privacy issues; arranging money; answering the door; offering moral approval and support; ensuring safety; preparing his body; creating a physical environment conducive to sex; and 'being around' during the exchange, in case anything went wrong. In addition, some men also talked to their PA, sharing their experiences post-purchase, which they could not do with family and friends. Without this crucial sexual support, several male informants may not have had the opportunity to purchase sex. This highlights that, while there is a significant deficit in statutory and voluntary support services recognising and supporting disabled people's desire for sexual expression (see Wotton and Isbister 2010), this deficit does not always extend, as this section suggests, to individual PAs, who were fully supportive of their clients' wishes and central to sex purchases taking place.

For example, Abram saw his (male) PA as crucial to his decision to purchase sex. Prior to purchase, Abram said that he had discussed sex work with his PA '*a lot*'. Not only did his PA's lack of surprise confirm to Abram that his desires were not inappropriate or out of reach, but his PA, as someone who knows Abram's body and its capabilities intimately, offered helpful advice about the physical practicalities of managing foreplay and intercourse with the sex worker. So important was his PA's approval that, if it had not been present, Abram said that he would not have gone on to purchase sex:

ABRAM: I don't think I'd want to disrupt my relationship with him. Life's complicated enough without causing a scene with someone you live with day to
day. With his support, I decided that yeah – I'd go through with it.

Abram's assertion here reveals the difficult power dynamics that can occur
within the relationships between PAs and disabled people. For example, in order
for Abram's desire for sex to be fulfilled, the (moral) sanction of his PA was
essential. Shakespeare *et al.* (1996: 38) suggest that 'PAs have a responsibility
to ensure that assistance is exactly that, assistance, and that no judgements are
made about the nature of the assistance required'. However, this is problematic
in that when it comes to matters of sexual and intimate life – particularly commercial sex – PAs *do* have the right to object and thus not facilitate (for fear of
supporting potentially illegal activity), making the disabled person's access to
this form of sexual expression dependent upon the consent of another person
who may not be willing to support it. Past this, Shakespeare *et al.*'s somewhat
utilitarian prescriptions propose the PA and disabled person as two discreet, dis-
entangled bodies and isolated selves, which leaves little space to consider the
intimacies between them that likely contribute to negotiations around accessing
sex. As Kelly Fritsch (2010: 1) reminds us, even when steeped in the everyday –
the seeming mundanity of personal care, shopping, feeding – the PA and a disabled person can experience 'a leaking of their identities, a mingling of their
sexualities, and multiple intimate slippages of their bodies'; thus together they
form an intimate assemblage (Fritsch 2010). In her research, Earle (1999:
312–313) found that PAs often made 'moral judgements' and behaved in ways
that did not 'benefit or support the person they are working for'; thus sexual
support, for some, was withheld (see also Browne and Russell 2005). Bahner
(2013: 4) suggests that the structure of intimate caring labour plays a role –
namely, its 'low levels of standardization and high levels of flexibility and indi-
viduality, with few prescribed instructions for how to execute tasks'. Thus, there
are no established guidelines of how to react, respond or support, although in
some institutional care contexts this is changing (Sexuality Alliance 2015).
Should Abram's PA have objected, he could have requested another PA, but his
account here (and wider story) indicates that this settled relationship is not only
vital to his daily functioning, but also that, because his PA lived with him, he
had become as much a friend, companion and housemate as a contracted worker
– emphasising the intimate assemblage in practice (Fritsch 2010). Thus, not
wanting to '*disrupt the relationship*' is as much based on maintaining personal
and intimate relations as professional ones, revealing the deep complexities of
care, desire and sexual expression.

In addition to providing moral endorsement, PAs were essential to male
informants' preparing themselves and their bodies for an encounter:

MARK: I can spend whole days dedicating them to prostitutes, like don't drink a
few hours beforehand, don't eat too much 'cause it makes my heart beat fast
so ... I try to get my PA to make my flat a bit cleaner, help me with

washing, make sure that if I do pee, to wash myself afterwards, make sure there's no trace of pee, and spray some perfume on me, on the sheet.

The above set of practicalities – which Mark called his '*ritual*' – was important to him feeling comfortable and sexually confident, particularly in terms of how he looks and smells. Mark said that PAs would undress him (or put him in loose clothing which could be easily removed) prior to the sex worker arriving, so that she did not struggle with moving, handling or undressing him. Sanders (2007) found that sex workers with disabled clients welcomed this PA assistance. According to Mark and Abram, PAs also had to answer the door, welcome the sex worker and escort the sex worker into the bedroom. PAs were also useful for obtaining the money to pay the sex worker and for safety during the purchase:

ABRAM: I basically told [PA] to shut the door, shut my door, ask her to wait for a moment in the living room and say to her 'okay, you can come through in a moment'. Then she came in – kind of, sort of, laughing, 'hi'. She was laughing at the fact that [PA] had just looked at her and said 'he's all yours' [laughs].

TERRY: Erm, there is ways of safeguarding – by, you know, having a PA nearby who can see what's going on inside.

Having a PA close by was also purposeful towards managing a crisis, should one have arisen. Abram said that during the sex worker's visit, his (electric) bed broke and his PA had to step in and mend the bed before they could continue.

Abram's experience of sex with a sex worker led him to think about how much he wants to have greater control over his care arrangements:

ABRAM: I think I would be a bit more specific now about my requirement on a carer [PA]. At the moment he comes from an agency that the social services fund directly. And that's my choice, because I didn't want to get into this whole Direct Payments business. And maybe I don't need to immediately change to Direct Payments in terms of employing my new people, but maybe there'll come a point when I do, just so that I can be sure that I'm getting people that are cool with these sorts of choices. How I would bring it up I don't know. Obviously my dad would be involved to some degree in making sure that I had carers [PAs] sorted out. I'd like to think that I'd inter-view them myself completely privately, but – yeah, it's the sort of thing where I don't think you can put much down on paper – and kind of contract it, so … But yeah, I definitely feel like I need to explore a lot more about myself. And I want these carers to understand too, to help me with that.

Mona (2003: 217) suggests that 'one of the most integral parts of receiving assistance with sexual expression is identifying a PA who is comfortable with assisting these activities'. Abram's account reveals that, even under the Direct Payments system (where recipients use government funds to broker their own personal assistance), reaching a joint understanding with the PA about the expectations of care may still be complicated (see Glasby and Littlechild 2009). Agreeing to facilitate sexual life via supporting sex purchases is currently, within a UK social care context, not something that can be put into a formal Care Plan, despite the fact sexual support is funded in other countries (Kulick and Rydström 2016). For example, Bahner (2012: 339) draws our attention to Danish Ministry of Social Affairs (Socialministeriet) guidelines, in which it is stated that 'it is the personnel's duty to facilitate service users' sexuality, whether it concerns assistance in order to have sex with a partner, to masturbate or to contact a prostitute'. Bahner (2012: 339) contrasts this with Sweden, where 'as personal assistance services are indirectly funded by the state, and the purchase of sexual favors is prohibited, sexual facilitation within personal assistance is interpreted as purchase of sexual services', showing the (legal and moral) discrepancies even between neighbouring countries (see Kulick and Rydström 2015 for a detailed account of such discrepancies).

In the UK, the personalisation agenda – an approach to social care where people are deemed to 'have maximum choice, control and power over the support services they receive' (Department of Health 2007: 3) through participating in the writing of their own Care Plan (which requires the approval of a social worker) – proffers that disabled people *may* be able to include sexual fulfilment as part of their personal and social 'goals' within the Plan, although there have been no known cases of this happening. The subsequent introduction of individual budgets (a development of direct payments), an allocation of a sum of money to eligible individuals for them to decide to spend as they wish on a 'package of support' (Beresford 2008: 9) – heralded as a 'transformation agenda' – also hasn't offered the choice, control and freedoms, sexual or otherwise, signalled at their introduction by an excitable Labour government. Thus, one is given the freedom and choice to create a unique package of personalised support, but said package must fit prescribed criteria about what constitutes care and support – thus, a bounded freedom at best. In the contexts of the prevailing desexualisation of disabled people, an endemic 'professional neglect of disabled sexual identities' (Earle 2001: 433), the perceived ethical ambiguity and illegality of commercial sex transactions, and now massive austerity in the UK, it is likely that such desires will remain highly difficult to voice, enact and claim in contexts of welfare for the foreseeable future.

Assisted masturbation

Existing research suggests that PAs can be very unsure of how to deal with the sexual desires of their clients (Browne and Russell 2005; Whyte 2000); and that this is despite 'problems with managing men's sexual behaviour' being well identified within a care context (Chivers and Mathieson 2000: 75; Thompson *et al.* 1994). For those in my research who had received it, negotiating the assistance of a PA with masturbation – either through supporting a man's hand on his penis or masturbating him – could be very difficult. While

Kadeem saw his PA masturbating him as a regular, unproblematic arrangement – '*when it gets to a couple of weeks and when it gets too much she [PA] just does it for me'* – Abram's story revealed just how contentious the negotiation could be:

ABRAM: I miss having female carers now for company and [pause] I mean, sexually as well. I mean there were times I used to try and judge how the female carers would be towards things like masturbation, things like that...

KIRSTY: How did you do that?

ABRAM: I would try and just ask for help to different degrees. And just see how they would react. Some of them were actually very good like that and didn't seem to have a problem. Erm ... a couple of them did get offended by it...

KIRSTY: So some of the carers obliged?

ABRAM: Yeah. I mean one of them – she was a young German girl. We had people from all over the world. And she's the one that stands out as a person that genuinely wanted to help as much as she could. And, erm, up to the point where, if I wanted to masturbate, she would pull back the foreskin, put my fingers on my penis and ... She seemed quite – she didn't seem to have a problem with doing that at all. So that was good for me. And a couple of the other people were okay, you know, just to put my hand down there and – you know.

KIRSTY: So they would facilitate?

ABRAM: Yeah. And other people [PAs] were kind of doing it but very kind of reluctantly...

Abram's account clearly illustrates how problematic (and risky) situations where he '*sees how they react*' can be, and his description of PAs as '*doing it reluctantly*' reveals the complexity of the situation. Trans-exclusionary radical feminist (TERF) Sheila Jeffreys (2008: 333–334) states that facilitated sex constitutes 'a form of unwanted and potentially highly distasteful activity within the ordinary expectations in male dominated societies that women should be accessible to men and sexually service them' and a practice whereby disabled men 'demand masturbation from poor migrant women who will be in no position to defend themselves against demands by their clients for such services' (see also Raymond 2004). While PAs might be made vulnerable by their gender, race, immigration status and/or class position (see Fritsch 2010), rather than the belligerent 'demand' that Jeffreys suggests, Abram describes his negotiation for assisted masturbation as potentially highly perilous and precarious. Browne and Russell (2005: 381) report that many informants (particularly women) in their study were 'too shy to ask' for help with masturbation, but said that it 'would be a great relief if they could feel comfortable enough to ask carers to help them to masturbate', suggesting that it may be a practice that is desired by women far more than it is 'demanded'.

While Jeffreys' (2008) writings on disabled sexualities are, I argue, inherently dis/ableist in that they overlook the lived realities of disabled sexualities and lack empathy and understanding of what it means to be disabled in a dehumanising neoliberal-able culture (Goodley 2014; see Liddiard 2014a), the extent to which assisted masturbation and certain forms of sexual support more generally are embedded in gendered ideologies and relations of power must be recognised. The male sex drive discourse (Hollway 1984, 1996), for example, means that PAs (a predominantly female workforce) are more likely to offer this service, or reluctantly agree to it, based on socially constructed ideas of male 'relief'. Or, as Fritsch (2010: 9) suggests, it is 'generally assumed that women are better equipped to deal with bodily substances, are sympathetic, can provide for others emotionally, [and] enjoy this kind of work'. Moreover, Chivers and Mathieson (2000: 75) state that conventionally gendered discourses of assisted masturbation are reproduced in PA training and practice: 'staff may consider that young men need sexual release and therefore plan to teach about masturbation; but rarely are young women's sexual needs considered within an individual planning process'.

Further underlining the gendered problematics of assisted masturbation, such experiences were completely absent from female informants' care stories. This was either because women did not speak of it, or (perhaps more likely) because, as with paying for sex, these avenues of expression weren't available for disabled women. This absence speaks volumes. Such services, or forms of care, are likely seldom *offered* to disabled women (by either male or female PAs) because there is assumed to be less of a (physiological) 'need' for 'indolent' female sexualities (Chivers and Mathieson 2000). Nor are these forms of support *requested* by disabled women due to conflicts with narrow notions of femininity and female desire as embedded within romantic coupledom. In particular, male PAs are less likely to offer assistance with masturbation to disabled women (than female PAs are to disabled men) based on constructions of disabled women as always-vulnerable to sexual abuse and constructions of men as always-potentially-abusive (and male PAs as abusers). Thus, 'concern with the risk of sexual abuse and exploitation may go some way to explain this neglect' (Earle 2001: 436). Another reason the practice is more common between female PAs and disabled men is because of the (female) PA's identity as a pleasure provider; for example, disabled men did not talk of making such requests from male PAs. While this may have been about not disturbing heterosexual masculine performances, or the fact that the care industry is made up predominantly of female workers, it also demonstrates that the act itself is not purely mechanical (otherwise it wouldn't matter who 'did it') and thus that the gender identity and gendered body of the PA is central to the practice taking place.

Blurred boundaries

While relationships between disabled men and their male PAs were very much platonic and based on typical male friendships, for some male informants this was not the case in relationships with female PAs, and such relationships were considered potential sites of sexual relationships. This is possibly because, as I have shown in other chapters, the PA/disabled person caring relationship can have blurred boundaries. For example, Browne and Russell (2005: 386) found in their research that PAs and disabled clients had 'different understandings of what is "work" and what is "personal"'. While Neal (1999) argues that it is the responsibility of the professional to maintain boundaries in care relationships, many of my informants (men and women) stipulated that maintaining boundaries was equally their responsibility. This was emphasised by many when it came to matters of sexuality; for example, one male participant said of his relationship with his female PA: '*It [care] is not sexual, and carries no ulterior motives or emotions other than to get a job done*'. However, other male informants found it more difficult. For example, while Mark asserted strongly that he doesn't '*ask for them [PAs] for extra [e.g. a sexual service]*', he did say that he regularly fell in love with female PAs and that employing them was a primary way for him to meet women:

MARK: I used to think that a way of getting a girlfriend could be to get a few up from the agencies [female PAs] and then you fall in love etcetera and everything else [...] Ok, falling in love is a natural thing but, this is three different girls [PAs] ... and I fell in love with each one ... but I guess ... sometimes I get so desperate, like really searching for a girlfriend, that I look for the easiest way to get a girlfriend and try to get enough contact [with PAs] and [then] maybe something [may] happen [...] I guess you hope that it means something more than just a physical task and that they'd have the same feelings as well...

Getting '*a few up from the agencies*' shows Mark's attitude as an employer (similar to the power of a sex purchaser) and the ways in which power can be used to objectify personal assistants. This strategy has been found in other research; for example, Browne and Russell (2005: 384) report one of their informants 'specifically hired carers around his own age, making attraction "more likely"'. The contested meanings of the '*physical task*' (washing, bathing, etc.) add to the ambiguity of the relationship for Mark: the carrying out of personal care has more of an embodied and sensual meaning for him than for a PA, to whom Mark's body may be merely a site of work. It also echoes, from the previous section, the desire for the sex workers' labour to be 'genuine', for the meaning of the work to go beyond a job or financial transaction. Thus, even where sexual support and assisted masturbation *aren't* present, the male/female caring relationship can still be inscribed with typical gendered heterosexual scripts. To avoid this situation, Mark stressed that he now only hires male PAs.

Kadeem (and a couple of other male informants) also said that they could obtain sexual pleasure from a PA's touch during routine personal care: '*it can feel too good sometimes*'. Similarly, Kadeem said of one female PA who assisted him in masturbation that she '*looked like she was getting turned on*' when carrying out the act, but that another deliberately avoided washing his genitals because he would get an erection (suggesting that she wasn't comfortable with this reaction). Feeling pleasure and embodying the routine touch of a PA shows that the customary 'body work' carried out by PAs is a contentious space of multiple meanings of which the PA may have little control. Wolkowitz (2006: 147) defines body work as 'employment which takes the body as its immediate site of labour, involving intimate, messy contact with the (frequently supine or naked) body, its orifices or products through touch or close proximity'. However, Siebers (2008: 145–146; original emphasis) states that 'as long as staff *act* professionally, they do not consider themselves responsible for sexual side effects, and yet they cross erotic boundaries constantly, with little regard for the consequences of their actions'.

Moreover, the changes to adult social care over the last decade that I mentioned earlier (personalisation agenda and individual budgets) may exacerbate the potentially difficult boundaries between PAs and disabled people where love, sex and desire are concerned. Such changes position disabled people as purchasers of their own care and thus, in many cases, direct employers of their PAs. This empowerment is of particular concern if an employment contract is dependent upon assisting masturbation. As one male informant admitted, whether he hired a PA or not was based on her willingness to carry out masturbation and her level of attractiveness. Furthermore, the disabled person as the bearer of the money a PA earns may also have an impact, because money is, as Zelizer (1989: 343) argues, 'interdependent with historically variable systems of meanings and structures of social relation'. Thus, far from being a genderless commodity, money has links with masculinity and masculine power (Zelizer 1989). For example, men's labour has a higher value within the capitalist system (Williams *et al.* 2010), making 'wealth relatively masculine' (Williams *et al.* 2010: 17). The majority of money for care provision now being brokered by disabled people themselves (rather than the state), specifically to foster disabled people's empowerment, precisely recognises that money brings social value, autonomy and power, constructing the ideal neoliberal citizen in times of advanced capitalism (Braidotti 2012). This, combined with the notion that disabled people may prefer more informal paid caring arrangements and unqualified and unskilled workers who can be trained to meet their specific needs and requirements, as Morris (1993) found in her research, may increase arrangements whereby there are no employment contracts, meaning that PAs within such arrangements have little or no employment rights (Ungerson 1997).

Conclusion

To conclude, this chapter has shown how informants' experiences of commercial sex and certain forms of sexual support are problematically entrenched in conventional ideologies of gender, heteronormativity and heterosexuality. The general acceptance of the marginalisation of disabled women's experiences, both from debates about the place of forms of sex work and sexual support for disabled people, and from such practices themselves, reveals the extent to which these remain highly gendered practices. Women's absences also show the way in which such practices *reproduce* a heteronormativity that requires female passivity and asexuality – meaning disabled women (and others) are largely unable to act in the same way. Fittingly, analysis has shown that disabled men are more able to locate themselves within normative masculinities through such heteronormative narratives and practices (although this is a fairly precarious identity that is easily disrupted).

Therefore, the sexual stories in this chapter emphasise, as others have, that disabled people are seldom stripped of gender identity and subjectivity. Rather, disabled informants' gendered identities, and associated oppressions, are a variant of prevailing gendered discourse that both empowers and restricts the sexualities of (non-disabled) men and women. Because discourses of sexual rights and 'needs' are gendered in ways that privilege men's constructed sexual 'need' and deny women's sexual agency, they legitimate men's opportunities for claiming sexual access, regardless of its form. Notably, neither the women nor the men in my study were able to articulate the rights of disabled women to access, for example, sex with a sex worker or assisted masturbation. This is partly because female sexuality is so tightly constructed around romantic desires that exclude commercial (and other) forms of sex and pleasure that there is an absence of any substantial market in commercial sex work for women. Therefore, it is pertinent at this juncture not to forget that both claims for and access to sexual rights, regardless of their foci, get determined by other facets of identity – most explicitly by gender (Oriel 2005; see also Petchesky 2000). Thus, a vital reason to question the very inclusion of access to commercial sex and particular forms of sexual support (such as assisted masturbation) within broader claims for disabled sexual citizenship is because of the implications these have for disabled female and queer sexual citizenship. This has not been helped by the routine gender neutrality within public, activist and (some) academic discourses of disability and commercial sex (see Wotton and Isbister 2010), nor the marked gender neutrality within discussions of sexual rights to pleasure more generally (Oriel 2005; Petchesky 2000).

Therefore, rather than making the case for increased access to similar sexual opportunities for disabled women, which fails to account for the very nature of heteronormativity and risks inadvertently endorsing heteronormative frameworks that are deeply problematic for all people (as I have tentatively argued throughout this book), it is crucial to consider the meanings of such findings within disabled people's burgeoning sexual and intimate citizenship. For example, analysis has shown that male informants' experiences of purchasing sex and sexual surrogacy were seldom about satiating male 'need' or sexual gratification, echoing findings from research with non-disabled men (Campbell 1998; Sanders 2008). Instead, it was found that male informants articulated multiple and complex reasons for their sex purchases which were, for the most part, shaped by both their social and political positioning as disabled men *and* – as with the motivations of non-disabled men – by hegemonic masculinity and normative sexuality. This counters the inherent naturalisation of disabled (male) sexualities, a conceptualisation of desire that offers little towards challenging the very structural, institutional and systemic dis/ableist discourses that desexualise disabled people – forms of oppression which constitute equally significant chapters in both men's and women's sexual stories. Thus, the dangers of not extending disabled sexualities an intellection beyond pre-social modes of sexuality inevitably divorces sexual agency and access from social and political power and civil citizenship (which are the fundamental underpinnings of sexual citizenship politics), serving to recreate the problematic historical division of public and private oppressions within past disability rights movements (Shakespeare *et al.* 1996) (see Chapter 1).

Further, male informants' interactions with their sex workers have revealed the complex power dynamics that can subsist between disabled male sex purchasers and non-disabled female sex workers. Through their role as a consumer of commercial sex, male informants could claim considerable power over sex workers. This could be through scrutinising their physical bodies, or denigrating their racial ethnic groups, social background, femininity and chasteness; through disobeying set contract rules; and expecting (without wanting to pay) 'genuine' effortful work requiring the appearance of the suspension of a worker's own identity and subjectivity. Again, these findings arguably complicate common simplistic (ableist and sexist) cultural constructions of disabled male sexuality as anguished, tormented and in despair (see Califia 1994); as 'risky' and 'dangerous' to others if not satiated (see Jeffreys 2008); and as detrimental to health and well-being if not affirmed (Browne and Russell 2005). Men's multifaceted motivations to purchase sex have shown that consigning disabled male sexuality to notions of victimhood or as subject to an insatiate sex drive is not only inaccurate and unhelpful, but does little to challenge or disrupt the governing constructions of sexual normalcy, traditional gendered sexual power relations or hegemonic masculinity – ableist aspects of sexual and intimate life that have long been positioned as acutely oppressive for disabled people (Shakespeare *et al.* 1996; Siebers 2008; Tepper 2000).

Note

1 I purposefully haven't stipulated the country from which Harjit and his parents have emigrated due to concerns around revealing his identity.

8   Drawing some conclusions

Accessible summary

- In this chapter I draw some conclusions from the research findings sketched out in, across and between the chapters of this book.
- I lay these out in an Accessible Summary of Key Findings (below) and demarcate my own definition of sexual ableism and its relation to self, body and gender.
- I weave together original findings with some recent theoretical explorations that rethink the category of the human through disability.
- I draw out some key tensions within and across findings, before applying a DisHuman lens as a means to make sense of these contradictions.
- I end by critically questioning the ways in which the DisHuman invokes alternative kinds of citizenship and ways of being in the world; and ultimately, might pave new ways of imagining and advocating for disabled people's sexual and intimate futures.

Being disabled is not a tragedy but a possibility, an affirmation, a queer or Crip space for rethinking what it means to be human, to live a quality life and a life with quality.

(Goodley 2014: 160)

I long for futures where disability is not rendered illegible or absent, but rather where disability and impairment are perceived to enhance, not spoil, life, including conceptions of sexuality and reproduction. Or, to paraphrase the hip-hop duo Salt-n-Pepa, we can talk about how sex is, how it could be, how it was, and more important how it should be.

(Gill 2015: 194)

At the heart of my research project lies an ethics that respects vulnerability while actively constructing horizons of hope.

(Braidotti 2013: 22)

Each of the quotes above speaks to my political engagement with the research centred in this book. Each account centres hope, change, justice and a desire or will for something different: a recognition that disability, vulnerability and the crip body can bring forth new ways of coming to know humanness, humanity, sexuality and selfhood. In drafting this concluding chapter, I must first confess that the 'collective story' that emerges from my research is not one I expected (nor wanted) to tell. In exploring the complex relationships between disability, body, sexuality and gender, the thematic analysis of informants' sexual stories detailed through this book has affirmed disability as synonymous with sexual oppression, suppression and repression, at least with regards to informants' own lived understandings and storytelling. Disabled people in my research have spoken of striving, fighting and intensely labouring to gain entry only to normative categories of sex and gender that serve to exclude, oppress or violate them. Many have articulated the need to carry out extensive forms of sexual, survival and self-advocacy work within a variety of spaces and across multiple interactions in their sexual and intimate lives. Almost all have experienced extensive psycho-emotional disablism as routine within intimate life at some time or another. This sounds deeply discouraging, and I state this here starkly not to detract in any way from informants' resistance to or skilled negotiations of ableism and disablism, but because it is precisely at this nexus between desired and actual findings that interesting distinctions can be made.

As a result, through this chapter I weave in some recent theoretical explorations that I have been doing as part of ProjectDisHuman,[1] 'a collective of people who are committed to rethinking the category of the human through disability' (Project-DisHuman, forthcoming; see also Goodley *et al*. 2015). I do so because the original conclusion to my doctoral thesis – the original draft of this chapter – always felt unfinished: there were tensions of which I could not make sense in time for submission, and lingering critical questions of my research and its findings that needed to be explored and re-theorised through further scholarship and study. Following (Re) Telling Sexual Stories, a postdoctoral activist-scholarship project to communicate, translate and disseminate new knowledges from my doctoral research outside of the Academy to disabled people, their organisations and communities – a public sociology (Burowoy 2013) endeavour that could only have been carried out at the wonderful School of Disability Studies, Ryerson University, Toronto – I returned to theorising these stories once again to publish my work (Liddiard 2013, 2014a, 2014b, 2014c; Goodley, Runswick-Cole and Liddiard 2015; Liddiard and Goodley 2016; Liddiard and Slater 2017) and to begin writing this book. By this time, I was living back in England being seduced by the offers of posthuman theory to disabled lives – particularly Rosi Braidotti's work on the posthuman condition (Braidotti 2003, 2006, 2013) – and the later emergence of posthuman disability studies (Goodley, Runswick-Cole, Lawthom and Liddiard in press b).

This emerging postconventional scholarship began from collective recognition of the reality that disabled people have seldom ever been treated as 'fully human' (Goodley *et al*. in press a) and that the borders of what constitutes the 'human' in neoliberal times is purposefully narrow, and *narrowing*. An exclusive category, where only a privileged few feel the security of its boundaries, or are granted its tremendous social, political, cultural and economic power. As Rosi Braidotti (2013: 65) herself posits, 'humanity (the archetypal human) is very much a male of the species: it is a he'. This 'Universal "Man"', she continues, is 'implicitly assumed to be masculine, White, urbanised, speaking a standard language, heterosexually inscribed in a reproductive unit and full citizen of a recognised polity' (Braidotti 2013: 65). According to Goodley *et al.* (in press a), this vision of the human has at its core a Eurocentrism as well as imperialist tendencies, 'meaning that many of those outside of Europe (including in the colonies) become known as less than human or inhuman'. In short, some of us are considered more human than others. At the intersections of ableism, neoliberalism and austerity, disability brings something politicised and critical to posthuman theory.

But a DisHuman analysis offers something even more, as I demarcate later in the chapter. In making use of what Braidotti (2012: 54) calls 'affirmative politics', which 'combines critique with creativity in the pursuit of alternative visions and projects', disability can be viewed for its productive, creative and disruptive potential. Or, as Braidotti (2012: 37) says of the posthumanist perspective, disability offers 'alternative ways of conceptualizing the human subject'. To clarify, the DisHuman is a mode of understanding that simultaneously acknowledges the possibilities offered by disability to trouble, reshape and refashion the human (crip and posthuman ambitions) while at the same time asserting disabled people's humanity (normative and humanistic desires):

> Our sense is that disabled people will continue to fight to be recognised as humans (in the humanist sense and register of humanism) but equally (and simultaneously) are already enacting forms of activism, art and relationality that push us all to think imaginatively and critically about a new epoch that we might term the posthuman.
>
> (Goodley *et al.* 2014b: 358)

Thus, throughout this chapter I draw in and upon the posthuman and DisHuman – and, later, play with something I have come to call the DisSexual – knitting these delicately to capture the complex interplay between disability, sexuality and the social world. I do so because each proposes a new lens with which to understand informants' stories. As a beginning, however, I first offer an accessible summary of the key findings from the research, grouped by themes. I hope this is helpful, rather than repetitive. Next, I unpack these findings in relation to existing literature, research, theory and activism, revealing their value to the (still) emerging field of disability and sexuality studies. Later, I pull out some key tensions in the findings, before applying a DisHuman lens (Goodley *et al.* in press a) as a means to make sense of these contradictions. I end by critically questioning the ways in which the DisHuman invokes alternative kinds of citizenship and ways of being in the world – and, ultimately, might pave new ways of imagining and advocating for disabled people's sexual and intimate futures.

Accessible summary of key findings

Heteronormative sexuality as disempowering disabled men and women

- Heteronormative sexuality was experienced by my informants as much a form of oppression in their lived experiences of sexual and intimate life as the routine dis/ableist constructions of asexuality and sexual inadequacy cast upon their lives and bodies.
- Normative gender categories and heterosexuality were upheld and privileged by informants as given, natural and fixed, leaving space *only* for disability and impairment to be conceptualised as disruptive and highly conflicting to a heteronormative sexual life.
- There were very complicated and contradictory implications of heteronormative discourse for disabled men and women.

Heteronormativity, masculine privilege and (disabled) male power

- Heteronormativity was found to create different outcomes and opportunities for (disabled) men and women. Thus, heteronormativity, as a male-serving discourse, worked *for* disabled men through spaces where it did not for disabled women.
- As such, male informants generally had more manoeuvrability within, as well as opportunities to negotiate, normative sexual and gender identities than female informants.

Impairment as part of the experience

- For all informants, experiences of sexual opportunities, identities and intimate relationships were mediated by the lived experience of impairment. Impairment, for the most part, was the primary means through which disabled informants conceptualised their sexual and gendered selves.
- The 'hard physical realities' (Wendell 1996: 45) of impairment were very important to informants and had significant impact upon the ability to engage in sexual encounters.
- However, many informants managed the bodily realities of impairment through devising management strategies that ensured that their bodies could be sites of sexual pleasure and enjoyment.

Managing and negotiating sexual life

- Analysis has illustrated the 'complex invisible 'work' performed by disabled people in every day/night life' (Church *et al.* 2007: 1). Informants carried out a variety of forms of work, negotiation and management within multifarious spaces of their private and intimate lives.

- Informants' labour was diverse and served a variety of purposes within the construction of a sexual self.
- Much of informants' work and labour was rooted in, and thus indicative of, the oppressive and inherent inequalities of ableist culture.

Psycho-emotional selves

- Informants were Othered and desexualised through heteronormative discourse, and were denied autonomy, agency and sexual freedom through their engagement with particular ableist social institutions and an ableist cultural imaginary.
- Psychoemotional disablism was experienced through a variety of 'known agents' within disabled people's own networks (Reeves 2002). Informants reported being bullied, abused, manipulated, exploited, chastised, ridiculed, humiliated and shamed in various intimate spaces.
- Through internalising heteronormative and ableist discourse, some informants devalued themselves and became complicit in their own experiences of psycho-emotional disablism (see Reeve 2004).
- Many informants' strategies were what I identify as harmful and constituted significant psycho-emotional disablism. Additionally, much of the work carried out often involved performing to ableist 'demanding publics' (Goodley 2011a: 93).

Sexual ableism: the power of normalcy

A significant amount of storytelling that masquerades as disability is not really about impairment or disablement, the 'real' story being told is about ableism.

(Campbell 2009: 197)

To make use of Fiona Kumari Campbell's assertion above, an unforeseen finding to emerge from the research has been the extent to which normative heterosexual discourse serves as a central tenet of ableism. It is safe to say that my original focus at the outset was upon the ways in which disabled people managed disablist constructions or depictions of their sexual lives, as 'asexual, or oversexed, innocents or perverts', to return to Brown's (1994: 125) early framings (see Chapter 1). In hindsight, I was interested in ways in which such tropes are inscribed on disabled bodies and minds, the impact they have, and the ways in which disabled people live with or come to resist and/or contest such tropes. I imagined these depictions to serve as a kind of sexual disablism; their production and proliferation across mass media, law, civil society, popular culture and public institutions generated forms of unequal and oppressive treatment that are direct, tangible and measureable (see Campbell 2009). At that time, I didn't view heteronormativity or heterosexuality as inherently oppressive, nor deeply ableist institutions.[2] Yet, crucially, informants' stories have emphasised sexual oppression to be far broader.

That ableist sexual normativity, or sexual ableism – the impossibility of sexual normalcy for myriad bodies and minds – is a root cause of the (sexual) oppression of disabled people (and many others that don't fit), of which sexual disablism is just one part. Mike Gill (2015: 151) defines sexual ableism as 'the system of imbuing sexuality with determinations of qualification to be sexual based on criteria of ability, morality, physicality, appearance, age, race, social acceptability, and gender conformity'. He argues that sexual ableism inherently denies 'an understanding of disability as a valuable difference that yields unique perspectives of personhood, competence, sexuality, agency and ability' (Gill 2015: 3). In this section, I sketch out my own definition of sexual ableism written from informants' stories, and demarcate its relationship to heterosexuality and heteronormativity as institutions that govern social and sexual life.

Storying sexual ableism

For me, sexual ableism has been clearly defined through the varied sexual stories told in this book. To recap previous chapters for a moment: (i) sexual stories privileged normative sexuality as a central theme: normative gender categories and heterosexuality were upheld and privileged as given, natural and fixed; (ii) intimate relationships and coupledom were strongly desired and seen to affirm a sense of intimate citizenship (Plummer 2003), as well as confirm worth and desirability; (iii) sexual expression and gratification were understood as inherently natural (particularly in the context of male bodies) and obtaining pleasure served to proffer social value, evidence ones humanness and 'constitute full subjectivity' (Shuttleworth 2000: 280); (iv) normative bodily aesthetics were revered and strived for (most notably by women); and (v) the prescribed phallocentric and orgasmic 'mechanics' of heteronormative practice remained the immovable embodied norms from which other alternative sexual methods, interactions and pleasures were judged.

Importantly, such privileging of sexual normalcy bore significant weight on informants' lived experiences of sexual opportunities, identities and intimate relationships, which only left space for disability to be lived and experienced as troublesome towards meeting heteronormative ideals – a product of sexual ableism. For most, the realities and practicalities of the impaired body and the cultural ascription of a desexualised identity came to be experienced as highly conflicting towards maintaining a heteronormative sexual life and convincing and meaningful (and always repetitive) performances of the (desired) heterosexual subject (Butler 1990). Powerfully, this seldom negated the desire to achieve sexual normalcy in the *right* ways, or consciously view the prescriptiveness of heterosexual practice as the problem. This illustrates the ways in which heteronormativity continues to shape the sexual subjectivities of, and have psycho-emotional consequences for, those who are excluded from its narrow boundaries, as found in other research – for example, on female sexual dysfunction (Cacchioni 2007) and people with HIV/AIDS (see Dune and Shuttleworth 2009). Thus, heterosexuality as an institution serves as a 'showcase for able-bodied performance' (McRuer

2006a: 9) and, in ways similar to compulsory able-bodiedness (McRuer 2006a), sexual ableism propagates a level of normalcy, a perfection of body, self and pleasure, that no one, in reality, ever achieves. Sexual ableism, I propose, merely serves to marginalise a diversity of bodies and minds and guard the boundaries of, as Shildrick (2007b: 221; original emphasis) puts it, 'the contested question of who is to count as a *sexual* subject'.

As such, the psycho-emotional consequences of heteronormative discourse were extensive: informants were routinely Othered, denied autonomy, sexual agency and sexual freedom through an ableist cultural imaginary that promulgates normative embodiment and autonomous sexual selfhood. Not surprisingly, many informants internalised such discourse, devaluing themselves and experiencing what Donna Reeve (2008: 1; emphasis added) calls the 'barriers in *here*'. Thus, quite often, disabled people in my research were complicit in their own experiences of psycho-emotional disablism and would contain and regulate themselves and their behaviour accordingly. This is, of course, not to attribute blame, but to show that devaluing the self – particularly in relation to the non-disabled Other – was part of the disabled sexual psyche for most informants (see Chapter 5). For example, low sexual self-esteem and self-worth, feelings of inadequacy and low body confidence were common and constituted significant psycho-emotional disablism. Individual stories have shown, I suggest, the extent to which this could impact upon the realising of an affirmative sexual selfhood, as well as the deployment of strategies and labour to negotiate and manage the sexual dis/ableism routine to sexual and intimate life.

Importantly, informants' experiences were also mediated by the very complex and contradictory relationships between disability, impairment and heteronormative discourse. These were shown through the experiences of informants who – in certain spaces – *could* negotiate gender categories and transgress the strict boundaries of normative sexuality *at the same time as* upholding these boundaries as natural and normal. Thus, these breaches were seldom understood as anything but Other, lesser and abnormal, rather than creative expansions of sexual behaviour and the opening up of 'new (sexual) horizons' (Shildrick 2009: 36; see also Siebers 2008). Thus, informants didn't label or consciously crip the productive deviations from sexual normalcy that they did experience as such – this *revision* was left unclaimed – causing the meaning of this disavowal to represent (to them) little else but Other, which had further psycho-emotional consequences through legitimising feelings of abnormality. Such findings serve as an interesting comparison to similar research exploring the intersections of impairment and heteronormativity that has largely reported disability as a moment to redefine oneself against cultural norms of sexiness and sexual practice (see Guldin 2000; O'Toole 2000; Potgieter and Khan 2005).

To clarify with an example, in her research on the ways in which disabled people self-claim sexuality, Guldin (2000: 234–235) found that informants' assertions about orgasms 'demonstrate that they do not reject cultural notions altogether, indeed, in some cases they accept those meanings and values, more common, however, was for them to redefine how orgasms might be interpreted

or experienced relative to their own bodies'. Guldin (2000: 237) asks the difficult question, then, of 'who defines sexual resistance and who defines a political
act?' In my research, disabled informants' expansions of sexual normalcy – the
spaces where their bodies *did* contravene the rules of heterosex – did not automatically equate to crip sexual emancipation (see Rembis 2010). Thus, informants' sexual practices were not, for the most part, knowingly or consciously
subversive, nor were their sexual practices understood or lived as transgressive
acts. Rather, their experiences of sexual life were determined primarily through
lived experiences of impairment and interactions with normative heterosexual
and ableist discourse. As Guldin (2000: 237–238) says of her own findings, 'all
four men in this study were engaging in sexual acts, thoughts, or behaviours that
I would interpret as political, yet they would say they were simply living their
lives of which sexuality is a part'. This simultaneous claiming of normalcy at the
very same time as disrupting or disobeying it – this push and pull – is quintes-
sentially DisHuman. I return to this key tension later in the chapter.

Labouring for the norm

Sexual ableism also emphasises disability as synonymous with labour, work and
performance: that being a disabled sexual subject in a dis/ableist world requires
undertaking a multitude of labours. For most informants, a variety of forms of
work were executed across multiple spaces of their sexual and intimate lives.
Disabled informants regularly took on the roles of teacher, negotiator, manager,
mediator, performer, survivor, educator and resistor through a wide variety of
strategies. Thus, these sexual stories have made visible 'the telling, hiding,
keeping up, waiting, teaching, networking and negotiating' (Church *et al.* 2007:
10) required of disabled people. Inevitably, analysis has shown that the *necessity*
to carry out work cannot be separated from the oppressive and inherent inequalities of ableist culture, and that the requirement to labour in one's intimate life
has marked psycho-emotional consequences. It has also revealed the extent to
which forms of work required were embedded in informants' daily realities,
highlighting once again the need to privilege or value the more mundane,
everyday and routine aspects of the disability experience within theorisations of
disability life. Informants' labour was diverse and served a variety of purposes
within the construction of the sexual self. For example, some types of work were
routine within the context of the disability experience; such as managing the
non-disabled gaze (see Chapter 4) and the bodily realities of impairment (see
Chapter 6) and carrying out the oft-extensive emotional work involved as a
receiver of care (see Chapter 5). Some types of work served to reinforce rather
than challenge normative sexuality and ableist constructions of disability and a
significant amount of labour was performative in nature, involving displaying
and enacting appropriate and/or expected emotions and stereotypical characteristics of the disabled identity, such as passivity, submissiveness and timidity – the
good crip – often only for the benefit of close others and ableist 'demanding
publics' (Goodley 2011a: 93).

Not surprisingly, some informants' strategies and forms of work had substantial psycho-emotional consequences and constituted significant harm. For example, Chapter 5 revealed the extensive survival and emotional work required to both endure violence and abuse and stay in unhappy and unfulfilling relationships for the sake of being partnered. While I have conceptualised this particular form of work as constituting informants' resilience and survival, one cannot argue that these are strategies that fostered momentous emotional and physical harm. These forms of work act as painfully explicit examples that psycho-emotional disablism can be at its most acute when carried out by those close to us – our carers, allies and loved ones (Reeve 2002). Also worth noting here is that many informants reported being bullied, abused, manipulated, exploited, chastised, ridiculed, humiliated and shamed as routine across other intimate and familial spaces of their lives, which could impart a wealth of pain and hurt, deeply impacting self-esteem and self-love, as well as encouraging culturally imbued feelings of embarrassment and shame (see Stevens 2010). Importantly, then, much of the work employed by informants was located within social or interpersonal interactions with (non-disabled) others; for example, work took place with partners, PAs, in-laws, peers, (non-disabled/disabled) friends, doctors and other health professionals, strangers, PAs/carers, teachers, parents, families, partners, sex workers, bullies, fellow activists and prospective partners. Thus, everyday interactions have shown themselves to be constitutive of the disabled sexual self and psyche; that it is within these 'meaning laden interactions' (Brickell 2006: 416) that sexual identities were formed and reformed. This demonstrates the potential utility of a micro-social or symbolic interactionist approach towards theorising disabled sexualities, for an understanding of the ways in which disabled people's sexual agency and selfhood is contoured by relations with others in day-to-day interactions (see Weeks 1986).

While the discovery of such labour within disabled people's sexual and intimate lives – regardless of its outcome or efficacy – forcefully challenges the assumed passivity and docility of disabled people, reinforcing that disabled people are or have to be active, resourceful and creative within their sexual, intimate and erotic lives, it is crucial not to underestimate the sizeable extent to which this work is rooted in, and thus indicative of – or demanded by – the oppressive and inherent inequalities propagated in ableist culture. As I argued in Chapter 5, rather than overt transgressive resistance, much of informants' work and strategies were carried out through *necessity* – for example, to survive, to be loved, to be human, to be included, to *be* 'normal', to be sexual and to be valued – and thus is revealing of the psycho-emotional disablism, oppression and performances that disabled informants endured in order to be part of an ableist life world.

Embodying the norm

For all informants, experiences of sexual opportunities, identities and intimate relationships were touched by lived experiences of the body. Impairment was prominent within the collective sexual story and its 'hard physical realities' (Wendell 1996: 45) mediated the ways in which informants constructed and claimed gendered sexual selfhood. For the majority, the materiality of the body was very important because it had significant impact upon the ability to engage in sexual encounters at all. Impairment was routinely shrouded in negativity – an obstruction to a desired sexually embodied and human self. The lived and embodied realities of impairment – whether aspects related to function and thus how the impaired body *performed* (such as leakiness, pain, fatigue and immobility) or aesthetics, to how the impaired body *looked* (for example, non-normative embodiment such as scarring, 'deformity' and muscle wastage) – meant that it was foremost in people's minds when it came to physical sexuality, understood as the coming together of bodies.

Constructing a sexual self *through* embodiment in this way and in the shadows of impairment only as a negative bodily state is, of course, not surprising in the face of dominant ableist discourse that renders disability only as body problem (see Thomas 2002b). But this positionality also affirms the deep roots of heteronormativity, which delineate 'sex' as of the (normative) body and flesh (Tiefer 2001). Yet, as the sexual stories in Chapter 6 showed, many informants devised strategies to deal with the bodily difficulties that they considered impairment to bring and used 'different positions and various sexual aids to facilitate sexual fulfilment' (Shuttleworth 2010: 3). This suggests, then, that although impairment was deemed deeply problematic within the confines of the normative erotic body, informants' self-managed strategies ensured that their bodies could be experienced as sites of pleasure and enjoyment. Further to this, for some other informants (though very few), impairment offered a means to explore new forms of pleasure, illustrating its potential to radically shift conventional notions of pleasure – that disability can be artful where pleasure is concerned (Siebers 2008). This is another tension that I explore later through applying a DisHuman lens.

In order to attempt to diffuse the theoretical tensions outlined in Chapter 2 between critical realist requirements to 'mark' the realities of impairment and postmodern and poststructuralist perspectives which are argued to 'write-out' such realities (see Wendell 1996) (or least 'reduce' them to discourse), an analysis of sexual stories has affirmed the need for perspectives which mediate impairment as 'relational, constructed, and negotiable' (Goodley and Tregaskis 2006: 638) but also foreground the embodied, the psycho-emotional and the affective meanings of materiality to disabled people. For example, clear through most stories was the extent to which impairment was far more than a 'taken-for-granted fixed corporeality' (Meekosha 1998: 175), but customarily constituted a site of deep social, cultural and psychic meaning. To recap, Chapter 4 showed the ways in which impaired bodies, (per)forming sexual identity and intimate citizenship (Plummer 2003) come together in the social world. In Chapter 5, the impaired body emerged as integral within intimate relationships with others, particularly with regard to power relationships and the body as both sites of care and abuse; and in Chapter 6, impairment was centred as a 'troublesome presence' in the context of desired (hetero)sexual lives. In Chapter 7, the impaired body was rooted in disabled men's motivations to purchase sex and imbricated in their experiences of male sexual power. Thus, this shows the importance of recognising lived experiences of the body and impairment, their meanings and 'impairment effects' – 'the direct effects of impairment which differentiate bodily functioning from that which is socially construed to be normal or usual' (Thomas 2002b: 20) – within theorisations of disabled people's sexual, intimate and erotic lives.

Living intersectional lives: heteronormativity, masculine privilege and (disabled) male power

Ingraham (1996: 187) maintains that heterosexuality is 'the organising institution and ideology for gender'; thus, heteronormativity both depends upon and produces normative gender categories as a relation of power. It is perhaps not surprising, then, that informants' experiences of sexual and intimate life were further structured by the differential sexual power that heteronormative discourse affords men and women. As this chapter has argued so far, while heteronormative discourse was found to significantly disempower disabled men and women, in myriad ways, constituting sexual ableism, in this section I articulate the ways in which people's stories have revealed it to empower disabled men relative to disabled women. Due to informants' cisgender identities I speak in binary terms in this section. This is not to generalise or essentialise 'men's' and 'women's' experiences as discrete or in opposition, but to understand these categories in the contexts of disability and sexuality, in relation to one another and inclusive of their intersections. Inevitably, heteronormativity as a male-serving discourse often worked *for* disabled men through particular means and spaces where it didn't for disabled women, and thus created different outcomes and opportunities for disabled informants. At particular junctures, disabled men could enact a sexual dominance and exercise greater sexual agency because of their increased access to sexual power that (hegemonic) masculinity, heterosexuality and heteronormativity provided. Therefore, findings emphasise that, just as heteronormativity creates different sexual opportunities and identities for cisgender non-disabled men and women and proffers cisgender non-disabled men greater sexual power, the presence of disability and impairment seldom mitigates these differences.

Importantly, disabled men enacted and embodied a variety of masculinities within and through their stories, but generally had more manoeuvrability within, as well as opportunities to negotiate, sexual and gender identities than disabled women. Thus, many had access to multiple forms of social and sexual capital that are both the preserve of cisgender heterosexual men and valorised in heteronormative culture. As previous research suggests, independence, self-sufficiency, strength – as the necessary qualities of hegemonic masculinity – may be '(re) negotiated, relied upon, or resisted by disabled men' (Gibson *et al.* 2014: 96; see also Abbott 2012; Gibson *et al.* 2007; Sparkes and Smith 2002; Shakespeare

1999b; Shuttleworth 2000). Men's stories have shown that marginalisation from gendered sexual categories served (for some) as an opportunity to negotiate gender within sexual identity and practice. For example, some men could resist some of the most oppressive requirements of hegemonic sexuality, most notably its incessant phallocentrism, to access a more empowering sexual project whereby they excelled in non-penetrative practices (see Chapter 6). Gerschick and Miller (1995) label this category of disabled men 'rejecters', based upon their ability to reconstruct a masculine identity according to their own (sexual) abilities, instead of those outlined and revered in the dominant culture. Other male informants were avowed by partners to enact feminine characteristics or put on feminised performances without fear of judgement, what Phillips (2010: 117) calls 'becoming socially female' (see Garland-Thomson 2002) (see Chapter 6), and in some instances bodily impairment served as a release from the restrictive masculine requirements demanded of non-impaired male bodies (see Chapters 5 and 6).

It is critical to determine here, then, that disabled women in my research seldom experienced such manoeuvrability or freedom, and remained largely confined by conventional sex and gender norms. The majority of women did not have such agency when defining – or at least narrating – their sexual and gendered selves, and their sexual stories revealed few alternatives to normative categories that they could claim. Most clearly, disabled women remained painfully subject to their bodies. Their non-normative embodiment by no means excused them from the objectifying discourse surrounding women's bodies and thus it had significant psycho-emotional consequences. Women routinely hid their bodies (from themselves and partners), felt shame and disgust at their body's divergence from aesthetic bodily norms and (some) carried out extensive body projects to 'fix' their bodies according to idealised beauty aesthetics (see Chapter 6). Furthermore, despite many women's assertions that they desired a more active role within sex, most positioned their impairment as the primary reason why this couldn't be achieved, showing that they couldn't negotiate the body to a preferred or alternative sexual role in the same ways as (some) disabled men. In addition, the requirement (and desire) to adhere to normative femininity meant that women were not able to avail themselves of sexual opportunities available and accessible to disabled men, largely excluding them from purchasing sex from commercial sex work contexts and seeking other forms of sexual support (see Chapter 7).

These findings constitute a number of important contributions. First, they offer a powerful challenge to prevailing hetero/sexist ideas of male sexuality as more *impacted* by impairment and disability than female sexuality (see Murphy 1990); that the intersections of the cultural categories of 'masculine' and 'disabled' are more problematic and conflicting than femininity and disability (Shakespeare 1999b); and that disability 'erodes much, but not all, masculine privilege' (Gerschick 2000: 1265). At the same time, however, it is important to remember that access to privilege was by no means definitive. While some men *could* perceive hegemonic masculinity as 'less a total index of their desirability'

(Shuttleworth 2000: 227), meaning that they could 'draw on alternative ideals' (Shuttleworth 2000: 227), many others couldn't, and experienced substantial psycho-emotional disablism as a result of their inability to 'let go of restrictive notions of manhood' (Tepper 1999: 37).

Second, as most chapters have emphasised, these findings reveal the similarities of the experiences of disabled and non-disabled women, who occupy analogous subordinate positions within heteronormativity and heterosexuality. This illustrates – as other disabled feminists already have long suggested (Begum 1992; Garland-Thomson 2002; Ghai 2002, 2006; Keith 1990; Lonsdale 1990; Morris 1991, 1993, 1996; Schriempft 2001; Thomas 1999; Wendell 1996; Wilkerson 2002) – the need for mainstream ('hegemonic') feminism to be more inclusive of all types of women and thus broaden its contextualisation of the female experience which, while diverse, is unified by women's suppression under patriarchy and male (sexual) power. However, as Thomas (2006: 183) suggests, it is not enough for this to constitute 'exclusion by nominal inclusion' – including disabled women's experiences merely for the sake of doing so. Instead, 'more sustained analyses of the social and gendered character of disability and impairment both culturally and materially is required' (Thomas 2006: 183).

Finally, these findings affirm the importance of centring gender, as well as race, class, sexuality and nation, as lived categories when theorising disabled sexualities. Disabled people are intersectional subjects with intersectional lives: to paraphrase Audrey Lorde (1982, 2007), none of us live single-issue lives. Thus, gender categories and constructs are not merely lexicon but have embodied, social, cultural and economic meanings (see Bordo 1993), for those located both inside and outside of them. As informants' stories have shown, such categories socially organise the lives of heterosexual disabled men and women – they can't merely be cast away with ease, despite the undesirability of the binary. We might, then, ask critical questions of calls for emancipatory dis/abled sexual futures where normative gender binaries must be overcome. As Rembis (2010: 56) proposes, the 'problem' with current disability and sexuality research is that it doesn't work enough to 'reshape the very notion of gender, sex, sexuality, eroticism, desire, and disability, and to subvert the power relations and class structures that undergird the maintenance of these ideological constructions'. I agree of course (see Chapter 2), but speaking literally, or rather ethically, what do we do with – in this case – disabled people's gendered lives and experiences? Or more importantly, how their experiences of gender underpin lived experiences of psycho-emotional disablism, abuse and violence? And/or mediate access to the erotic and the claiming of pleasure? I'm aware that speaking in such terms paradoxically serves to affirm the binaries of male/female and masculine/feminine upon which the heterosexual matrix is based (Butler 1990) – the very ground that needs to be shattered – but anything else risks neglecting everyday gendered realities of individual and collective lives and selves. Inevitably, it's critical that the lived intersections of disabled people's lives are at the forefront of our work in disability and sexuality studies. This is yet another productive tension that serves as a helpful segue into the final section of this chapter, as I ask critical questions of DisHuman studies – a perspective which acknowledges the lived desires and realities of disabled people at the same time as making space to think otherwise.

DisHuman: which way to the future?

As a means to begin this section, I first want to introduce the DisHuman manifesto. While ProjectDisHuman has been working for a number of years, it came together in 2015 to explicitly articulate its DisHuman manifesto. The decision to produce a manifesto emerged from our collective aspiration to 'sketch out a version of the world that we think is worth drawing on in the everyday' as well from our mounting concerns around the *state* of humanity (for want of a more sophisticated phraseology) and thus our desire to '(re)claim humanity in a time when the world is increasingly dehumanising' (ProjectDisHuman forthcoming). Subsequently, the DisHuman Manifesto (ProjectDisHuman 2015) was born:

DisHuman manifesto:

* unpacks and troubles dominant notions of what it means to be human
* celebrates the disruptive potential of disability to trouble these dominant notions
* acknowledges that being recognised as a regular normal human being is desirable, especially for those people who been denied access to the category of the human
* recognises disability's intersectional relationship with other identities that have been considered less than human (associated with class, gender, sexuality, ethnicity, age)
* aims to develop theory, research, art and activism that push at the boundaries of what it means to be human and disabled
* keeps in mind the pernicious and stifling impacts of ableism, which we define as discriminatory processes that idealise a narrow version of humanness and reject more diverse forms of humanity
* seeks to promote transdisciplinary forms of empirical and theoretical enquiry that breaks disciplinary orthodoxies, dominances and boundaries
* foregrounds dis/ability as the complex for interrogating oppression and furthering a posthuman politics of affirmation.

In this section, then, I draw more explicitly upon the DisHuman to trouble some of the tensions identified in this chapter so far. It is here that I ask some critical questions – the very same ones I was left with following the submission of my doctoral thesis. The fact that such questions have ruminated over several years shows how we often *live* with theory, and that theory gets under our skin and just won't leave us be. Importantly, I suggest that a DisHuman lens offers new ways to understand tensions, and enables alternative ways forward when critically imagining disabled people's sexual and intimate futures. Selfishly, I apply a DisHuman lens here for the first time because I want to end this book centring hope and affirmation as the means to value, make visible and celebrate disabled lives and their disruptions in these precarious times of neoliberalism-ableism and advanced capitalism (Braidotti 2013; Goodley 2014). In this era we are all becoming vulnerable-but-responsibilised-subjects whose citizenship is conditional upon our ability to transform into a subject that can participate in and/or is desired by the market (see Scoular and O'Neill 2007); and, fittingly for disabled sexualities, these are times where new forms of precarity drive us, at best, back into the normative body and self, once again delineating disability as unliveable and unlovable. It is important for me state, however, that it is not my intention to apply new frameworks at this juncture in order to 'skim over' the findings I have discussed so far – to disregard informants' subjective and material realities – but rather the opposite: precisely because imagining otherwise is a way to raise consciousness and create the conditions for enacting change (see Hill-Collins 2000).

To bring my focus back to my core findings, then, I recap for a brief moment: in their sexual stories disabled people forcefully asserted a (naturalised) sexual subjectivity and made claims only for normative sexual citizenship, locating their rights, access, agency and embodied experiences of sex as central to their humanness. Desiring (and significantly labouring towards) a normalised, autonomous, independent and bounded sexual reality was a viable (but often precarious) means through which to humanise the self and served (see Chapter 4), for some, to gain entry into mainstream sexual cultures. Such complex and invisible labours were very purposeful towards feeling and enacting 'human' in the context of lives and selves consistently devalued and dehumanised. My critical questions are as follows:

- In light of informants' will for normalcy and desire for humanness, can there also be space to explore/acknowledge disability as radical and emancipatory in the context of sexual and intimate life?
- How do I not become yet another 'expert' voice appropriating the collective disabled sexual story? To return to Guldin's (2000: 237) earlier contention, 'who defines sexual resistance and who defines a political act?'
- How might positing disabled/crip sexualities as posthuman or DisHuman conflict with disabled people's own sexual politics and their calls for sexual citizenship?

Critically, to illuminate and unpack these questions, through the DisHuman position it becomes possible to 'recognise the norm, the pragmatic and political value of claiming the norm' (Goodley and Runswick-Cole 2014: 5) while always seeking to disrupt and contest it. The prefix of 'dis' is employed here to symbolise the 'necessity to critically question and – at certain junctures – disrespect and critique that which it precedes' (Goodley and Runswick-Cole 2014: 5). To offer an example, speaking about the lives of those with the label of intellectual impairment, Goodley and Runswick-Cole (2014: 2) clarify: 'Intellectual disability is always profound because it enlarges, pauses, questions and clarifies what it means to be human. Intellectual disability "disses" (or disrespects) the human but it also desires the human.' Therefore, as Goodley and Runswick-Cole (2014: 3–4) suggest:

> a dis/human[3] analysis allows us to claim (normative) citizenship (associated with choice, a sense of autonomy, being part of a loving family, the chance to labour, love and consume) while simultaneously drawing on disability to trouble, re-shape and re-fashion liberal citizenship

ultimately, then, to invoke alternative kinds of citizenship and ways of being in the world.

To clarify, a DisHuman analysis at once appreciates and understands disabled desires for sexual normalcy, comprehending the power of such a category, yet at the same time it avows a space for seeing otherwise, to appreciate the lived and everyday on an alternative register. It seeks 'more expanded, crip, [and] relational forms of the human' (Goodley *et al.* 2017), which, I suggest, pave new ways of imagining and advocating for disabled people's sexual and intimate futures. To tender an example, the disabled sexualities that have unfolded through this book – while striving for normalcy – have also showed themselves to be unquestionably non-normative, queered, cripped, and at points interdependent and radically relational – entities 'entangled in multiple assemblages' (Fritsch 2010: 3) – connected both inter/corporeally and sometimes literally with multiple technologies, bodies, services and power structures that dis/avow. Therefore, rather than abject, aberrant and asexual – as informants' own storytelling has largely maintained – disability has shown itself to be productive, radical and vital *because* of the ways it *already* surpasses and subverts the strict confines of the human and, by extension, human sexuality (Liddiard 2013). In short, thinking through the DisHuman illuminates the presence and power of disability to exceed and expand the confines of heteronormative sexuality and pleasure (which limit all sexual subjects) in ways that shift sexual desire and practice for dynamic and provocative effect.

To offer an example[4] in the context of an individual story, I would like to return to Terry's account from Chapter 4. Terry was talking about being placed in a specialist/segregated PSHE (personal, social and health education) class:

TERRY: 'Today we're going to learn how people with muscle weakness are going to put a condom on'. I remember saying – 'to be fair you're talking to someone who can't even open a chocolate wrapper, so I haven't got much hope, have I?' I remember it was almost like a shock because he [teacher] said 'does that mean you're not going to use contraception?!' and I said, 'well no, obviously I'd just ask the other person to put the condom on'.

In Chapter 4 Terry's account was used to show the ways in which disabled people's learning about sex can remain defined by its deviation from sexual normalcy and its practices and that a relentless focus on normative bodies and bodily experiences has the potential to alienate disabled young people when learning about sexuality, thus impeding their access to intimate citizenship (Plummer 2003). To reread this intimate 'problem' through a DisHuman lens would reveal the presence of disability (previously troublesome) as transformative: Terry's account embodies a moment where the (sexist) gendered politics of condom use are disrupted (as the man, who is often responsible for putting a condom on, Terry can't); a moment where dominant myths of the (masculine) sexual body as autonomous, in control and self-governing are contested (Terry's male sexual body requires support from his partner); and a moment where the (crip) sexual body emerges as a space of (embodied) relationality and interconnectedness, corporeally interwoven with other bodies and selves in creative assemblages (putting the condom on becomes a shared activity between partners). It is fair to say that these are deeply transformative sexual relations, especially in the context of youth (see Slater 2015).

To re/encounter informants' sexual stories through a DisHuman framework reveals a multitude of transgressions: actively displacing, decentring or demoting the orgasm as a marker of pleasure, dislodging it from heteronormative scripts as the 'natural outcome' (Cacchioni 2007: 306); queering heterosexual practices through exploration that facilitated discovery of a multitude of pleasures (tongues and fingers as cocks); expanding normative modes of pleasure through incorporating the visual, staring, fantasy, verbal sex and (sexual) technologies and enhancements, uncoupling human sexuality from its 'long-presumed biological essence' (Plummer 2015: 44); the discovery of new erogenous zones – orgasmic pleasures through stroking arms, shoulders and necks – queering the embodied norms of the conventional erotic body that dictates that orgasms, rather boringly, are bound only to genitals (Ostrander 2009; see also Liddiard and Goodley 2016); and through an acknowledgement that disability can welcome in multiple supports to disrupt the autonomous, independent, self-governing human subject as crip sexual bodies come to be collectively and collaboratively maintained by chosen others, such as partners, family, carers, sex workers and care professionals (see Earle 1999; see also Fritsch 2010). Without doubt, then, disability, by its very nature, offers possibilities for opening up new ontologies of pleasure and alternative economies of desire. Despite routine and persistent disqualification through sexual ableism, crip erotics exist, persist, survive and thrive.

Elsewhere, I have called this transformative space the DisSexual (Goodley *et al.* 2015). Echoing DisHuman politics, the DisSexual is a mode through which disabled people can claim their humanness through conventional modes of sexuality and gender if they so choose, yet simultaneously defy, crip and exceed such boundaries (see Goodley *et al.* 2015). The DisSexual is an idea that I am still working with – it is likely too early to mention it in the confines of this (concluding) chapter. I do so because its bifurcated position provides ways to negotiate tensions and think through the push/pull I mentioned in an earlier section – the simultaneity and connection of binaries produced through sexual ableism: normalised/Other, crip/queer, rejected/desired, natural/technologised, autonomous/collaborative, intimate/commodified, private/exposed and orgasmic/non-orgasmic (not inorgasmic), as well as the liminal spaces between. I offer some examples from informants' sexual stories below:

- DisSexual can mean abandoning typically gendered sexual practices during sexual relations, while still subscribing to cisgender modes of being/privilege in everyday life.
- DisSexual could mean welcoming non-normative and queered pleasures and practices (that some impaired bodies often demand) into heterosexual sex.
- DisSexual could mean embracing myriad technologies to sustain a naturalised disabled sexual and reproductive life and self.
- DisSexual could mean that the autonomous, self-governing and unitary sexual subjects be collectively and collaboratively maintained by a range of supports.
- DisSexual could mean privileging normative modes of orgasmic and phallocentric sexuality while experiencing orgasm through non-erogenous zones of the body, and different forms of penetration either with/without genitals and/or with/without the support of (sexual) bodily technologies/enhancements (see Chapter 6).
- DisSexual might mean having intimate relationships through paid-for sexual encounters.

Each of these examples aspires to a dis/ableist human sexual normalcy while inherently being non-normative and – in part – non-human. Each claims the normative sexualised self as a marker of humanity yet revises human sexuality as we know it. Each privileges the 'natural' through technologies, enhancements and extensive labour. Thus, each of these – I tentatively conclude – embodies the DisSexual. This is important, because, whilst the majority of disabled people in my research expressed their desires for sex and intimacy that might be deemed as illustrative of a typically sexually functioning and normatively gendered human subject, the input of personal assistants, technologies and, sometimes, sex workers, as well as the opening up of the totality of the body and impairment as sites of multifarious pleasure, reconfigures how we think of and enact sex, desire and intimacy.

To end, then, what I've tried to do in this latter section is ponder the possibilities of a posthuman disabled sexual subject, as well as locate these in the context of everyday lived lives of disabled people. The DisSexual is, I argue, a means through which to do so theoretically – but also ethically, faithfully and honourably – in ways that stay true to informants' own constructed sexual subjective realities. Thus, the beauty of a DisHuman analysis is that it reframes what would otherwise be a problematic desire for the norm – a yearning to fit into binaries, a longing for sameness and a will to be included into the category of the human (see Chapter 2). At the same time, it encourages thinking *with* crip (McRuer 2006b), even if the majority of disabled people's lived and conscious realities are not quite there yet – largely because sexual ableism suppresses *access* to crip, and therefore sexual liberation for disabled people (and many others). Rather than call, then, for the total splintering of the human, of binaries, and of normalcy – risky projects in times where disabled people remain marginalised, impoverished and excluded – the DisHuman and DisSexual enable access to the power, relative security and social (and sexual) capital of the human, while always holding these categories to account.

To end where I began, if I were in that Toronto bar – pissed but not too pissed (possibly having just consumed a cheeky Malibu or three) – with someone asking me to explain this research, this project, this book, I would say this: as a disabled woman, having opportunities to hear, live with and write through the stories of disabled others has been an incredible gift. I have learned copious amounts, and I hope I have conveyed as much between these covers. When people let you into their lives in such ways, into their intimate spaces, thoughts, feelings – exposing themselves – to give voice to that which, for most, is deeply intimate, often painful, shameful and baring, you understand how important it is for stories to be treated faithfully and in line with an ethics of care that acknowledges both the preciousness and power of such stories and the truly collaborative nature of storytelling. I hope this book contributes to activism, advocacy and theory, and to ways of thinking about disability, sexuality, humanness and the social world, but most of all I hope that disabled people can take something from this work if they so choose. Loosing sexual stories into the world, as Plummer (1995) maintains, encourages a community of stories that make social and sexual justice – in this case for disabled people – imaginable and tenable. In this vein, storytelling is, I believe, a route to sexual and intimate futures where we can just *be* – loving others and ourselves in equal measures.

Notes

1 Project DisHuman includes the following researchers: Dr Kirsty Liddiard (University of Sheffield), Professor Katherine Runswick-Cole (Manchester Metropolitan University), Professor Rebecca Lawthom (Metropolitan University) and Professor Dan Goodley (University of Sheffield).
2 This is perhaps not surprising for a cisgender woman in a long-term heterosexual partnership!
3 In earlier work, ProjectDisHuman has applied a forward slash (i.e. 'dis/human') to recognise the interplay of disability and humanity. However, we now use 'DisHuman' in order to 'break the binarised fusion of the dis/human and move towards a more melded conception of the DisHuman' (Goodley *et al.* 2015: 6). As Goodley and Runswick Cole (2014: 3) state, 'we desire a time when dis/human becomes dishuman: when any thought about the human has in mind what disability does to it. It is not simply the case that we want to jettison the "/" because we find it ungainly, we want to move to a time when thinking about the human will always involve thinking about disability.'
4 Taken from Goodley *et al.* (2015).

Bibliography

Abberley, P. (2002) 'Work, Disability, Disabled People and European Social Theory'. In C. Barnes *et al.* (eds) *Disability Studies Today*. Cambridge: Polity Press

Abbott, D. W. F. (2012) 'Other Voices, Other Rooms: Reflections on Talking to Young Men with Duchenne Muscular Dystrophy (DMD) and their Families about Transition to Adulthood', *Children & Society*, 26: 3, 241–250

Abbott, D. (2015) 'Love in a Cold Climate: Changes in the Fortunes of LGBT Men and Women with Learning Disabilities?' *British Journal of Learning Disabilities*, 43: 2, 100–105

Abeyesekera, S. (1997) 'Activism for Sexual and Reproductive Rights: Progress and Challenges', *Health and Human Rights*, 2: 3, 39–43

Abu-Habib, L. (1997) *Gender and Disability: Women's Experiences in the Middle East*. UK and Ireland: Oxfam

Adams, R. (2001) *Sideshow USA: Freaks and the American Cultural Imagination*. Chicago: University of Chicago Press

Adams, T. E. (2006) 'Seeking Father: Relationally Reframing a Troubled Love Story', *Qualitative Inquiry*, 12: 4, 704–723

Adams, T. E. (2008) 'A Review of Narrative Ethics', *Qualitative Inquiry*, 14: 2, 175–194

Addlakha, R. (2007) 'How Young People with Disabilities Conceptualize the Body, Sex and Marriage in Urban India: Four Case Studies', *Sexuality and Disability*, 25: 3, 111–123

Albrecht, G., Seelman, K. and Bury, M. (2001) *The Handbook of Disability Studies*. Thousand Oaks, CA: Sage

Allen, L. (2006) ' "Looking at the Real Thing": Young Men, Pornography, and Sexuality Education', *Discourse: Studies in the Cultural Politics of Education*, 27: 1, 69–83

Aloni, R. and Katz, S. (2003) *Sexual Difficulties after Traumatic Brain Injury and Ways to Deal with It*. Springfield, IL: Charles C. Thomas

Anderson, E. M. and Clarke, L. (1982) *Disability in Adolescence*. London: Methuen

Anderson, P. and Kitchen, R. (2000) 'Disability, Space and Sexuality: Access to Family Planning Services', *Social Science & Medicine*, 51, 1163–1173

Aphramor, L. (2009) 'Disability and the Anti-Obesity Offensive', *Disability & Society*, 24: 7, 897–909

Appleby, Y. (1992) 'Disability and "Compulsory Heterosexuality"', *Feminism and Psychology*, 2: 3, 502–505

Appleby, Y. (1994) 'Out on the Margins', *Disability & Society*, 9: 1, 13–32

Arber, S. and Gilbert, G. N. (1992) *Women and Working Lives: Divisions and Change*. London: Macmillan

Ariotti, L. (1999) 'Social Construction of Anangu Disability', *Australian Journal of Rural Health*, 7, 216–222

Arksley, H. and Knight, P. (1999) *Interviewing for Social Scientists: An Introductory Resource with Examples*. London and Thousand Oaks, CA: Sage Publications

Armer, B. (2007) 'Eugenetics: A Polemical View of Social Policy in the Genetic Age', *New Formations*, 60, 89–103

Arnot, M. and Dillabough, J. (2000) *Challenging Democracy: Feminist Perspectives on the Education of Citizens*. London: Taylor & Francis

Arundell, T. (1997) 'Reflections on the Researcher–Researched Relationship: A Woman Interviewing Men', *Qualitative Sociology*, 20: 3, 341–368

Asch, A., and Fine, M. (1985) 'Disabled Women: Sexism without the Pedestal'. In M. K. Deegan and N. A. Brooks (eds) *Women and Disability: The Double Handicap*. New Brunswick, NJ: Transaction Books

Asch, A., and Fine, M. (1997) 'Nurturance, Sexuality and Women with Disabilities: The Example of Women and Literature'. In L. J. Davis (ed.) *The Disability Studies Reader*. New York: Routledge

Atchison, C., Fraser, L. and Lowman, J. (1998) 'Men Who Buy Sex: Preliminary Findings of an Exploratory Study'. In J. Elias, V. Bullough, V. Elias and J. Elders (eds) *Prostitution: On Whores, Hustlers, and Johns*. New York: Prometheus Books

Bahner, J. (2012) 'Legal Rights or Simply Wishes? The Struggle for Sexual Recognition of People with Physical Disabilities Using Personal Assistance in Sweden', *Sexuality and Disability*, 30: 3, 337–356, doi: 10.1007/s11195-012-9268-2

Bahner, J. (2013) 'The Power of Discretion and the Discretion of Power: Personal Assistants and Sexual Facilitation in Disability Services', *Vulnerable Groups & Inclusion*, 4: 1, 20673–20673, doi: 10.3402/vgi.v4i0.20673

Balderston, S. (2014) 'Victimised Again? Intersectionality and Injustice in Disabled Women's Lives after Hate Crime and Rape. Gendered Violence: Macro and Micro Settings', *Advances in Gender Research*, 18, 17–51

Bailey, R. (1996) 'Prenatal Testing and the Prevention of Impairment: A Woman's Right to Choose?' In. J. Morris (ed.) *Encounters with Strangers: Feminism and Disability*. London: Women's Press

Ball, K. F. (2002) 'Who'd Fuck an Ableist?' *Disability Studies Quarterly*, 22: 4, 166–172

Banks, M. and Kaschak, E. (2003) *Women with Visible and Invisible Disabilities: Multiple Intersections, Multiple Issues, Multiple Therapies*. London: Routledge

Barbara, G., Facchin, F., Meschia, M. and Vercellini P. (2015) ' "The First Cut is the Deepest": A Psychological, Sexological, and Gynecological Perspective on Female Genital Cosmetic Surgery', *Acta Obstetricia et Gynecologica Scandinavica*, doi: 10.1111/aogs.12660

Baril, A. (2015) 'Needing to Acquire a Physical Impairment/Disability: (Re)Thinking the Connections between Trans and Disability Studies through Transability', *Hypatia* 30: 1, 30–48

Barnes, C. (1991) *Disabled People in Britain*. London: Hurst and Company

Barnes, C. (1992) *Disabling Imagery*. Derby: BCDODP

Barnes, C. (1998) 'The Social Model of Disability: A Sociological Phenomenon Ignored by Sociologists'. In T. Shakespeare (ed.) *The Disability Reader: Social Science Perspectives*. London: Continuum

Barnes, C. (2003) 'What a Difference a Decade Makes: Reflections on Doing "Emancipatory" Disability Research', *Disability & Society*, 18: 1, 3–17

Barnes, C. and Mercer, G. (1997) *Doing Disability Research*. Leeds: The Disability Press

Barnes, C. and Mercer, G. (2003) *Disability: Key Concepts*. Cambridge: Polity Press

Barnes, C. and Mercer, G. (2004) *Implementing the Social Model of Disability: Theory and Research*. Leeds: The Disability Press

Barnes, C. *et al.* (2002) *Disability Studies Today*. Cambridge: Polity Press

Barnes, H. (2009) *Disabled Women who Pay for Sex*. BBC Ouch: Disability Talk. Online. Available from: www.bbc.co.uk/ouch/features/disabled_women_who_pay_for_sex.shtml [accessed 2/9/2011]

Baron, K. (1997) 'The Bumpy Road to Womanhood', *Disability & Society*, 12: 2, 223–240

Barrett, S., Komarony C., Robb M. and Rogers A. (2004) *Communication, Relationships and Care: A Reader*. London: Routledge

Bartky, S. L. (1990) *Femininity and Domination: Studies in the Phenomenology of Oppression*. New York: Routledge

Barton, L. (ed.) (1996) *Disability and Society: Emerging Issues and Insights*. Harlow: Longman

Barton, L. (2003) 'Challenging Perspectives on Disability and Inclusion'. In K. Heggen *et al.* (eds) *Marginalization and Social Exclusion*. Volda: Volda University College

Barton, L. (2005) 'Emancipatory Research and Disabled People: Some Observations and Questions', *Educational Review*, 57: 3, 317–327

Barton, L. and Oliver, M. (1997) *Disability Studies: Past, Present, and Future*. Leeds: The Disability Press

Beazley, S., Moore, M. and Benzie, S. (1997) 'Involving Disabled People in Research: A Study of Inclusion in Environmental Activities'. In. C. Barnes and G. Mercer (eds) *Doing Disability Research*. Leeds: The Disability Press, 15–31

Begum, N. (1992) 'Disabled Women and the Feminist Agenda', *Feminist Review*, 40, 70–84

Bell, C. (2010) 'Is Disability Studies Actually White Disability Studies?' In L. Davis (ed.) *The Disability Studies Reader*. New York: Routledge

Bendelow, G. and Williams, S. J. (1998) *Emotions in Social Life: Critical Themes and Contemporary Issues*. London: Routledge

Bennet deMarrais, K. (1998) *Inside Stories: Qualitative Research Reflections*. London: Routledge

Beresford, P. (2008) 'Whose Personalisation?' *Soundings*, 40, 8–17

Beresford, P., Harrison, C. and Wilson, A. (2002) 'Mental Health Service Users and Disability: Implications for Future Strategies', *Policy and Politics*, 30, 387–396

Beresford, P., Nettle, M. and Perring, R. (2010) *Towards a Social Model of Madness and Distress? Exploring What Service Users Say*. London: Joseph Rowntree Foundation

Bernstein, E. (2007) *Temporarily Yours: Intimacy, Authenticity and the Commerce of Sex*. Chicago: University of Chicago Press

Bewley, C. and Glendinning, C. (1994) *Involving Disabled People In Community Care Planning*. London: Joseph Rowntree Foundation

Blackburn, M. (2002) *Sexuality & Disability*, 4th ed. Oxford: Butterworth-Heinemann

Bland, L. and Doan, L. (1998) *Sexology Uncensored: The Documents of Sexual Science*. Cambridge: Polity Press

Blumenreich, M. (2004) 'Avoiding the Pitfalls of "Conventional" Narrative Research: Using Poststructural Theory to Guide the Creation of Narratives of Children with HIV', *Qualitative Research*, 4: 1, 77–90

Blumer, H. (1969) *Symbolic Interactionism: Perspective and Method*. Englewood Cliffs, NJ: Prentice Hall

Blyth, C. (2010) 'Members Only: The Use of Gay Space(s) by Gay Disabled Men'. In R. Shuttleworth and T. Sanders (eds) *Sex and Disability: Politics, Identity, and Access*. Leeds: The Disability Press

Blyth, C. and Carson, I. (2007) 'Sexual Uncertainties and Disabled Young Men: Silencing Difference Within the Classroom', *Journal of Pastoral Care in Education*, 25: 3, 34–38

Bolton, S. and Boyd, C. (2003) 'Trolley Dolly or Skilled Emotion Manager? Moving on from Hochschild's Managed Heart'. *Work, Employment & Society* 17: 2, 289–308

Bone, K. M. (2017) 'Trapped behind the Glass: Crip Theory and Disability Identity', *Disability & Society*, http://dx.doi.org/10.1080/09687599.2017.1313722

Bonnie, S. (2004) 'Disabled People, Disability and Sexuality'. In. J. Swain (ed.) *Disabling Barriers, Enabling Environments*. London: Sage Publications

Bordo, S. (1993) *Unbearable Weight: Feminism, Western Culture, and the Body*. Berkeley: University of California Press

Boris, E., Gilmore, S. and Parreñas, R. (2010) 'Sexual Labors: Interdisciplinary Perspectives Toward Sex as Work', *Sexualities*, 13: 2, 131–137

Bourdieu, P. and Wacquant, L. (1992) *An Invitation to Reflexive Sociology*. Chicago: University of Chicago Press

Braidotti, R. (2003) 'Becoming Woman: Or Sexual Difference Revisited', *Theory, Culture and Society*, 20: 3, 43–64

Braidotti, R. (2006) *Transpositions: On Nomadic Ethics*. London: Polity Press

Braidotti, R. (2012) *Nomadic Theory: The Portable Rosi Braidotti*. New York: Columbia University Press

Braidotti, R. (2013) *The Posthuman*. UK: Polity Press

Branfield, F. (1998) 'What Are You Doing Here? "Non Disabled" People and the Disability Movement: A Response to Robert F. Drake', *Disability & Society*, 13: 1, 143–144

Brechin, A., Liddiard, P. A. and Swain, J. (1981) *Handicap in a Social World*. London: Open University Press/Tavistock Publications

Breckenridge, C. A. and Vogler, C. (2001) 'The Critical Limits of Embodiment: Disability's Criticism', *Public Culture*, 13: 3, 349–357

Bricher, G. (2000) 'Disabled People, Health Professionals and the Social Model of Disability: Can There Be a Research Relationship?' *Disability & Society*, 15: 5, 781–793

Brickell, C. (2006) 'A Symbolic Interactionist History of Sexuality?' *Rethinking History*, 10: 3, 415–432

Brockmeier, J. and Carbaugh, D. (2001) *Narrative and Identity: Studies in Autobiography, Self, and Culture*. Amsterdam and Philadelphia: John Benjamins

Brook Advisory Service (2010) *Sex and Disability*. Online. Available from: www.brook.org.uk/my-rights/sex-relationships-and-your-rights/sex-and-disability [accessed 2/12/11]

Brown, H. (1994) '"An Ordinary Sexual Life?" A Review of the Normalisation Principle as It Applies to the Sexual Options of People with Learning Disabilities', *Disability & Society*, 9: 2, 123–144

Brown, H., Stein, J. and Turk, V. (1995) 'The Sexual Abuse of Adults with Learning Disabilities: Report of a Second Two Year Incidence Survey', *Mental Handicap Research*, 8: 1, 1–22

Browne, J. and Russell, S. (2005) 'My Home, Your Workplace: People with Physical Disability Negotiate Their Sexual Health Without Crossing Professional Boundaries', *Disability & Society*, 20: 4, 375–388

Brownworth, V. A. and Raffo, S. (1999) *Restricted Access: Lesbians on Disability*. Berkeley, CA: Seal Press

Bruner, J. (1986) *Actual Minds, Possible Worlds*. Cambridge, MA: Harvard University Press

Bryant, J. and Schofield, T. (2007) 'Feminine Sexual Subjectivities: Bodies, Agency and Life History', *Sexualities*, 10: 3, 321–340

Bryman, A. (2004) *Social Research Methods*. Oxford: Oxford University Press

Bryman, A. (2008) *Social Research Methods*, 3rd ed. Oxford: Oxford University Press

Bullard, D. G. and Wallace, D. H. (1978) 'Peer Educator-Counsellors in Sexuality for the Disabled', *Sexuality and Disability*, 1: 2, 147–152

Bullough, V. (1994) *Science in the Bedroom*. New York: Basic Books

Bulmer, M. (1982) *Social Research Ethics: An Examination of the Merits of Covert Participant Observation*. London: Macmillan

Burkitt, I. (2012) 'Emotional Reflexivity: Feeling, Emotion and Imagination in Reflexive Dialogues', *Sociology*, 46: 3, 458–472

Burowoy, M. (2013) 'Public Sociology: The Task and the Promise'. In K. Gould and T. Lewis (eds) *Ten Lessons in Introductory Sociology*. Oxford: Oxford University Press

Bury, M. (1996) 'Defining and Researching Disability: Challenges and Responses'. In C. Barnes and G. Mercer (eds), *Exploring the Divide: Illness and Disability*. Leeds: The Disability Press

Bury, M. (2001) 'Illness Narratives: Fact or Fiction?' *Sociology of Health & Illness*, 23: 3, 263–285

Butler, J. (1990) *Gender Trouble*. London: Routledge

Butler, J. (1993) *Bodies that Matter: On the Discursive Limits of Sex*. London: Routledge

Butler, J. (1997) *Excitable Speech: A Politics of the Performative*. London: Routledge

Carr, S. (2004) *Has Service User Participation Made a Difference to Social Care Services?* London: Social Care Institute for Excellence

Cacchioni, T. (2007) 'Heterosexuality and "the Labour of Love": A Contribution to Recent Debates on Female Sexual Dysfunction', *Sexualities*, 10: 3, 299–320

Califia, P. (1994) *Public Sex: The Culture of Radical Sex*. Pittsburgh: Cleis Press

Campbell, F. K. (2001) 'Inciting Legal Fictions: Disability's Date with Ontology and the Ableist Body of the Law'. *Griffith Law Review*, 10, 42–62

Campbell, F. K. (2008) 'Refusing Able(ness): A Preliminary Conversation about Ableism'. *M/C Journal*. Online. Available from: http://journal.media-culture.org.au/index.php/mcjournal/article/view/46 [accessed: 6/7/2017]

Campbell, F. K. (2009) *Contours of Ableism: Territories, Objects, Disability and Desire*. London: Palgrave Macmillan

Campbell, J. and Oliver, M. (1996) *Disability Politics: Understanding Our Past, Changing Our Future*. London: Routledge

Campbell, R. (1998) 'Invisible Men: Making Visible Male Clients of Female Prostitutes in Merseyside'. In J. Elias, V. Bullough, V. Elias and J. Elders (eds) *Prostitution: On Whores, Hustlers, and Johns*. New York: Prometheus Books

Cambridge, P. (1996) 'Men with Learning Disabilities Who Have Sex with Men in Public Places: Mapping the Needs of Services and Users in South East London', *Journal of Intellectual Disability Research*, 40: 3, 241–251

Campos, L. N. *et al.* (2008) 'HIV, Syphilis, and Hepatitis B and C Prevalence Among Patients with Mental Illness: A Review of the Literature', *Cad Saude Publica*, 24 Supplement 4, S607–S620

Carroll, K. (2012) 'Infertile? The Emotional Labour of Sensitive and Feminist Research Methodologies', *Qualitative Research*, 12, 1–16

Chan, N .K. and Gillick, A. C. (2009) 'Fatness as a Disability: Questions of Personal and Group Identity', *Disability & Society*, 24: 2, 231–243

Chang, J. C. (2003) 'Helping Women with Disabilities and Domestic Violence: Strategies, Limitations, and Challenges of Domestic Violence Programs and Services', *Journal of Women's Health*, 12: 7, 699–708

Chapkis, W. (1986) *Beauty Secrets: Women and the Politics of Appearance*. South End: South End Press

Chapkis, W. (1997) *Live Sex Acts: Women Performing Erotic Labour*. London: Cassell

Chauncey, G. (1995) *Gay New York: Gender, Urban Culture, and the Making of the Gay Male World, 1890–1940*. New York: Basic Books

Cheausuwantavee, T. (2002) 'Sexual Problems and Attitudes Toward the Sexuality of Persons With and Without Disabilities in Thailand', *Sexuality and Disability*, 20: 2, 125–134

Chesser, E. (1950) *Sexual Behaviour: Normal and Abnormal*. London: Hutchinson

Chivers, J and Mathieson, S. (2000) 'Training in Sexuality and Relationships: An Australian Model', *Sexuality and Disability*, 18: 1, 73–80

Church, K., Frazee, C., Panitch, M., Luciani, T. and Bowman, V. (2007) *Doing Disability at the Bank: Discovering the Work of Learning/Teaching Done by Disabled Bank Employees Public Report*. Toronto: Ryerson RBC Foundation Institute for Disability Studies Research and Education

Clarke, H., and McKay, S. (2008) *Exploring Disability, Family Formation and Break-Up: Reviewing the Evidence*. Norwich: Department for Work and Pensions

Clare, E. (1999) *Exile and Pride: Disability, Queerness, and Liberation*. Cambridge, MA: South End Press

Clayton, A. H. and Balon, R. (2009) 'Continuing Medical Education: The Impact of Mental Illness and Psychotropic Medications on Sexual Functioning: The Evidence and Management (CME)', *Journal of Sexual Medicine*, 6: 5, 1200–1211

Cockram, J. (2003) *Silent Voices: Women with Disabilities and Family and Domestic Violence*. Nedlands, Australia: People with Disabilities (WA) Inc.

Coffey, A. and Atkinson, P. (1996) *Making Sense of Qualitative Data: Complementary Research Strategies*. London: Sage Publications

Cohen, J. J. (2015) 'Queer Crip Sex and Critical Mattering', *GLQ: A Journal of Lesbian and Gay Studies*, 21: 1, 153–162

Connell, R. W. (1995) *Masculinities*. Cambridge: Polity Press

Cooper, C. (1997) 'Can a Fat Woman Call Herself Disabled?' *Disability & Society*, 12: 1, 31–42

Corbett, J. (1994) 'A Proud Label: Exploring the Relationship Between Disability Politics and Gay Pride', *Disability & Society*, 9: 3, 343–357

Corker, M. (1998) *Deaf and Disabled or Deafness Disabled*. Buckingham: Open University Press

Corker, M. (1999) 'Differences, Conflations and Foundations: The Limits to "Accurate" Theoretical Representation of Disabled People's Experience?' *Disability & Society*, 14: 5, 627–642

Corker, M. and Shakespeare, T. (2002) *Disability/Postmodernity: Embodying Disability Theory*. London: Continuum

Corker, M. and Thomas, C. (2002) 'A Journey Around the Social Model'. In M. Corker and T. Shakespeare (eds) *Disability/Postmodernity: Embodying Disability Theory*. London: Continuum

Corlyon, J. and McGuire, C. (1997) *Young Parents in Public Care*. London: National Children's Bureau

Costa, L., Voronka, J., Landry, D., Reid, J., McFarlane, B., Reville, D. *et al.* (2012) 'Recovering our Stories: A Small Act of Resistance', *Studies in Social Justice*, 6, 85–101

Courvant, D. (1999) 'Coming Out Disabled: A Transsexual Woman Considers Queer Contributions to Living with Disability', *Journal of Gay, Lesbian, and Bisexual Identity*, 4: 1, 97–105

Crabtree, L. (1997) 'Charcot-Marie-Tooth Disease: Sex, Sexuality and Self-Esteem', *Sexuality and Disability*, 15: 4, 293–306

Craig, L. A. *et al.* (2006) 'Treating Sexual Offenders with Learning Disabilities in the Community: A Critical Review', *International Journal of Offender Therapy and Comparative Criminology*, 50: 4, 369–390

Crenshaw, K. (1989) 'Demarginalizing the Intersection of Race and Sex: A Black Feminist Critique of Antidiscrimination Doctrine, Feminist Theory and Antiracist Politics', *University of Chicago Legal Forum*, 140, 139–167

Crenshaw, K. (1991) Mapping the Margins: Intersectionality, Identity Politics, and Violence against Women of Color, *Stanford Law Review*, 43: 6, 1241–1299

Crow, L. (1996) 'Rippling Raspberries: Disabled Women and Sexuality'. Unpublished MSc dissertation, South Bank Polytechnic, London

Crow, L. (2015) *Figures*. UK: Roaring Girl Productions

Csapo, M. and L. Goguen (1989) 'Special Education Across Canada: Challenges for the 90s Vancouver'. Vancouver: Centre for Human Development and Research, 199–218

Curry, M. A., Hassouneh-Phillips, D. and Johnston-Silverberg, A. J. (2001) 'Abuse of Women with Disabilities: An Ecological Model and Review'. *Violence Against Women*, 7, 60–79

Davidson, D. (2011) 'Reflections on Doing Feminist Research Grounded in my Experience of Perinatal Loss: From Auto/biography to Autoethnography', *Sociological Research Online*, 16: 1. Available from: www.socresonline.org.uk/16/1/6.html

Davies, D. (2000) 'Sharing Our Stories, Empowering Our Lives: Don't Dis Me!' *Sexuality and Disability*, 18: 3, 179–186

Davis, L. J. (1995) *Enforcing Normalcy: Disability, Deafness, and the Body*. New York: Verso

Davis, L. J. (1997) *The Disability Studies Reader*. New York: Routledge

Davis, L. J. (2000) 'Go to the Margins of the Class: Hate Crimes and Disability'. In L. Francis and A. Silvers (eds) *Americans with Disabilities: Exploring Implications of the Law for Individuals and Institutions*. New York: Routledge

Davis, L. J. (2002) *Bending Over Backwards: Disability, Dismodernism, and Other Difficult Positions*. New York: New York University Press

Davy, Z. (2010) 'A Psycho-social Exploration of (Trans) Gender, Sexual Citizenship and Disability: A Case Study'. In R. Shuttleworth and T. Sanders (eds) *Sex and Disability: Politics, Identity, and Access*. Leeds: The Disability Press

Deal, M. (2003) 'Disabled People's Attitudes Toward Other Impairment Groups: A Hierarchy of Impairments', *Disability & Society*, 18: 7, 897–910

Deegan, M. (1995) 'Multiple Minority Groups: A Case Study of Physically Disabled Women'. In. M. J. Deegan and N. A. Brooks (eds) *Women and Disability: A Double Handicap*. New Brunswick, NJ: Transaction Publishers

Deegan, M. and Brooks, M. (1985) *Women and Disability: The Double Handicap*. New Brunswick, NJ: Transaction Books

De Graeve, K. (2010) 'The Limits Of Intimate Citizenship: Reproduction Of Difference In Flemish-Ethiopian 'Adoption Cultures', *Bioethics*, 24: 4, 365–372

Dei, G. J. S. and Johal, G. S. (2005) *Critical Issues in Anti-Racist Research Methodologies*. New York: Lang plc

DeLoach, C., Wilkins, R. And Walker, G. (1983) *Independent Living, Philosophy, Process and Services*. Baltimore: University Park Press

Denov, M. (2003) 'The Myth of Innocence: Sexual Scripts and the Recognition of Child Sexual Abuse by Female Perpetrators', *Journal of Sex Research*, 40: 3, 303–314

Department for Education and Skills (2001) *Special Education Needs Code of Practice*, Para 9:51. London: Department for Education and Science

Department of Health (2007) *Putting People First: A Shared Vision and Commitment to the Transformation of Adult Social Care*. London: Department of Health

Descartes, R. (1974) *The Philosophical Works of Descartes*, trans. E. Haldene, and G. Ross. Cambridge: Cambridge University Press

DeVault, M. L. (1999) 'Comfort and Struggle: Emotion Work in Family Life', *The Annals of the American Academy of Political and Social Science*, 561, 52–63

Dewsbury, G. *et al.* (2004) 'The Anti-social Model of Disability', *Disability & Society*, 19: 2, 145–158

Dickson-Smith, V. *et al.* (2009) 'Researching Sensitive Topics: Qualitative Research as Emotion Work', *Qualitative Research*, 9: 1, 61–79

Disability Now (2005) 'Results of Time to Talk: Sex Survey', *Disability Now*, May

Drench, M. (1992) 'Impact of Altered Sexual Function in Spinal Cord Injury', *Sex and Disability*, 10, 3–14

Duckett, P. S. and Pratt, R. (2001) 'The Researched Opinions on Research: Visually Impaired People and Visual Impairment Research', *Disability & Society*, 16: 6, 815–835

Dukes, E. and McGuire, B. E. (2009) 'Enhancing Capacity to Make Sexuality-Related Decisions in People with an Intellectual Disability', *Journal of Intellectual Disability Research*, 53: 8, 727–734

Duncombe, J. and Marsden, D. (1998) '"Stepford Wives" and "Hollow Men"? Doing Emotion Work, Gender and "Authenticity" in Intimate Relationships'. In G. Bendelow and S. J. Williams (eds) *Emotions in Social Life: Critical Themes and Contemporary Issues*. London: Routledge

Dune, T. M. and Shuttleworth, R. P. (2009) '"It's Just Supposed to Happen"': The Myth of Sexual Spontaneity and the Sexually Marginalized', *Sexuality and Disability*, 27, 97–108

Earle, S. (1999) 'Facilitated Sex and the Concept of Sexual Need: Disabled Students and Their Personal Assistants', *Disability & Society*, 14: 3, 309–323

Earle, S. (2001) 'Disability, Facilitated Sex and the Role of the Nurse', *Journal of Advanced Nursing*, 36: 3, 433–440

Egharevba, I. (2001) 'Researching an-"Other" Minority Ethnic Community: Reflections of a Black Female Researcher on the Intersections of Race, Gender and Other Power Positions on the Research Process', *International Journal Social Research Methodology*, 4: 3, 225–241

Elias, J., Bullough, V., Elias, V. and Elders, J. (1998) *Prostitution: On Whores, Hustlers, and Johns*. New York: Prometheus Books

Ellis, H. (1927) *Studies in the Psychology of Sex*, vol. 3, *Analysis of the Sexual Impulse, Love and Pain, The Sexual Impulse in Women*. Philadelphia: D. A. Davies

Engelsrud, G. (2005) 'The Lived Body as Experience and Perspective: Methodological Challenges', *Qualitative Research*, 5: 3, 267–284

England, K. V. L. (1994) 'Getting Personal: Reflexivity, Positionality, and Feminist Research', *Professional Geographer*, 46: 1, 80–89

Erevelles, N. (2005) 'Understanding Curriculum as Normalising Text: Disability Studies Meets Curriculum Theory', *Journal of Curriculum Studies*, 37: 4, 421–439

Evans, M. and Lee, E. (2002) *Real Bodies: A Sociological Introduction.* Basingstoke, Hampshire: Palgrave Macmillan

Exley, C. and Letherby, G. (2001) 'Managing a Dirupted Lifecourse: Issues of Identity and Emotion Work', *Health*, 5: 1, 112–132

Fanon, F. (1993) *Black Skin, White Masks.* London: Pluto Press

Fetterman, D. M. (1991) *Using Qualitative Methods in Institutional Research.* San Francisco: Jossey-Bass

Finch, J. and Groves, D. (1983) *A Labour of Love: Women, Work and Caring.* London: Routledge & Kegan Paul

Fine, M. and Asch, A. (1988) *Women with Disabilities: Essays in Psychology, Culture, and Politics.* Philadelphia: Temple University Press

Finger, A. (1992) 'Forbidden Fruit'. *New Internationalist*, 233: 8–10

Finkelstein, V. (1980) *Attitudes and Disabled People: Issues for Discussion.* New York: World Rehabilitation Fund

Foucault, M. (1976) *The History of Sexuality*, vol. 1, *The Will to Knowledge.* Harmondsworth: Penguin

Foucault, M. (1985) *The History of Sexuality*, vol. 2, *The Use of Pleasure.* Harmondsworth: Penguin

Foucault, M. (1986) *The History of Sexuality*, vol. 3, *The Care of the Self.* Harmondsworth: Penguin

Francis, L. and Silvers, A. (2000) *Americans with Disabilities: Exploring Implications of the Law for Individuals and Institutions.* New York: Routledge

Frank, A. W. (1995) *The Wounded Storyteller: Body Illness, and Ethics.* Chicago and London: University of Chicago Press

Fraser, M. (1999) 'Classing Queer: Politics in Competition', *Theory, Culture and Society*, 16: 2, 107–131

French, S. (1993) *Disabling Barriers – Enabling Environments.* London: Sage

Friedman, S. H., and Loue, S. (2007) 'Incidence and Prevalence of Intimate Partner Violence by and Against Women with Severe Mental Illness', *Journal of Women's Health*, 16: 4, 471–480

Fritsch, K. (2010) 'Intimate Assemblages: Disability, Intercorporeality, and the Labour of Attendant Care'. *Critical Disability Discourse*, 2, 1–14

Fritsch, K., Heynen, R. Ross, A. and van der Meulen, E. (2016) 'Disability and Sex Work: Developing Affinities through Decriminalization', *Disability & Society*, 31: 1, 84–99

Frogatt, K. (1998) 'The Place of Metaphor and Language in Exploring Nurses' Emotional Work', *Journal of Advanced Nursing*, 28: 2, 332–338

Gabel, S. and Peters, S. (2004) 'Presage of a Paradigm Shift? Beyond the Social Model of Disability Toward Resistance Theories of Disability', *Disability & Society*, 19: 6, 585–600

Gagnon, J. and Simon, W. (1973) *Sexual Conduct: The Social Sources of Human Sexuality.* Piscataway, NJ: Transaction

Galvin, R. D. (2005) 'Researching the Disabled Identity: Contextualising the Identity Transformations Which Accompany the Onset of Impairment', *Sociology of Health & Illness*, 27: 3, 393–413

Galvin, R. (2006) 'A Genealogy of the Disabled Identity in Relation to Work and Sexuality', *Disability & Society*, 21: 5, 499–512

Garbutt, R. (2010) 'Exploring the Barriers to Sex and Relationships for People with Learning Difficulties'. In R. Shuttleworth and T. Sanders (eds) *Sex and Disability: Politics, Identity, and Access.* Leeds: The Disability Press

Garland-Thomson, R. (2002) 'Integrating Disability, Transforming Feminist Theory', *Feminist Formations*, 14: 3, 1–32

Gerschick, T. J. (2000) 'Toward a Theory of Disability and Gender', *Signs: Journal of Women in Culture and Society*, 25: 4, 1263–1268

Gerschick T. J. and Miller A. S. (1995) 'Coming to Terms'. In D. Sabo and D. Gordon (eds) *Men's Health and Illness*. London: Sage

Ghai, A. (2002) 'Disabled Women: An Excluded Agenda of Indian Feminism', *Hypatia*, 17: 3, 49–66

Ghai, A. (2006) '*(Dis)embodied Form: Issues for Disabled Women*. Delhi: Shakti Books

Gibson, B. E., Mistry, B., Smith, B., Yoshida, K. K., Abbott, D., Lindsay, S. and Hamdani, Y. (2014) 'Becoming Men: Gender, Disability, and Transitioning to Adulthood', *Health*, 18: 1, 95–114

Gibson, B. E., Young, N. L., Upshur, R. E. G., *et al.* (2007) 'Men on the Margin: A Bourdieusian Examination of Living into Adulthood with Muscular Dystrophy'. *Social Science & Medicine*, 65 (3): 505–517

Giddens, A. (1992) *The Transformation of Intimacy: Sexuality, Love and Eroticism in Modern Societies*. Cambridge: Polity Press

Gill, M. (2015) *Already Doing It: Intellectual Disability and Sexual Agency*. Minneapolis and London: University of Minnesota Press

Gillespie-Sells, K., Hills, M. and Robbins, B. (1998) *She Dances to Different Drums*. London: King's Fund

Glasby, J. and Littlechild, R. (2009) *Direct Payments and Personal Budgets: Putting Personalisation into Practice*. Bristol: Policy Press

Goffman, E. (1963) *Stigma: Notes on the Management of Social Identity*. Harmondsworth: Penguin

Goodley, D. (1999) 'Disability Research and the "Researcher Template": Reflections on Grounded Subjectivity in Ethnographic Research', *Qualitative Research*, 5: 1, 24–46

Goodley, D. (2011a) *Disability Studies: An Interdisciplinary Introduction*. London, California, New Delhi and Singapore: Sage Publications

Goodley, D. (2011b) 'Social Psychoanalytic Disability Studies', *Disability & Society*, 26: 6, 715–728

Goodley, D. (2014) *Dis/ability Studies. Theorising Disablism and Ableism*. London: Routledge

Goodley, D. (2016) *Disability Studies: An Interdisciplinary Introduction*, 2nd ed. London: Sage

Goodley, D. and McLaughlin, J. (2011) *Does Every Child Matter, Post-Blair? The Interconnections of Disabled Childhoods*. ESRC End of Award Report, RES-062–23–1138. Swindon: ESRC

Goodley, D. and Runswick-Cole, K. (2011a) *Does Every Child Matter, Post-Blair? Accessible End of project Report*. Online. Available from: www.rihsc.mmu.ac.uk/post-blairproject/ [accessed 10/12/11]

Goodley, D. and Runswick-Cole, K. (2011b) *Does Every Child Matter, Post-Blair? The Interconnections of Disabled Childhoods Website*. Online. Available from: http://post-blair.posterous.com/pages/publications [accessed 13/12/11]

Goodley, D. and Runswick-Cole, K. (2012). 'Reading Rosie. The Postmodern Disabled Child'. *Journal of Educational and Child Psychology*, 29: 2, 53–66

Goodley, D. and Runswick Cole, K. (2014) Becoming Dishuman: Thinking about the Human Through Dis/ability, *Discourse: Cultural Politics of Education*. 36: 1, 1–15. doi:1080/01596306.2014.930021

Goodley, D. and Tregaskis, C. (2006) 'Storying Disability and Impairment: Retrospective Accounts of Disabled Family Life'. *Qualitative Health Research*, 16: 5, 630–646

Goodley, D. Lawthom, R. and Runswick-Cole, K. (2014a) 'Dis/ability and Austerity: Beyond Work and Slow Death', *Disability & Society*, 29: 6, 980–984

Goodley, D., Lawthom, R., and Runswick-Cole, K. (2014b) 'Posthuman Disability Studies', *Subjectivity*, 7: 4, 342–361, DOI: 10.1057/sub.2014.15

Goodley, D., Runswick-Cole, K. and Liddiard, K. (2015) 'The DisHuman Child', *Discourse: Studies in the Cultural Politics of Education*, Special Issue Fabulous Monsters: Alternative Discourses of Childhood in Education, 37: 5, doi: 10.1080/01596306. 2015.1075731

Goodley, D. Lawthom, R., Goodley, R. and Goodley, R. (2017) *Them and Us: Brexit and the Logics of Neoliberal-ableism*. Online. Available from www.humanactivism.org/ assets/images/Them%20and%20us.pdf [accessed 21/5/2017]

Goodley, D., Lawthom, R., Liddiard, K., and Runswick-Cole, K. (in press a) 'Posthuman Disability and Dishuman Studies'. In R. Braidotti and M. Hlavajova (eds) *Posthuman Glossary*. London: Bloomsbury Academic

Goodley, D., Lawthom, R., Liddiard, K. and Runswick Cole, K. (in press b) 'Towards a DisHuman Civil Society'. In B. Watermeyer, J. McKenzie and L. Swartz (eds) (2017) *Disability and Citizenship: Critical perspectives on diversity and belonging*. London: HSRC

Graham, H. (1983) 'Caring: A Labour of Love'. In J. Finch and D. Groves (eds) *A Labour of Love: Women, Work and Caring*. London: Routledge & Kegan Paul

Griffiths, M. (2006) 'Sex: Should We All Be at it? A Study into the Struggles of Disabled People's Fight for Sexual Expression, and the Implications of Using Prostitutes and Surrogates to Facilitate This Sexual Expression'. Dissertation, University of Leeds

Guldin, A. (2000) 'Self-Claiming Sexuality: Mobility Impaired People and American Culture', *Sex and Disability*, 18: 4, 233–238

Hahn, H. (1981) 'The Social Component of Sexuality and Disability: Some Problems and Proposals', *Sexuality and Disability*, 4: 4, 220–233

Hahn, H. (1988) 'Can Disability be Beautiful?' *Social Policy*, 18: 3, 26–32

Hales, G. (1995) *Beyond Disability*. London: Sage

Halperin, D. (1995) *Saint Foucault: Towards a Gay Hagiography*. Oxford: Oxford University Press

Hamam, N., McCluskey, A. and Shuttleworth, R. (2009) 'Sexual Adaptation in Adults with Physical Impairment'. Inaugural Conference for OT Australia NSW-ACT, Sydney, Australia

Hamilton, C. A. (2009) '"Now I'd Like to Sleep with Rachael' – Researching Sexuality Support in a Service Agency Group Home', *Disability & Society*, 24: 3, 303–315

Haraway, D. (1988) 'Situated Knowledges: The Science Question in Feminism and the Privilege of Partial Perspective', *Feminist Studies*, 14: 3, 575–599

Haraway, D. (1991) *Simians, Cyborgs and Women: The Reinvention of Nature*. London: Free Association Books

Hassouneh-Phillips, D. and McNeff, E. (2005) '"I Thought I Was Less Worthy": Low Sexual and Body Esteem and Increased Vulnerability to Intimate Partner Abuse in Women with Physical Disabilities', *Disability and Sexuality*, 23: 4, 227–240

Hawkes, G. (1996) *A Sociology of Sex and Sexuality*. Buckingham: Open University Press

Heggen, K. *et al.* (2003) *Marginalization and Social Exclusion*. Volda: Volda University College

Henderson, A. (2001) 'Emotional Labour and Nursing: An Under-Appreciated Aspect of Caring Work', *Nursing Inquiry*, 8: 2, 130–138

Henriques, J., Hollway, W., Venn, C. and Walkerdine, V. (1984) *Changing the Subject: Psychology, Social Regulation and Subjectivity.* New York: Methuen

Hevey, D. (1992) *The Creatures Time Forgot: Photography and Disability Imagery.* London: Routledge

Hicks, S. (1981) 'Relationship and Sexual Problems of the Visually Handicapped'. In A. Brechin, P. A. Liddiard and J. Swan (eds) *The Handicapped Person in the Community.* London: Open University Press/Tavistock Publications

Hill-Collins, P. (2000) *Black Feminist Thought: Knowledge, Consciousness, and the Politics of Empowerment*, 2nd ed. New York and London: Routledge

Hochschild, A. R. (1979) 'Emotion Work, Feeling Rules, and Social Structure', *American Journal of Sociology*, 85: 3, 551–575

Hochschild, A. R. (1983) *The Managed Heart: Commercialization of Human Feeling.* Berkeley, Los Angeles and London: University of California Press

Hodge, N. (2008) 'Evaluating Lifeworld as an Emancipatory Methodology', *Disability & Society*, 23: 1, 29–40

Høigård, C. and Finstad, L. (1992) *Backstreets: Prostitution, Money, and Love.* University Park: Pennsylvania State University Press

Holland, J., Ramazanoglu, C., Sharpe, S. and Thomson, R. (1998) *The Male in the Head: Young People, Heterosexuality and Power.* London: Tuffnell Press

Hollomotz, A. (2010) 'Sexual "Vulnerability" of People with Learning Difficulties: A Self-Fulfilling Prophecy', In R. Shuttleworth and T. Sanders (eds) *Sex and Disability: Politics, Identity, and Access.* Leeds: The Disability Press

Hollomotz, A. (2011) *Learning Difficulties and Sexual Vulnerability.* London: Jessica Kingsley

Hollway, W. (1984) 'Gender Difference and the Production of Subjectivity'. In J. Henriques, W. Hollway, C. Venn and V. Walkerdine (eds) *Changing the Subject: Psychology, Social Regulation and Subjectivity.* New York: Methuen

Hollway, W. (1996) 'Gender Difference and the Production of Subjectivity'. In S. Jackson and S. Scott (eds) *Feminism and Sexuality: A Reader.* New York: Columbia University Press

Holt, T. J. and Blevins, K. R. (2007) 'Examining Sex Work from the Client's Perspective: Assessing Johns Using On-Line Data', *Deviant Behavior*, 28, 333–354

Holzman, H. R. and Pines, S. (1982) 'Buying Sex: The Phenomenology of Being a John', *Deviant Behavior*, 4, 89–116

hooks, bell (1981) *Ain't I a Woman: Black Women and Feminism.* Cambridge, MA: Southend Press

Howland, C. A. and Rintala, D. H. (2001) 'Dating Behaviors of Women with Physical Disabilities', *Sexuality and Disability*, 19: 1, 41–70

Huang, S. and Yeoh, B. S. A. (2007) Emotional Labour and Transnational Domestic Work: The Moving Geographies of "Maid Abuse" in Singapore', *Mobilities*, 2: 2, 195–217

Hughes, B. and Paterson, K. (1997) 'The Social Model of Disability and the Disappearing Body: Towards a Sociology of Impairment', *Disability & Society*, 12: 3, 325–340

Hughes, B., McKie, L., Hopkins, D. and Watson, N. (2005) 'Love's Labours Lost? Feminism, the Disabled People's Movement and an Ethic of Care', *Sociology*, 39: 2, 259–275

Hughes, E. and Gray, R. (2009) 'HIV Prevention for People with Serious Mental Illness: A Survey of Mental Health Workers' Attitudes, Knowledge and Practice', *Journal of Clinical Nursing*, 18: 4, 591–600

Humphreys, C. and Thiara, R. (2003) 'Mental Health and Domestic Violence: "I Call it Symptoms of Abuse"', *British Journal of Social Work*, 33: 2, 209–226

Hunt, P. (1981) 'Settling Accounts with the Parasite People: A Critique of *A Life Apart* by E. J. Miller and G. V. Gwynne'. *Disability Challenge*, 1: 37–50

Ignagni, E., Fudge-Schormans, A., Liddiard, K. and Runswick-Cole, K. (2016) 'Some People Aren't Allowed to Love: Intimate Citizenship in the Lives of People Labelled with Intellectual Disabilities', *Disability & Society*, doi: 10.1080/09687599.2015. 1136148

Ingraham, C. (1996) 'The Heterosexual Imaginary'. In S. Seidman (ed.) *Queer Theory/ Sociology*. Oxford: Blackwell, 168–193

Intimaterider.com (2011) *Intimate Rider*. Online. Available from: www.intimaterider. com/ [accessed 14/12/11]

Jackson, S. (1999) *Heterosexuality in Question*. London: Sage

Jackson, S. and Scott, S. (1996) *Feminism and Sexuality: A Reader*. New York: Columbia University Press

Jackson, S. and Scott, S. (1997) 'Gut Reactions to Matters of the Heart: Reflections on Rationality, Irrationality and Sexuality', *Sociological Review*, 45: 4 551–575

Jackson, S. and Scott, S. (2010) *Theorizing Sexuality*. Berkshire: Open University Press

James, N. (1992) 'Care=Organisation+Physical Labour+Emotional Labour', *Sociology of Health and Illness*, 14: 4, 488–509

Janesick, V. J. (1998) 'A Journal About Journal Writing as a Qualitative Research Technique: History, Issues, and Reflections', *Qualitative Inquiry*, 5: 4, 505–524

Jeffreys, J. (1994) 'The Queer Disappearance of Lesbians: Sexuality in the Academy', *Women's Studies International Forum*, 17: 5, 459–472

Jeffreys, S. (2008) 'Disability and the Male Sex Right', *Women's Studies International Forum*, 31, 327–335

Jennes, V. (1990) 'From Sex as Sin to Sex as Work: COYOTE and the Reorganization of Prostitution as a Social Problem', *Social Problems*, 37: 3, 403–420

Jewkes, Y. (2003) *Dot.Cons: Crime, Deviance And Identity on the Internet*. Cullompton: Willan Publishing

Johnson-Bailey, J. (1999) 'The Ties that Bind and the Shackles that Separate: Race, Gender, Class, and Color in a Research Process', *Qualitative Sociology*, 12: 6, 659–670

Jokinen, E. (2004) 'The Makings of Mother in Diary Narratives', *Qualitative Inquiry*, 10: 3, 339–359

Kafer, A. (2003) 'Compulsory Bodies: Reflections on Heterosexuality and Able-Bodiedness', *Journal of Women's History*, 15: 3, 77–89

Kafer, A. (2013) *Feminist Queer Crip*. Bloomington and Indianapolis: Indiana University Press

Kang, M. (2010) *The Managed Hand: Race, Gender, and the Body in Beauty Service Work*. Berkeley: University of California Press

Kanguade, G. (2010) 'Advancing Sexual Health of Persons with Disabilities through Sexual Rights: The Challenge'. In R. Shuttleworth and T. Sanders (eds) *Sex and Disability: Politics, Identity, and Access*. Leeds: The Disability Press

Kantola, J. and Squires, J. (2004) 'Discourses Surrounding Prostitution Policies in the UK', *European Journal of Women's Studies*, 11: 1, 77–101

Kaufman, M., Silverberg, C. and Odette, F. (2003) *The Ultimate Guide to Sex and Disability: For All of Us Who Live with Disabilities, Chronic Pain and Illness*. San Francisco, CA: Cleis Press

Keith, L. (1990) 'Caring Partnership', *Community Care*, 22 February, v–vi

Keith, L. (1996) 'Encounters with Strangers: The Public's Responses to Disabled Women and how this Affects our Sense of Self'. In J. Morris (ed.) *Encounters with Strangers: Feminism and Disability*. London: Women's Press

Keith, L. and Morris, J. (1995) 'Easy Targets: A Disability Rights Perspective on the "Children as Carers" Debate'. In J. Morris (ed.) *Encounters with Strangers: Feminism and Disability*. London: Women's Press

Kelly, M. P. and Field, D. (1996) 'Medical Sociology, Chronic Illness and the Body', *Sociology of Health and Illness*, 18: 2, 241–257

Kent, D. (2002) 'Beyond Expectations: Being Blind and Becoming a Mother', *Sexuality and Disability*, 20: 1, 81–88

Kennedy, E. L. and Davis, M. D. (1993) *Boots of Leather, Slippers of Gold: The History of a Lesbian Community*. New York: Routledge

Kenway, J. and McLeod, J. (2004) 'Bourdieu's Reflexive Sociology and "Spaces of Points of View": Whose Reflexivity, Which Perspective?' *British Journal of Sociology of Education*, 25: 4, 525–544

Kim, E. (2011) 'Asexuality in Disability Narratives', *Sexualities*, 14: 4, 479–493

Kimmel, M. (2007) *The Sexual Self: The Construction of Sexual Scripts*. Nashville: Vanderbilt University Press

Kinsey, A. C. (1953) *Sexual Behavior in the Human Female*. London: W. B. Saunders

Kinsey A. C., Pomeroy W. B. and Martin C. E. (1948) *Sexual Behavior in the Human Male*. Philadelphia: W. B. Saunders

Kitchen, R. (2000) 'The Researched Opinions on Research: Disabled People and Disability Research', *Disability & Society*, 15: 1, 25–47

Kitchin, R. (2000) 'The Researched Opinions on Research: Disabled People and Disability Research', *Disability & Society*, 15: 1, 25–47

Kitchin, R. (2001) 'Using Participatory Action Research Approaches in Geographical Studies of Disability: Some Reflections', *Disability Studies Quarterly*, 24: 4, 61–69

Kleinman, S. and Copp, M. A (1993) *Emotions and Fieldwork*. Chapel Hill: University of North Carolina Press

Koch, T. (2000) 'Life Quality vs the "Quality of Life": Assumptions Underlying Prospective Quality of Life Instruments in Health Care Planning', *Social Science & Medicine*, 51: 3, 419–427

Kohrman, M. (2008) 'Grooming Quezi: Marriage Exclusion and Identity Formation Among Disabled Men in Contemporary China', *American Ethnologist*, 26: 4, 890–909

Kolárová, K. (2010) 'Performing the Pain: Opening the (Crip) Body for (Queer) Pleasures', *Review of Disability Studies*, 6: 3, 44–52

Komisaruk, B. R., Beyer, C. and Whipple, B. (2006) *The Science of the Orgasm*. Liverpool: Johns Hopkins University Press

Korczynski, M. (2003) 'Communities of Coping: Collective Emotional Labour in Service Work', *Organization*, 10: 1, 55–79

Krafft-Ebing, R. V. (1899) *Psychopathia Sexualis: With Especial Reference to Antipathetic Sexual Instincts: A Medico-Forensic Study*. London: Rebman

Krotoski, D. M., Nosek, M. A. and Turk, M. A (eds) (1996) *Women with Physical Disabilities: Achieving and Maintaining Health and Well-being*. Baltimore, MD: Paul H. Brooks

Kulick, D. and Rydström, J. (2015) *Loneliness and its Opposite: Sex, Disability and the Ethics of Engagement*. Durham: Duke University Press

Lancaster, R. N. (2003) *The Trouble with Nature: Sex in Science and Popular Culture*. Berkeley: University of California Press

Langellier, K. (2001) ' "You're Marked": Breast Cancer, Tattoo and the Narrative Performance of Identity.' In J. Brockmeier and D. Carbaugh (eds) *Narrative and Identity: Studies in Autobiography, Self, and Culture.* Amsterdam and Philadelphia: John Benjamins

Laurier, E. and Parr, H. (1999) 'Emotions and Interviewing, Environment', *Ethics and Place*, 3: 1, 98–102

Laws, J. L. and Schwartz, P. (1977) *Sexual Scripts: The Social Construction of Female Sexuality.* Hinsdale, IL: Dryden

Laxton, C. and Goldworthy, A. (2008) *Up Close and Personal: A Report into Disabled and Non Disabled People's Attitudes and Experiences of Relationships in the UK.* London: Leonard Cheshire Disability

LeCompte, M. D. (1993) 'A Framework for Hearing Silence: What Does Telling Stories Mean When We are Supposed to be Doing Science?' In D. McLaughlin and W. G. Tierney (eds) *Naming Silenced Lives: Personal Narratives and Processes of Educational Change.* New York: Routledge, 9–28

LeFrançois, F., Menzies, R. and Reaume, G. (2013) *Mad Matters: A Critical Reader in Canadian Mad Studies.* Toronto: Canadian Scholars' Press

LeMoncheck, L. (1997). *Loose Women, Lecherous Men: A Feminist Philosophy of Sex.* New York: Oxford University Press

Leder, D. (1990) *The Absent Body.* Chicago and London: University of Chicago Press

Lee, O. E. K. and Heykyung, O. (2005) 'A Wise Wife and Good Mother: Reproductive Health and Maternity Among Women with Disability in South Korea', *Sexuality and Disability*, 23: 3, 121–144

Lee, R. M. (1993) *Doing Research on Sensitive Topics.* London: Sage Publications

Lee, R. and Renzetti, C. (1993) *Researching Sensitive Topics.* London: Sage Publications

Lee, S. (2016) 'Changing Position: An Exploration of the Meaning of Sexual Well-being for Physically Disabled People'. PhD thesis, Bournemouth University, Faculty of Health & Social Sciences

Lee-Treweek, G. (1996) 'Emotion Work, Order and Emotional Power in Care Assistant Work', in V. James and J. Gabe (eds) *Health and the Sociology of Emotions.* Oxford: Blackwell

Lee-Treweek G. (1997) 'Women, Resistance and Care: An Ethnography of Nursing Auxiliary Work', *Work, Employment and Society*, 11: 1, 47–63

Lees, S. (2000) 'Sexuality and Citizenship Education'. In. M. Arnot and J. Dillabough (eds) *Challenging Democracy: Feminist Perspectives on the Education of Citizens.* London: Taylor & Francis

Leibowitz, R. Q. (2005) 'Sexual Rehabilitation Services after Spinal Cord Injury: What do Women Want? *Sexuality and Disability*, 23: 2, 81–107

Leonard Cheshire Disability (2011) *In Touch.* Online. Available from: www.lcdisability. org/?lid=9439 [accessed 4/9/11]

Levinson, J. (2010) *Making Life Work: Freedom and Disability in a Community Group Home.* Minneapolis: University of Minnesota Press

Li, C. M. and Yau, M. K. (2006) 'Sexual Issues and Concerns: Tales of Chinese Women with Spinal Cord Impairments', *Sexuality and Disability*, 24: 1, 1–26

Liddiard, K. (2013) 'Reflections on the Process of Researching Disabled People's Sexual Lives', *Social Research Online*, 18: 3, 10

Liddiard, K. (2014a) ' "I Never Felt Like She Was Just Doing it for the Money": The Intimate (Gendered) Realities of Purchasing Sexual Pleasure and Intimacy', *Sexualities*, 17: 7, 837–855

Liddiard, K. (2014b) 'Liking for Like's Sake: The Commodification of Disability on Facebook', *Journal of Developmental Disabilities*, 20: 3, 94–101

Liddiard, K. (2014c) 'The Work of Disabled Identities in Intimate Relationships', *Disability & Society*, 29: 1, 115–128, doi: 10.1080/09687599.2013.776486

Liddiard, K. and Goodley, D. (2016) 'The Mouth and Dis/Ability', *Community Dental Health*, special issue, 33, 152–155

Liddiard, K. and Goodley, D. (in press) 'Disability and Impairment'. In B. Turner *et al.* (eds) *Encyclopedia of Social Theory*. London: Wiley

Liddiard, K. and Jones, L. (2017) 'A Diversity of Crip Childhoods? Considering the Looked After Childhood'. In K. Runswick-Cole, T. Curran and K. Liddiard (eds) *The Palgrave Handbook of Disabled Children's Childhood Studies*. Basingstoke: Palgrave.

Liddiard, K. and Slater, J. (2017) ' "Like, Pissing Yourself is not a Particularly Attractive Quality, Let's be Honest": Learning to Contain through Youth, Adulthood, Disability and Sexuality', *Sexualities*, special issue, *Disability and Sexual Corporeality*

Light, R. (2000) 'Disability Theory: Social Model or Unsociable Muddle?' *Disability Tribune*, December/January, 10–13

Lindsay, W. R. *et al.* (1998) 'The Treatment of Six Men with a Learning Disability Convicted of Sex Offences with Children', *British Journal of Clinical Psychology*, 37: 1, 83–98

Lloyd, M. *et al.* (1996) 'Whose Project is it Anyway? Sharing and Shaping the Research and Development Agenda', *Disability & Society*, 11: 3, 301–315

Lloyd, M. (2001) 'The Politics of Disability and Feminism: Discord or Synbook?' *Sociology*, 35: 3, 715–728

Loach, K. (dir.) (2016) *I, Daniel Blake*. United Kingdom, France, Germany, Belgium: Sixteen Films, Why Not Productions, Wild Bunch

Löfgren-Mårtenson, L. (2009) 'The Invisibility of Young Homosexual Women and Men with Intellectual Disabilities', *Sexuality and Disability*, 27: 1, 21–26

Lonsdale, S. (1990) *Women and Disability: The Experience of Disability Among Women*. Basingstoke: Macmillan

Lorde, A. (1982) *Chosen Poems: Old and New*. New York: W. W. Norton Publishing

Lorde, A. (2007) *Sister Outsider: Essays & Speeches by Audre Lorde*. Berkeley: Crossing Press

Lunsky, Y. *et al.* (2007) 'Sexual Knowledge and Attitudes of Men with Intellectual Disability who Sexually Offend', *Journal of Intellectual and Developmental Disability*, 32: 2, 74–81

Lupton, D. (1996) 'Constructing the Menopausal Body: The Discourses on Hormone Replacement Therapy', *Body and Society*, 2: 1, 91–97

McCabe, M. P., Cummins, R. A. and Deeks, A. A. (2000) 'Sexuality and Quality of Life Among People with Physical Disability', Sexuality *and Disability*, 18: 2, 115–123

McCabe, M. P. and Taleporos, G. (2003) 'Sexual Esteem, Sexual Satisfaction, and Sexual Behavior Among People with Physical Disability', *Archives of Sexual Behavior*, 32: 4, 359–369

McCarthy, M. (1996) 'The Sexual Support of People with Learning Disabilities: A Profile of Those Referred to Sex Education', *Sexuality and Disability*, 14: 4, 265–279

McCarthy, M. (1998) 'Interviewing People with Learning Disabilities about Sensitive Topics: A Discussion of Ethical Issues', *British Journal of Learning Disabilities*, 24: 4, 140–145

McCarthy, M. (1999) *Sexuality and Women with Learning Disabilities*. London: Jessica Kingsley Publishers

McCarthy, M. (2009) 'Contraception and Women with Intellectual Disabilities', *Journal of Applied Research in Intellectual Disabilities*, 22, 363–369

McCarthy, M. and Thompson, D. (1996) 'Sexual Abuse by Design: An Examination of the Issues in Learning Disability Services', *Disability & Society*, 11: 2, 205–217

McClelland, A., Flicker, S., Nepveux, D., Nixon, S., Vo, T., Wilson, C. *et al.* (2012) 'Seeking Safer Sexual Spaces: Queer and Trans Young People Labeled with Intellectual Disabilities and the Paradoxical Risks of Restriction', *Journal of Homosexuality* 59: 6, 808–819

McCorkel, J. A. and Myers, K. (2003) 'What Difference Does Difference Make? Position and Privilege in the Field', *Qualitative Sociology* 26, 199–232

McCormick, N. B. (1999) 'When Pleasure Causes Pain: Living with Interstitial Cystitis', *Sexuality and Disability*, 17: 1, 7–18

McKeganey, N. and Barnard, M. (1996) *Sex Work on the Streets*. Buckingham: Open University Press

McLaughlin, D. and Tierney, W. G. (1993) *Naming Silenced Lives: Personal Narratives and Processes of Educational Change*. New York: Routledge

McRuer, R. (2002) 'Critical Investments: AIDS, Christopher Reeve, and Queer/Disability Studies', *Journal of Medical Humanities*, 23: 3, 221–237

McRuer, R. (2006a) *Crip Theory: Cultural Signs of Queerness and Disability*. New York and London: New York University Press

McRuer, R. (2006b) 'We Were Never Identified: Feminism, Queer Theory, and a Disabled World', *Radical History Review*, 94, 148–154

Mairs, N. (1996) *Waist-High in the World: A Life Among the Nondisabled*. Boston: Beacon

Marks, D. (1997) 'Models of Disability', *Disability and Rehabilitation*, 19: 3, 85–91

Marks, D. (1999) 'Dimensions of Oppression: Theorising the Embodied Subject', *Disability & Society*, 14: 5, 611–626

Marshall, B. and Katz, S. (2002) 'Forever Functional: Sexual Fitness and the Ageing Male Body', *Body & Society*, 8; 4, 43–70

Martino, A. S. (2017) Cripping Sexualities: An Analytic Review of Theoretical and Empirical Writing on the Intersection of Disabilities and Sexualities', *Sociology Compass*, 11: 5, 1–15

Mason, M. (1992) 'A Nineteen-Parent Family'. In J. Morris (ed.) *Alone Together: Voices of Single Mothers*. London: Women's Press

Masters, W. H. and Johnson V. E. (1966) *Human Sexual Response*. Boston, MA: Little, Brown

Masters, W. H. and Johnson, V. E. (1974) *The Pleasure Bond*. Toronto and New York: Bantam Books

Masters, W. H. and Johnson, V. E. (1986) *On Sex and Human Loving*. Boston, MA: Little, Brown

Meadows-Klue, D. (2008) 'Opinion Piece: Falling in Love 2.0: Relationship Marketing for the Facebook Generation', *Journal of Direct, Data and Digital Marketing Practice*, 9, 245–250

Meekosha, H. (1998) 'Body Battles: Bodies, Gender and Disability'. In T. Shakespeare (ed.) *The Disability Reader*. London: Continuum

Meekosha, H. and Shuttleworth, R. (2009) 'What's so "Critical" about Critical Disability Studies?' *Australian Journal of Human Rights*, 15: 1, 47–76

Meekosha, H. and Soldatic, K. (2011) 'Human Rights and the Global South: The Case of Disability', *Third World Quarterly*, 32: 8, 1383–1397

Merleau-Ponty, M. (1962) *The Phenomenology of Perception*. London: Routledge

Michalko, R. (2002) *The Difference that Disability Makes.* Philadelphia, PA: Temple University Press

Michie, A. M. *et al.* (2006) 'A Test of Counterfeit Deviance: A Comparison of Sexual Knowledge in Groups of Sex Offenders with Intellectual Disability and Controls', *Sexual Abuse: A Journal of Research and Treatment*, 18: 3, 271–278

Milberger S., Israel N., LeRoy B., and Martin A. (2003) 'Violence against Women with Physical Disabilities', *Violence and Victims*, 18: 5, 581–591

Milligan, M. and Neufeldt, A. (2001) 'The Myth of Asexuality: A Survey of Social and Empirical Evidence', *Sexuality and Disability*, 4, 91–109

Mills, C. (in press). ' "Dead People Don't Claim": A Psychopolitical Autopsy of UK Austerity Suicides'. *Critical Social Policy*

Millward, L. J. (1995) 'Contextualising Social Identity in Considerations of What it Means to be a Nurse', *European Journal of Psychology*, 25, 303–324

Mona, L. R. (2003) 'Using Personal Assistance Services for Sexual Expression'. In M. Banks and E. Kaschak (eds) *Women with Visible and Invisible Disabilities: Multiple Intersections, Multiple Issues, Multiple Therapies.* London: Routledge

Mona, L. R., Gardos, P. S. and Brown, R. C. (1994) 'Sexual Self Views of Women with Disabilities: The Relationship Among Age-of-Onset, Nature of Disability and Sexual Self-Esteem', *Sexuality and Disability*, 12: 4, 261–277

Monto, M. A. (2000) 'Why Men Seek out Prostitutes'. In R. Weitzer (ed.) *Sex for Sale.* London: Routledge

Morris, J. (1989) *Able Lives: Women's Experience of Paralysis.* London: Women's Press

Morris, J. (1991) *Pride Against Prejudice: Transforming Attitudes to Disability.* Philadelphia, PA: New Society Publishers

Morris, J. (1992) *Alone Together: Voices of Single Mothers.* London: Women's Press

Morris, J. (1993) *Independent Lives? Community Care and Disabled People.* London: Macmillan

Morris, J. (1996) *Encounters with Strangers: Feminism and Disability.* London: Women's Press

Morris, J. (1997) 'Care or Empowerment? A Disability Rights Perspective', *Social Policy and Administration*, 31: 1, 54–60

Morris, J. (1998) 'Feminism, Gender and Disability'. Paper presented at a seminar in Sydney, Australia: February. Available from: http://pf7d7vi404s1dxh27mla5569.wpengine.netdna-cdn.com/files/library/morris-gender-and-disability.pdf

Morris, J. (2001) 'Impairment and Disability: Constructing an Ethics of Care That Promotes Human Rights', *Hypatia*, 16: 4, 1–16

Murphy, R. (1990) *The Body Silent.* New York: W. W. Norton

Neal, S. (1999) 'Researching Powerful People from a Feminist and Anti-racist Perspective: A Note on Gender, Collusion and Marginality', *British Educational Research Journal*, 21: 4, 517–531

Nelson, D. (2007) 'Women, Sex and Disability – A Triple Taboo', *Disability Knowledge and Research*, 1–2, London: HealthLink Worldwide

Nicolson, N. and Burr, J. (2003) 'What is "Normal" about Women's (Hetero)Sexual Desire and Orgasm? A Report of an in-Depth Interview Study', *Social Science & Medicine*, 57, 1735–1745

Noonan, R .J. (1984) 'Sex Surrogates: A Clarification Of Their Functions'. MA dissertation, New York University, Department of Health Education, School of Education, Health, Nursing, and Arts Professions

Nosek, M. (2001) 'Vulnerabilities for Abuse Among Women with Disabilities', *Sexuality and Disability*, 19: 3, 177–190

O'Brien, M. (1990) 'On Seeing a Sex Surrogate', *The Sun*, May, no. 174

O'Callaghan, A. C. and Murphy, G. H. (2007) 'Sexual Relationships in Adults with Intellectual Disabilities: Understanding the Law', *Journal of Intellectual Disability Research*, 51: 3, 197–206

O'Connell-Davidson, J. (1998) *Prostitution, Power and Freedom*. Cambridge: Polity

O'Connell-Davidson, J. (2002) 'The Rights and Wrongs of Prostitution', *Hypatia*, 17: 2, 84–98

O'Connell-Davidson, J. (2003) 'Sleeping with the Enemy'? Some Problems with Feminist Abolitionist Calls to Penalise those who Buy Commercial Sex', *Social Policy and Society*, 2: 1, 55–64

O'Toole, C. J. (2000) 'The View from Below: Developing a Knowledge Base About an Unknown Population', *Sexuality and Disability*, 18: 3, 207–224

O'Toole, C. (2002) 'Sex, Disability and Motherhood: Access to Sexuality for Disabled Mothers', *Disability Studies Quarterly*, 22: 4, 87–108

O'Toole, C. J. and Doe, T. (2002) 'Sexuality and Disabled Parents with Disabled Children', *Sexuality and Disability*, 20; 1, 89–101

Oakley, A. (1993) *Essays on Women, Medicine and Health*. Edinburgh: Edinburgh University Press

Ogbonna, E. and Harris, L. C. (2004) 'Work Intensification and Emotional Labour Among UK University Lecturers: An Exploratory Study', *Organization Studies*, 25: 7, 1185–1203

Ogden, C. (2013) 'Surveillance of the Leaky Child. No-body's Normal but That Doesn't Stop Us Trying'. In C. Ogden and S. Wakeman. (eds) *Corporeality: The Body and Society*. Chester: Chester University Press

Oleksy, E. H. (2009) *Intimate Citizenships: Gender, Sexualities, Politics*. London: Routledge

Oliver, M. (1990) *The Politics of Disablement*. Basingstoke: Macmillian

Oliver, M. (1992) 'Changing the Social Relations of Research Production', *Disability & Society*, 11, 115–120

Oliver, M. (1996) *Understanding Disability: From Theory to Practice*. Basingstoke: Macmillan

Oliver, M. (1997) 'Emancipatory Research: Realistic Goal or Impossible Dream?' In C. Barnes and G. Mercer (eds) *Doing Disability Research*. Leeds: The Disability Press

Oliver, M. and Barnes, C. (1997) 'All We Are Saying is Give Disabled Researchers a Chance', *Disability & Society*, 12: 5, 811–813

Olkin, R. (2002) 'Could you Hold the Door for Me? Including Disability in Diversity', *Cultural Diversity and Ethnic Minority Psychology*, 8: 2, 130–137

Olsen, R. and Clarke, H. (2003) *Parenting and Disability: Disabled Parents' Experiences of Raising Children*. Bristol: Policy Press

Oriel, J. (2005) 'Sexual Pleasure as a Human Right: Harmful or Helpful to Women in the Context of HIV/AIDS?' *Women's Studies International Forum*, 28, 392–404

Ostrander, N. (2009) 'Sexual Pursuits of Pleasure Among Men and Women with Spinal Cord Injuries', *Sexuality and Disability*, 27, 11–19

Outshoorn, J. (2001) 'Debating Prostitution in Parliament: A Feminist Analysis', *European Journal of Women's Studies*, 8: 4, 472–490

Outsiders (2011) *Free Speech Campaign 2009*. Online. Available from: www.outsiders.org.uk [accessed 23/11/11]

Overboe, J. (2007) 'Disability and Genetics: Affirming the Bare Life (the State of Exception)', *Canadian Review of Sociology and Anthropology*, 44: 2, 220–235

Parckar, G. (2008) *Disability Poverty in the UK*. London: Leonard Cheshire Disability

Parker, G. (1993) 'A Four-Way Stretch? The Politics of Disability and Caring'. In J. Swain *et al.* (eds) *Disabling Barriers: Enabling Environments*. London: Sage

Parker, M. G. and Yau, M. K. (2012) 'Sexuality, Identity and Women with Spinal Cord Injury', *Sexuality and Disability*, 30: 1, 15–27

Pateman, C. (1988) *The Sexual Contract*. Cambridge: Polity

Paterson, K. and Hughes, B. (1999) 'Disability Studies and Phenomenology: The Carnal Politics of Everyday Life', *Disability & Society*, 14: 5, 597–610

Patsavas, A. (2014) 'Recovering a Cripistemology of Pain: Leaky Bodies, Connective Tissue, and Feeling Discourse', *Journal of Literary & Cultural Disability Studies*, 8, 203–218

Pearson, V. and Klook, A. (1989) 'Sexual Behaviour Following Paraplegia: An Exploratory Study in Hong Kong', *Disability & Society*, 4: 4, 285–295

Peng, Y. W. (2007) 'Buying Sex: Domination and Difference in the Discourses of Taiwanese Piao-ke', *Men and Masculinities*, 9: 3, 315–336

Perry, B. L. and Wright, E. R. (2006) 'The Sexual Partnerships of People with Serious Mental Illness', *Journal of Sex Research*, 43: 2, 174–181

Petchesky, R. P. (2000) 'Rights and Needs: Rethinking the Connections in Debates over Reproductive and Sexual Rights', *Health and Human Rights*, 4: 2, 17–29

Phillips, S. (2010) 'Disability, Masculinity, and Sexuality in Post-Soviet Ukraine'. In R. Shuttleworth and T. Sanders (eds) *Sex and Disability: Politics, Identity, and Access*. Leeds: The Disability Press

Pierce, J. L. (1995) *Gender Trials: Emotional Lives in Contemporary Law Firms*. Berkeley: University of California Press

Plummer, K. (1975) *Sexual Stigma: An Interactionist Account*. London: Routledge & Kegan Paul

Plummer, K. (1995) *Telling Sexual Stories: Power, Change and Social Worlds*. London: Routledge

Plummer, K. (2003) *Intimate Citizenship: Private Decision and Public Dialogues*. Seattle and London: University of Washington Press

Plummer, K. (2008) 'Studying Sexualities for a Better World? Ten Years of Sexualities', *Sexualities*, 11: 1–2, 7–22

Plummer, K. (2015) *Cosmopolitan Sexualities: Hope and the Humanist Imagination*. Cambridge: Polity Press

Pole, C. J. and Lampard, R. (2002) *Practical Social Investigation: Qualitative and Quantitative Methods in Social Research*. Essex: Pearson

Potts, A. (2000) ' "The Essence of the Hard On": Hegemonic Masculinity and the Cultural Construction of "Erectile Dysfunction" ', *Men and Masculinities*, 3: 1, 85–103

Potgieter, C. A. and Khan, G. (2005) 'Sexual Self-esteem and Body Image of South African Spinal Cord Injured Adolescents', *Sex and Disability*, 23: 1, 1–20

Pothier, D. and Devlin, R. (2006) *Critical Disability Theory: Essays in Philosophy, Politics, Policy, and Law*. London: UBC Press

Poulton, E. (2012) ' "If You Had Balls, You'd Be One of Us!" Doing Gendered Research: Methodological Reflections on Being a Female Academic Researcher in the Hyper-Masculine Subculture of "Football Hooliganism" ', *Sociological Research Online*, 17: 4, 4. Available from: www.socresonline.org.uk/17/4/4.html

Powers, L. E., Curry, M. A., Oschwald, M., Maley, S., Saxton, M. and Eckels, K. (2002) 'Barriers and Strategies in Addressing Abuse: A Survey of Disabled Women's Experiences', *Journal of Rehabilitation*, 68: 1, 4–13

Prillelltensky, O. (2003) 'A Ramp to Motherhood: The Experiences of Mothers with Physical Disabilities', *Sexuality and Disability*, 21: 1, 21–47

ProjectDisHuman (2015) *A DisHuman Manifesto*. Online. Available from https://dishuman.com/dishuman-manifesto-elaborated-version/ [accessed 22/7/2017]

ProjectDisHuman (forthcoming) 'A DisHuman Manifesto'. In R. Garland-Thompson, M. Kent, K. Ellis and R. Robertson (eds) *Manifestos for the Future of Critical Disability Studies*. Abingdon: Routledge

Quarmby, K. (2011) *Scapegoat: Why We Are Failing Disabled People*. London: Portobello Press

Ramazanoglu, C. (1993) *Up Against Foucault*. London: Routledge

Raymond, J. G. (2004) 'Prostitution on Demand: Legalizing the Buyers as Sexual Consumers', *Violence Against Women*, 10: 10, 1156–1186

Razack, S. (1998) *Looking White People in the Eye: Gender, Race, and Culture in Courtrooms and Classrooms*. Toronto: University of Toronto Press

Reeve, D. (2002) 'Negotiating Psycho-emotional Dimensions of Disability and their Influence on Identity Constructions', *Disability & Society*, 17: 5, 493–508

Reeve, D. (2004) 'Psycho-emotional Dimensions of Disability and the Social Model'. In C. Barnes and G. Mercer (eds) *Implementing the Social Model of Disability: Theory and Research*. Leeds: The Disability Press

Reeve, D. (2008) 'Negotiating Disability in Everyday Life: The Experience of Psycho-Emotional Disablism', PhD thesis, Lancaster University

Reich, J. A. (2003) 'Pregnant with Possibility: Reflections on Embodiment, Access, and Inclusion in Field Research', *Qualitative Sociology*, 26: 3, 351–367

Reinharz, S. (1992) *Feminist Methods in Social Research*. Cary, NC: Oxford University Press

Reiter, R. (1975) *Toward an Anthropology of Women*. New York: Monthly Review Press

Rembis, M. A. (2010) 'Beyond the Binary: Rethinking the Social Model of Disabled Sexuality', *Sexuality and Disability*, 28, 51–60

Renzetti, C. M. (1993) *Researching Sensitive Topics*. California: Sage Publications

Reynolds, D. (2007) 'Disability and BDSM: Bob Flanagan and the Case for Sexual Rights', *Sexuality Research & Social Policy*, 4: 1, 40–52

Reynolds, P. (2010) 'Disentangling Privacy and Intimacy: Intimate Citizenship, Private Boundaries and Public Transgressions', *Human Affairs*, 20, 33–42

Rice, C. (2009). 'Imagining the Other? Ethical Challenges of Researching and Writing Women's Embodied Lives', *Feminism & Psychology*, 19: 2, 245–266

Rice, C., Chandler, E., Harrison, E. Liddiard, K. and Ferrari, M. (2015) 'Project Re•Vision: Disability at the Edges of Representation', *Disability & Society*, 30: 4, 513–527

Rice, C., Chandler, E., Harrison, E. Liddiard, K. and Rinaldi, J. (2016) 'Pedagogical Possibilities for Unruly Bodies', *Gender and Education* online. doi: 10.1080/09540253.2016.1247947

Rice, C., Chandler, E., Rinaldi, J., Changfoot, N., Liddiard, K., Mykitiuk, R., Mundel, I. (2017) 'Imagining Disability Futurities', *Hypatia*, 32: 2, 213–229

Rich, A. (1989) 'Compulsory Heterosexuality and Lesbian Existence'. In L. Richardson and V. Taylor (Eds) *Feminist Frontiers II: Rethinking Sex, Gender and Society*. New York: Random House

Richardson, D. (1996) *Theorising Sexuality*. Buckingham, UK: Open University

Richardson, D. (1998) 'Sexuality and Citizenship', *Sociology*, 32: 1, 83–100

Richardson, D. (2000) 'Constructing Sexual Citizenship: Theorizing Sexual Rights', *Critical Social Policy*, 20: 1, 105–135

Richardson J. T. (1996) *Handbook of Qualitative Research Methods for Psychology and the Social Sciences*. Leicester: BPS Books

Richardson, L. and Taylor, V. (1989) *Feminist Frontiers II: Rethinking Sex, Gender and Society*. New York: Random House

Riessman, C, K. (2003) 'Narrative Analysis', In M. S. Lewis-Beck, A. Bryman and T. Futing Liao (eds) *The Sage Encyclopedia of Social Science Research Methods*, vol. 3. London: Sage

Rintala, D.H. *et al.* (1997) 'Dating Issues for Women with Physical Disabilities', *Sexuality and Disability*, 15: 4, 219–242

Rioux, M. and Bach, M. (1994) *Disability is Not Measles: New Directions in Disability*. Ontario: L'Institut Roeher

Roberts, H. (1981) *Doing Feminist Research*. London: Routledge & Kegan Paul

Rock, P. J. (1996) 'Eugenics and Euthanasia: A Cause for Concern for Disabled People, Particularly Disabled Women', *Disability & Society*, 11: 1, 121–127

Rogers, C. (2009) '(S)excerpts from a Life Told: Sex, Gender and Learning Disability', *Sexualities*, 12: 3, 270–288

Rohleder, P., Swartz, L., Kalichman, S.and Simbayi, L. (2009). *HIV/AIDS in South Africa 25 Years on: Psychosocial Perspectives*. New York: Springer

Rohrer, J. (2005) 'Toward a Full-Inclusion Feminism: A Feminist Deployment of Disability Analysis', *Feminist Studies*, 31: 1, 34–63

Rose, N. (1998) *Inventing Our Selves: Psychology, Power, and Personhood*. Cambridge: Cambridge University Press

Rose, N. (2001) 'The Politics of Life Itself', *Theory, Culture and Society* 18: 6, 1–30

Rossi, L. M. (2007) Outdoor Pornification: Advertising Heterosexuality on the Streets'. In S. Paasonen, K. Nikunen and L. Saarenmaa (Eds), *Pornification: Sex and Sexuality in Media Culture*. Oxford: Berg

Roulstone, A., Thomas, P. and Balderston, S. (2011) 'Between Hate and Vulnerability: Unpacking the British Criminal Justice System's Construction of Disablist Hate Crime', *Disability & Society*, 26: 3, 351–364

Rubin, G. (1975) 'The Traffic in Women: Notes on the "Political Economy" of Sex'. In R. Reiter (ed.) *Toward an Anthropology of Women*. New York: Monthly Review Press

Runswick-Cole, K., Curran, T. and Liddiard, K. (eds) (in press) *The Palgrave Handbook of Disabled Children's Childhood Studies*. Basingstoke: Palgrave Macmillan

Ryan, G. W. and Bernard, H. R. (2003) 'Techniques to Identify Themes', *Field Methods*, 15, 85–109

Ryan-Flood, R. and Gill, R. (2009) *Secrecy and Silence in the Research Process: Feminist Reflections*. Abingdon and New York: Routledge

Sabo, D. and Gordon, D. (1995) *Men's Health and Illness*. London: Sage

Sakellariou, D. (2006) 'If not the Disability, Then What? Barriers to Reclaiming Sexuality Following Spinal Cord Injury', *Sexuality and Disability*, 24, 101–111

Sakellariou, D. and Algado, S. A. (2006) 'Sexuality and Disability: A Case of Occupational Injustice', *British Journal of Occupational Therapy*, 69: 2, 69–76

Sakellariou, D. and Sawada, Y. (2006) 'Sexuality After Spinal Cord Injury: The Greek Male's Perspective', *American Journal of Occupational Therapy*, 60, 311–319

Samuels, E. (2002) 'Judith Butler's Body Theory and the Question of Disability', *NWSA Journal*, 14: 3, 58–76

Sandahl, C. (2003) 'Queering the Crip or Cripping the Queer? Intersections of Queer and Crip Identities in Solo Autobiographical Performance', *GLQ: A Journal of Lesbian and Gay Studies*, 9: 1, 25–56

Sanders, T. (2005) *Sex Work: A Risky Business*. Cullompton: Willan Publishing

Sanders, T. (2007) 'The Politics of Sexual Citizenship: Commercial Sex and Disability', *Disability & Society*, 22: 5, 439–455

Sanders, T. (2008) *Paying for Pleasure: Men Who Buy Sex*. Cullompton: Willan Publishing

Sanders, T. (2010) 'Sexual Citizenship, Sexual Facilitation and the Right to Pleasure'. In R. Shuttleworth and T. Sanders (eds) *Sex and Disability: Politics, Identity, and Access*. Leeds: The Disability Press

Sandoval, C. (1991) 'US Third World Feminism: The Theory and Method of Oppositional Consciousness in the Postmodern World', *Genders*, 10, 1–24

Scarry, E. (1985) *The Body in Pain*. Oxford: Oxford University Press

Scherrer, K. S. (2008) 'Coming to an Asexual Identity: Negotiating Identity, Negotiating Desire', *Sexualities*, 1: 5, 621–641

Schilt, K. (2011) *Just One of the Guys? Transgender Men and the Persistence of Gender Inequality*. Chicago: University of Chicago Press

School of ICASA (2011) *Fear of Intimacy*. Online. Available from: www.icasa.co.uk/ [accessed 14/11/11]

Schriempft, A. (2001) '(Re)fusing the Amputated Body: An Interactionist Bridge for Feminism and Disability', *Hypatia*, 16: 4, 53–79

Schuchardt, M. (2012) 'Pornification of Everyday Life'. In M. Kosut (ed.) *Encyclopedia of Gender in Media*. New York: SAGE Publications

Scoular, J. and O'Neill, M. 2007, 'Regulating Prostitution: Social Inclusion, Responsibilisation and the Politics of Prostitution Reform', *British Journal of Criminology*, 47: 5, 764–778

Seidler, V. J. (1992) *Men, Sex and Relationships: Writings from Achilles Heel*. Abingdon: Routledge

Sexual Freedom Coalition (2008) *Sexual Freedom Coalition*. Online. Available from: www.sfc.org.uk/about-2/ [accessed 4/12/11]

Sexual Health and Disability Alliance (2011) *Sexual Health and Disability Alliance*. Online. Available from: www.shada.org.uk/ [accessed 1/12/11]

Sexual Offences (Amendment) Act 2000 (c. 44) UK: Stationery Office Limited

Sexual Offences (Amendment) Act 2003 (c. 42) UK: Stationery Office Limited

Sexuality Alliance (2015) *Talking About Sex, Sexuality and Relationships: Guidance and Standards. For Those Working with Young People with Life-Limiting or Life-Threatening Conditions*. London: Open University/Together for Short Lives

Seymour, W. S. (2001) 'In the Flesh or Online? Exploring Qualitative Research Methodologies', *Qualitative Research*, 1: 2, 147–168

Seymour, J. (1994) '"It's Different from Being Loving": Disablement, Caring and Marriage', BSA Conference paper

Shah, S., Tsitsou, L. and Woodin, S. (2016) 'Hidden Voices: Disabled Women's Experiences of Violence and Support Over the Lifecourse', *Violence Against Women*, 22: 10, 1189–1210

Shakespeare, T. (1994) 'Cultural Representation of Disabled People: Dustbins for Disavowal?' *Disability & Society*, 9: 3, 283–299

Shakespeare, T. (1996) 'Power and Prejudice: Issues of Gender, Sexuality and Disability'. In L. Barton (ed.) *Disability and Society: Emerging Issues and Insights*. Harlow: Longman

Shakespeare, T. (1997) 'Researching Disabled Sexuality'. In. C. Barnes and G. Mercer (eds) *Doing Disability Research*. Leeds: The Disability Press

Shakespeare, T. (1998) *The Disability Reader: Social Science Perspectives*. London: Continuum

Shakespeare, T. (1999a) '"Losing the Plot'? Medical and Activist Discourses of Contemporary Genetics and Disability', *Sociology of Health and Illness*, 21: 5, 669–688

Shakespeare, T. (1999b) 'The Sexual Politics of Disabled Masculinity', *Sex and Disability*, 17, 53–64

Shakespeare, T. (2000) 'Disabled Sexuality: Toward Rights and Recognition', *Sexuality and Disability*, 18: 3, 159–166

Shakespeare, T. (2001) 'Cultural Representation of Disabled People: Dustbins for Disavowal?' *Disability & Society*, 9: 3, 283–299

Shakespeare, T. and Corker, M. (2002) *Disability/Post-modernity: Embodying Disability Theory*. London: Continuum

Shakespeare, T. and Richardson, S. (forthcoming) 'The Sexual Politics of Disability, Twenty Years on', *Scandinavian Journal of Disability Research*

Shakespeare, T. and Watson, N. (1997) 'Defending the Social Model', *Disability & Society*, 12: 2, 293–300

Shakespeare T. and Watson, N. (2001) 'Making the Difference: Disability, Politics and Recognition'. In G. Albrecht, K. Seelman and M. Bury (eds) *The Handbook of Disability Studies*. Thousand Oaks, CA: Sage

Shakespeare, T. and Watson, N. (2002) 'The Social Model of Disability: An Outdated Ideology?' *Research in Social Science and Disability*, 2, 9–28

Shakespeare, T., Gillespie-Sells, K. and Davies, D. (1996) *Untold Desires: The Sexual Politics of Disability*. London and New York: Cassell

Shapiro, L. (2002) 'Incorporating Sexual Surrogacy into the Ontario Direct Funding Program', *Disability Studies Quarterly*, 22: 4, 72–81

Sharma, U. and Black, P. (2001) 'Look Good, Feel Better: Beauty Therapy as Emotional Labour', *Sociology*, 35: 4, 913–931

Sharp, K. and Earle, S. (2003) 'Cyberpunters and Cyberwhores: Prostitution on the Internet'. In Y. Jewkes (ed.) *Dot.Cons: Crime, Deviance and Identity on the Internet*. Cullompton: Willan Publishing

Shaw, B. (1994) *The Ragged Edge: The Disability Experience from the Pages of the First Fifteen Years of the Disability Rag*. Louisville, KY: Avocado Press

Shearer, A. (1980) *Handicapped Children in Residential Care: A Study of Policy Failure*. London: Bedford Square Press

Sheldon, A. *et al.* (2007) 'Disability Rights and Wrongs?' *Disability & Society*, 22: 2, 209–234

Sheppard, E. (2017) 'Kinked and Crippled: Disabled BDSM Practitioners' Experiences and Embodiment of Pain', PhD thesis, Edge Hill University, Ormskirk

Sheppard, M. and Mayo, J. B., Jr (2013) 'The Social Construction of Gender and Sexuality: Learning from Two Spirit Traditions', *Social Studies*, 104: 6, 259–270, doi: 10.1080/00377996.2013.788472

Sherry, M. (2004) 'Overlaps and Contradictions Between Queer Theory and Disability Studies', *Disability & Society*, 19: 7, 769–783

Shildrick, M. (2002) *Embodying the Monster: Encounters with the Vulnerable Self*. London: Sage

Shildrick, M. (2004) 'Queering Performativity: Disability after Deleuze', *SCAN: Journal of Media Arts Culture*. Available from: http://scan.net.au/scan/journal/display. php?journal_id=36 [accessed 23/6/2017]

Shildrick, M. (2007a) Contested Pleasures: The Sociopolitical Economy of Disability and Sexuality', *Sexuality Research and Social Policy: Journal of NSRC*, 3: 3, 51–75

Shildrick, M. (2007b) 'Dangerous Discourse: Anxiety, Desire and Disability', *Studies in Gender and Sexuality*, 8: 3, 221–244

Shildrick, M. (2009) *Dangerous Discourse of Disability, Subjectivity and Sexuality*. New York: Palgrave Macmillan

Shildrick, M. and Price, J. (1996) 'Breaking the Boundaries of the Broken Body: Mastery, Materiality and ME', *Body and Society*, 2: 4, 93–113

Shilling, C. (2003) *The Body and Social Theory 2nd Edition*. London, Thousand Oaks, New Delhi: Sage Publications

Shue, K. L. and Flores, A. (2002) 'Whose Sex is it Anyway? Freedom of Exploration and Expression of Sexuality of an Individual Living with Brain Injury in a Supported Independent Living Environment', *Disability Studies Quarterly*, 22: 4, 59–72

Shuttleworth, R. (2000) 'The Search for Sexual Intimacy for Men with Cerebral Palsy', *Sexuality and Disability*, 18: 4, 263–282

Shuttleworth, R. (2002) 'Dufusing the Adverse Context of Dsability and Desirability as a Practice of the Self for Men with Cerebral Palsy'. In M. Corker and T. Shakespeare (eds) *Disability/Postmodernity: Embodying Disability Theory*. London: Continuum

Shuttleworth, R. (2010) 'Towards an Inclusive Disability and Sexuality Research Agenda', In R. Shuttleworth and T. Sanders (eds) *Sex and Disability: Politics, Identity, and Access*. Leeds: The Disability Press

Shuttleworth, R. and Sanders, T. (eds) (2010) *Sex and Disability: Politics, Identity, and Access*. Leeds: The Disability Press

Siebers, T. (2001) 'Disability in Theory: From Social Constructionism to the New Realism of the Body', *American Literary History*, 13: 4, 737–754

Siebers, T. (2008) *Disability Theory*. Ann Arbor: University of Michigan Press

Simon, W. and Gagnon, J. (1969) 'Psychosexual Development: Men and Women Play the Sexual Drama According to a Post-Freudian Script', *Society*, 6: 5, 9–17

Sinecka, J. (2008) ' "I am Bodied". "I am Sexual". "I am Human". Experiencing Deafness and Gayness: A Story of a Young Man', *Disability & Society*, 23: 5, 475–484

Slater, J. (2015) *Youth and Dis/ability: A Challenge to Mr Reasonable. Interdisciplinary Disability Studies*. Farnham: Ashgate

Slater, J. (2016) 'The (Normal) Non-Normativity of Youth'. In: R. Mallett, C. Ogden and J. Slater (eds) *Theorising Normalcy and the Mundane: Precarious Positions*. Chester, University of Chester Press, 14–44

Smart, C. (1992) 'The Woman of Legal Discourse', *Social Legal Studies*, 1, 29–44

Smith, P. (1992) *The Emotional Labour of Nursing*. London: Macmillan

Smith-Rainey, S. (2010) *Love, Sex, and Disability: The Pleasures of Care*. Boulder, CO: Lynne Rienner Publishers

Smyth, C. (1992) *Lesbians Talk Queer Notions*. London: Scarlett Press

Smyth, L. (2009) 'Intimate Citizenship and the Right to Care: The Case of Breastfeeding'. In E. H. Oleksy (ed.) *Intimate Citizenships: Gender, Sexualities, Politics*. London: Routledge

Sobsey, D. (1994) *Violence and Abuse in the Lives of People with Disabilities: The End of Silent Acceptance?* Baltimore, MD: Paul H. Brookes

Sobsey, D. and Varnhagen, C. (1989) 'Sexual Abuse of People with Disabilities'. In M. Csapo and L. Goguen (eds) *Special Education Across Canada: Challenges for the 90's*. Vancouver: Centre for Human Development and Research, 199–218

Söder, M. (1984) *Economic and Industrial Democracy*. London: Sage Publications

Solomon, Y., Warin, J., Lewis, C. and Langford, W. (2002) 'Intimate Talk Between Parents and their Teenage Children: Democratic Openness or Covert Control', *Sociology*, 36: 4, 965–983

Solvang, P. (2007) 'The Amputee Body Desired: Beauty Destabilized? Disability Revalued?' *Sexuality and Disability*, 25, 51–64

Song, M. and Parker, D. (1995) 'Commonality, Difference and the Dynamics of Discourse in in-Depth Interviewing', *Sociology*, 29: 2, 241–256

Soorenian, A. (2016) 'Media, Disability and Human Rights'. In M. Gill and C. J. Schund-Vials (eds) *Disability, Human Rights and the Limits of Humanitarianism*. Farnham: Ashgate

Soothill, K. and Sanders, T. (2005) 'The Geographical Mobility, Preferences and Pleasures of Prolific Punters: A Demonstration Study of the Activities of Prostitutes' Clients', *Sociological Research Online*, 10: 1

Sparkes, A. C. and Smith, B. (2002) 'Sport, Spinal Cord Injuries, Embodied Masculinities, and the Dilemmas of Narrative Identity', *Men and Masculinities*, 4: 3, 258–285

Sparkes, A. C. and Smith, B. (2003) 'Men, Sport, Spinal Cord Injury and Narrative Time', *Qualitative Research*, 3: 3, 295–320

Stacey, C. L. (2005) 'Finding Dignity in Dirty Work: The Constraints and Rewards of Low-Wage Home Care Labour', *Sociology of Health and Illness*, 27: 6, 831–854

Stein, J. (2010) 'The Sex Factor', *Target MD*, Spring. London: Muscular Dystrophy Campaign

Steptoe, L., Lindsay, W. R., Forrest, D. and Power, M. J. (2006) 'Quality of Life and Relationships in Sex Offenders with Intellectual Disability', *Journal of Intellectual and Developmental Disability*, 31, 13–19

Stevens, B. (2010) 'Crip Sexuality: Sk(r)ewed Media Representation'. In R. Shuttleworth and T. Sanders (eds) *Sex and Disability: Politics, Identity, and Access*. Leeds: The Disability Press

Stevens, B. (2011) 'Politicizing Sexual Pleasure, Oppression and Disability: Recognizing and Undoing the Impacts of Ableism on Sexual and Reproductive Health'. In B. F. Waxman Fiduccia (ed.) *Papers on Women and Girls with Disabilities*. Center for Women Policy Studies

Stone, E. and Priestley, M. (1996) 'Parasites, Pawns and Partners: Disability Research and the Role of Non-Disabled Researchers', *British Journal of Sociology*, 47: 4, 699–716

Strazdin, L. (2000) 'Integrating Emotions: Multiple Role Measurement of Emotional Work', *Australian Journal of Psychology*, 52: 1, 41–50

Swain, J. (1996) ' "Just When You Think You Got it All Sorted…": Parental Dilemmas in Relation to the Developing Sexuality of Young Profoundly Disabled People', *Journal of Learning Disabilities*, 24: 2, 58–64

Swain, J. (2004) *Disabling Barriers, Enabling Environments*. London: Sage

Swain, J. and French, S. (2004) 'Disability and Communication: Listening is Not Enough'. In S. Barrett, C. Komarony, M. Robb and A. Rogers (eds) *Communication, Relationships and Care: A Reader*. London: Routledge

Swain, J., French, S., Barnes, C. and Thomas, C. (1993) *Disabling Barriers: Enabling Environments*. London: Sage

Taleporos, G. (2001) 'Sexuality and Physical Disability'. In E. Wood (ed.) *Sexual Positions: An Australian View*. Melbourne: Hill of Content Publishing

Taleporos, G. and McCabe, M. (2001) 'The Impact of Physical Disability on Body Esteem', *Sexuality and Disability*, 19, 293–308

Taleporos, G. and McCabe, M. (2002) 'Development and Validation of the Physical Disability Sexual and Body Esteem Scale'. *Sexuality and Disability*, 20, 159–176

Tamm, M. and Prellwitz, M. (1999) '"If I Had a Friend in a Wheelchair": Children's Thoughts on Disabilities', *Child: Care, Health and Development*, 27: 3, 223–240

Taylor, J. (2009) 'Cast Offs: The Verdict', *Independent*. Online. Available from: www. independent.co.uk/cast-offs-the-verdict-1826442.html [accessed 24/9/2011]

Tennille, J. *et al.* (2009) 'Elicitation of Cognitions Related to HIV Risk Behaviors in Persons with Mental Illnesses: Implications for Prevention', *Psychiatric Rehabilitation Journal*, 33: 1, 32–37

Tepper, M. S. (1999) 'Letting Go of Restricted Notions of Manhood: Male Sexuality, Disability and Chronic Illness', *Sexuality and Disability*, 17: 1, 37–52

Tepper, M. S. (2000) 'Sexuality and Disability: The Missing Discourse of Pleasure', *Sexuality and Disability*, 18: 4, 283–290

Tepper, M. (2002) 'Forbidden Wedding: Movie Review', *Disability Studies Quarterly*, 22: 4, 162–164

Thiara, R. *et al.* (2010) 'Disabled Women and Domestic Violence: Making the Links, a National UK Study', *Psychiatry, Psychology and Law*, 18: 1, 117–136

Thiara, R., Hague, G. and Mullender, A. (2011) 'Losing out on Both Counts: Disabled Women and Domestic Violence', *Disability & Society*, 26: 6, 757–771

Thiara, R. K., Hague, G., Ellis, B., Bashall, R. and Mullender, A. (2012) *Disabled Women and Domestic Violence: Responding to the Experiences of Survivors*. London: Jessica Kingsley

Thomas, C. (1997) 'The Baby and the Bath Water: Disabled Women and Motherhood in Social Context', *Sociology of Health & Illness*, 19: 5, 622–643

Thomas, C. (1998) 'The Body and Society: Impairment and Disability', paper presented at BSA Annual Conference on Making Sense of the Body, Edinburgh

Thomas, C. (1999) *Female Forms: Experiencing and Understanding Disability*. Buckingham: Open University Press

Thomas, C. (2002a) 'Disability Theory: Key Ideas, Issues and thinkers'. In. C. Barnes *et al.* (eds) *Disability Studies Today*. Cambridge: Polity Press

Thomas, C. (2002b) 'The Disabled Body'. In M. Evans and E. Lee (eds) *Real Bodies: A Sociological Introduction*. Hampshire: Palgrave

Thomas, C. (2004) 'Developing the Social Relational in the Social Model of Disability: A Theoretical Agenda'. In C. Barnes and G. Mercer (eds) *Implementing the Social Model of Disability: Theory and Research*. Leeds: The Disability Press, 32–47

Thomas, C. (2006) 'Disability and Gender: Reflections on Theory and Research', *Scandinavian Journal of Disability Research*, 8: 2–3, 177–185

Thomas, C. and Corker, M. (2002) 'Mapping the Terrain'. In M. Corker and Shakespeare, T. (eds) *Disability/Postmodernity: Embodying Disability Theory*. London: Continuum

Thompson, D., Clare, I., and Brown, H. (1994) 'Not Such an "Ordinary" Relationship: The Role of Women Support Staff in Relation to Men with Learning Disabilities Who Have Difficult Sexual Behaviour' *Disability & Society*, 12: 4, 573–592

Thompson, S. A., Bryson, M. and De Castell, S. (2001) 'Prospects for Identity Formation for Lesbian, Gay, or Bisexual Persons with Developmental Disabilities', *International Journal of Disability, Development and Education*, 48: 1, 53–65

Throsby, K. (2011) *Becoming a Channel Swimmer*. Online. Available from: www2. warwick.ac.uk/fac/soc/sociology/staff/academicstaff/throsby/homepage/channelswimmer/ [accessed 6/12/11]

Throsby, K. and Gimlin, D. (2009) 'Critiquing Thinness and Wanting to be Thin'. In R. Flood and R. Gill (eds) *Secrecy and Silence in the Research Process: Feminist Reflections*. Abingdon and New York: Routledge

Tiefer, L. (2001) 'A New View of Women's Sexual Problems: Why New? Why Now?' *Journal of Sex Research*, 38: 2, 89–96

TLC Trust (2011) *Welcome to the TLC Trust*. Online. Available from: www.tlc-trust.org. uk/ [accessed 27/11/11]

Touching Base (2008) *About Us*. Online. Available from: www.touchingbase.org.about. html [accessed 12/11/11]

Traustadóttir, R. (2006) 'Disability and Gender: Introduction to the Special Issue', *Scandinavian Journal of Disability Research*, 8: 2–3, 81–84

Tremain, S. (2000) 'Queering Disabled Sexuality Studies', *Sexuality and Disability*, 18: 4, 291–299

Tremain, S. (2002) 'On the Subject of Impairment'. In M. Corker and T. Shakespeare (eds) *Disability/Postmodernity: Embodying Disability Theory*. London: Continuum

Tremain, S. (2005) *Foucault and the Government of Disability*. Ann Arbor, MA: University of Michigan Press

Turk, V. and Brown, H. (1993) 'The Sexual Abuse of Adults with Learning Disabilities: Results of a Two-Year Incidence Survey', *Mental Handicap Research*, 6: 3, 193–216

Twigg, J. (2000) *Bathing: The Body and Community Care*. London: Routledge

Ungerson, C. (1997) 'Give Them the Money: Is Cash a Route to Empowerment?' *Social Policy & Administration*, 31: 1, 45–53

Vahldieck, A. (1999) 'Uninhibited', *Nerve*. Online. Available from: www.nerve.com/ PersonalEssays/Vahldieck/uninhibited/ [accessed 31/8/11]

Vasey, S. (1995) 'The Experience of Care'. In G. Hales (ed.) *Beyond Disability*. London: Sage

Vernon, A. (1996) 'A Stranger in Many Camps: The Experience of Disabled Black and Ethnic Minority Women'. In J. Morris (ed.) *Encounters with Strangers: Feminism and Disability*. London: Women's Press

Vernon, A. (1999) 'The Dialectics of Multiple Identities and the Disabled People's Movement', *Disability & Society*, 14: 3, 385–398

Villanueva, M. I. M. (1997) 'The Social Construction of Sexuality: Personal Meanings, Perceptions of Sexual Experience, and Females' Sexuality in Puerto Rico'. Unpublished book, Faculty of the Virginia Polytechnic Institute and State University

Wade, C. M. (1994) 'It Ain't Exactly Sexy'. In. B. Shaw (ed.) *The Ragged Edge: The Disability Experience from the Pages of the First Fifteen Years of the Disability Rag*. Louisville, KY: Avocado Press

Waerness, K. (1984) 'The Rationality of Caring'. In M. Söder (ed.) *Economic and Industrial Democracy*. London: Sage

Wainberg, M. L. *et al.* (2007) 'Targeted Ethnography as a Critical Step to Inform Cultural Adaptations of HIV Prevention Interventions for Adults with Severe Mental Illness', *Social Science & Medicine*, 65: 2, 296–308

Walby, S. (2011) 'The Impact of Feminism on Sociology', *Sociological Research Online*, 16: 3, 21. Available form: www.socresonline.org.uk/16/3/21.html

Warren, C. A. B. and Hackney, J. K. (2000) *Gender Issues in Ethnography*, 2nd ed. Thousand Oaks, CA: Sage

Warwick, D. P. (1982) 'Tearoom Trade: Means and Ends in Social Research'. In M. Bulmer (ed.) *Social Research Ethics: An Examination of the Merits of Covert Participant Observation*. London: Macmillan

Watermeyer, B. P. (2009) 'Conceptualising Psycho-Emotional Aspects of Disablist Discrimination And Impairment: Towards a Psychoanalytically Informed Disability Studies'. PhD dissertation, Stellenbosch University

Waxman, B. (1991) 'Hatred: The Unacknowledged Dimension in Violence Against Disabled People', *Sexuality and Disability*, 9: 3, 187–199

Waxman, B. (1994) 'Up Against Eugenics: Disabled Women's Challenge to Receive Reproductive Health Services', *Sexuality and Disability*, 12: 2, 185–171

Waxman Fiduccia, B. F. (1999) 'Sexual Imagery of Physically Disabled Women: Erotic? Perverse? Sexist?' *Sexuality and Disability*, 17: 3, 277–282

Waxman Fiduccia, B. (2000) 'Current Issues in Sexuality and the Disability Movement', *Sexuality and Disability*, 18: 3, 167–174

Waxman, B. F. and Finger, A. (1991) 'The Politics of Sexuality, Reproduction and Disability'. *Sexuality Update, National Task Force on Sexuality and Disability*, 4: 1, 1–3

Wazakili, M., Mpofu, R. and Devlieger, P. (2006) 'Experiences and Perceptions of Sexuality and HIV/AIDS Among Young People with Physical Disabilities in a South African Township: A Case Study', *Sexuality and Disability*, 24: 2, 77–88

Weatherall, A. and Priestly, A. (2001) 'A Feminist Discourse Analysis of Sex "Work"', *Feminism & Psychology*, 11: 3, 323–340

Weeks, J. (1985) *Sexuality and its Discontents: Meanings, Myths and Modern Sexualities*. London: Routledge

Weeks, J. (1986) *Sexuality*. Chichester: Ellis Horwood/Tavistock Publications

Weeks, J. (1998) 'The Sexual Citizen', *Theory, Culture and Society*, 15: 3, 35–52

Weinberg, M. *et al.* (1999) 'Gendered Sex Work in the San Francisco Tenderloin', *Archives of Sexual Behavior*, 28: 6, 503–521

Weitzer, R. (2000) *Sex for Sale*. London: Routledge

Weitzer, R. (2009) 'Sociology of Sex Work', *Annual Review of Sociology*, 35, 213–234

Wellings, K., Field, J., Johnson, A., and Wadsworth, J. (1994) *Sexual Behaviour in Britain*. London: Penguin

Welner, S. (1999) 'Contraceptive Choices for Women with Disabilities', *Sexuality and Disability*, 17: 3, 209–214

Wendell, S. (1996) *The Rejected Body: Feminist Philosophical Reflections on Disability*. London: Routledge & Kegan Paul

Whipple, B. *et al.* (1996) 'Sexual Response in Women with Complete Spinal Cord Injury'. In D. M. Krotoski, M. A. Nosek, and M. A. Turk (eds) *Women with Physical Disabilities: Achieving and Maintaining Health and Well-being*. Baltimore, MD: Paul H. Brookes

Whitaker, D. S. and Archer, L. (1994) 'Partnership Research and its Contributions to Learning and to Team-Building', *Social Work Education*, 13: 3, 39–60

Whitney, C. (2006) 'Intersections in Identity–Identity Development Among Queer Women with Disabilities', *Sexuality and Disability*, 24: 1, 39–52

Whyte, A. (2000) 'How Should Nurses Respond to Patients' Sexual Needs?' *Nursing Times*, 96, 35

Wilchins, R. (2004) *Queer Theory, Gender Theory*. Los Angeles: Alyson Books

Wilkerson, A. (2002) 'Disability, Sex Radicalism and Political Agency', *NSWA Journal*, 14: 3, 33–57

Williams, S. J. (1999) 'Is Anybody There? Critical Realism, Chronic Illness and the Disability Debate', *Sociology of Health and Illness*, 21: 6, 797–819

Williams M. J., Levy Paluck, E. and Spencer-Rodgers, J. (2010) 'The Masculinity of Money: Automatic Stereotypes Predict Gender Differences in Estimated Salaries', *Psychology of Women Quarterly*, 34, 7–20

Wilton, R. D. (2008) 'Workers with Disabilities and the Challenges of Emotional Labour'. *Disability and Society* 23: 4, 361–373

Wilton, R. and Schuer, S. (2006) 'Towards Socio-spatial Inclusion? Disabled People, Neoliberalism and the Contemporary Llabour Market', *Area*, 38: 2, 186–195

Wolbring, G. (2008) 'The Politics of Ableism', *Development*, 51, 252–258

Wolfe, P. S. (1997) 'The Influence of Personal Values on Issues of Sexuality and Disability', *Sexuality and Disability*, 15: 2, 69–90

Wolkowitz, C. (2006) *Bodies at Work*. London, Thousand Oaks, CA, and New Delhi: Sage

Women's Aid (2011a) *Topic: Emotional Abuse*. Online. Available from: www.womens aid.org.uk/domestic_violence_topic.asp?section=0001000100220042&sectionTitle= Emotional+abuse [accessed 28/02/2011]

Women's Aid (2011b) *Topic: Sexual Violence*. Online. Available from: www.womens aid.org.uk/domestic_violence_topic.asp?section=0001000100220022&sectionTitle= Sexual+violence [accessed 28/02/2011]

Wong, A. (2000) 'The Work of Disabled Women Seeking Reproductive Health Care', *Sexuality and Disability*, 18: 4, 301–306

Wood, C. (ed.) (2001) *Sexual Positions: An Australian View*. Melbourne: Hill of Content Publishing

Woodby, L., Williams, B. R., Wittich, A. R. and Burgio, K. L. (2011) 'Expanding the Notion of Researcher Distress: The Cumulative Effects of Coding', *Qualitative Health Research*, 21: 6, 830–838

Woodin, S. L. (2006) 'Social Relationships and Disabled People: The Impact of Direct Payments'. Unpublished PhD, University of Leeds

World Health Organization (2002) *Gender and Reproductive Rights: World Health Organization*. Online. Available from: www.who.int/reproductive-health/gender/ sexualhealth.html [accessed 23/9/11]

Wotton, R. and Isbister, S. (2010) 'A Sex Worker Perspective on Working with Clients with a Disability and the Development of Touching Base Inc.'. In R. Shuttleworth and T. Sanders (eds) *Sex and Disability: Politics, Identity, and Access*. Leeds: The Disability Press

Wouters, C. (1989) 'The Sociology of Emotions and Flights Attendants: Hochschild's Managed Heart', *Theory, Culture and Society*, 6, 95–123

Wright, E. R. *et al.* (2007) 'Stigma and the Sexual Isolation of People with Serious Mental Illness', *Social Problems*, 54: 1, 78–98

Yacoub, E. and Hall, I. (2009) 'The Sexual Lives of Men with Mild Learning Disability: A Qualitative Study', *British Journal of Learning Disabilities*, 37, 5–11

Yoshida, K. K., Li, A. and Odette, M. S. W. (1999) 'Cross-Cultural Views of Disability and Sexuality: Experiences of a Group of Ethno-Racial Women with Physical Disabilities', *Sexuality and Disability*, 17: 4, 321–337

Young, M. E., Nosek, M. A., Howland, C. and Chanpong, G. (1997) 'Prevalence of Abuse of Women with Physical Disabilities'. *Archives of Physical Medicine and Rehabilitation*, 78, 34–38

Zajano, N. C. and Edelsberg, C. M. (1993) 'Living and Writing the Researcher–Researched Relationship. *International Journal of Qualitative Studies in Education*, 6: 2, 143–15

Zarb, G. (1992) On the Road to Damascus: First Steps Towards Changing the Relations of Disability Research Production', *Disability, Handicap & Society*, 7: 2, 125–138

Zarb, G. (1997) 'Researching Disabling Barriers'. In C. Barnes and G. Mercer (eds) *Doing Disability Research*. Leeds: The Disability Press

Zavirsek, D. (2002) 'Pictures and Silences: Memories of Sexual Abuse of Disabled People', *International Journal of Social Welfare*, 11, 270–285

Zelizer, V. A. (1989) 'The Social Meaning of Money: "Special Monies"', *American Journal of Sociology*, 95: 2, 342–377

Index

Taylor & Francis eBooks

Helping you to choose the right eBooks for your Library

Add Routledge titles to your library's digital collection today. Taylor and Francis ebooks contains over 50,000 titles in the Humanities, Social Sciences, Behavioural Sciences, Built Environment and Law.

Choose from a range of subject packages or create your own!

Benefits for you
- » Free MARC records
- » COUNTER-compliant usage statistics
- » Flexible purchase and pricing options
- » All titles DRM-free.

Benefits for your user
- » Off-site, anytime access via Athens or referring URL
- » Print or copy pages or chapters
- » Full content search
- » Bookmark, highlight and annotate text
- » Access to thousands of pages of quality research at the click of a button.

REQUEST YOUR **FREE** INSTITUTIONAL TRIAL TODAY
Free Trials Available
We offer free trials to qualifying academic, corporate and government customers.

eCollections – Choose from over 30 subject eCollections, including:

Archaeology	Language Learning
Architecture	Law
Asian Studies	Literature
Business & Management	Media & Communication
Classical Studies	Middle East Studies
Construction	Music
Creative & Media Arts	Philosophy
Criminology & Criminal Justice	Planning
Economics	Politics
Education	Psychology & Mental Health
Energy	Religion
Engineering	Security
English Language & Linguistics	Social Work
Environment & Sustainability	Sociology
Geography	Sport
Health Studies	Theatre & Performance
History	Tourism, Hospitality & Events

For more information, pricing enquiries or to order a free trial, please contact your local sales team:
www.tandfebooks.com/page/sales